This is the most valuable compendium of information for ministers I have ever seen. If I had possessed it when I was starting my ministry, I would have been twice as effective as I was without it—no, three or four times. I commend it to all pastors—even those who may have only a few years remaining in which to employ its shining wisdom.

If it were possible to earn a PhD in pastoral insight, Bill Tuck would have at least three or four. An inveterate pastor who has served many churches, he has restlessly continued to review and improve his craft, so that he could easily be called the Dean of American Pastoral Studies. Now he has distilled in this highly readable book the essence of all his vast knowledge, so that any minister, at whatever stage of his or her life, can enjoy and profit from it.

—John Killinger
Former professor at
Vanderbilt Divinity School
Pastor and author of many books,
including *The Tender Shepherd* and
The Fundamentals of Preaching

Bill Tuck served as my homiletics professor in seminary. The same practical yet theoretical, thorough yet illustrative, framed yet visionary approach that I received to homiletics lives in every section of this book as well. We have needed an updated pastoral handbook for years, one that builds upon the insights of our predecessors, is born out of local church experience and takes into account the realities of our day. It has arrived. Pastors new to the ministry as well as those more seasoned will all benefit from Tuck's unique approach and style that have garnered him so many readers over the years. If you are not already, I encourage you to become one of Tuck's literary beneficiaries through the reading of these pages.

—Dr. C. Jeff Woods
Associate General Secretary
American Baptist Churches, USA

This is a marvelous book. *Star Thrower: A Pastor's Handbook* by William Tuck is so much more than a "how to" manual—it's a compassionate and guiding hand on the shoulders of men and women serving in pastoral "trenches" everywhere. (The first chapter alone, an empathetic review of the complex realities every pastor faces, is worth the price of the book.) After fifty years of pastoral ministry, Tuck writes with a still-obvious passion for the work to which he has given his life. His practical, theoretical, philosophical, and theological insights, combined with a rich collection of personal and anecdotal stories, are a welcome gift to every pastor.

—**Julie Pennington-Russell**
Pastor, First Baptist Church, Washington, DC

As an experienced pastor as well as a seminary professor, Bill Tuck is especially qualified to write this pastoral manual, which is a superb combination of practical guidance and theological depth. *Star Thrower: A Pastor's Handbook* is written in a conversational style and filled with helpful examples and marvelous illustrations. The book provides invaluable help in the daily tasks of pastoral ministry while also focusing on the inner life of the pastor. This comprehensive text of pastoral leadership will be a welcome addition to the library of ministerial students, young pastors, and seasoned ministers seeking to sharpen their skills and deepen their understanding of Christian ministry.

—**Thomas Graves**
President Emeritus, Baptist Theological
Seminary at Richmond

The pastoral office is a multi-faceted profession. While its responsibilities can be categorized into proclamation, administration, and pastoral care, within those categories are a myriad of tasks, each of which carries its unique demands. Pastors are, therefore, generalists, which does not come naturally for most of us. Fortunately, *Star Thrower: A Pastor's Handbook* offers comprehensive guidance and encouragement for those of us in pastoral ministry who may feel unqualified for certain aspects of our holy calling, but who realize that our effectiveness depends on our ability to do all pastoral things well. Readers will be grateful for how Bill Tuck draws from both his own experience in the pastorate and his years of study in the field of homiletics in order to give inspiration and instruction to those who may be overwhelmed by the enormity of the work, and with a needed reminder that the God who calls gives what is required so that we might be found faithful in what, despite its complexity, is the most rewarding work in the world.

—Doug Dortch
Pastor, Mountain Brook Baptist Church,
Birmingham, Alabama

Pastoral ministry is not for those who are faint of heart. Most pastors are generalists and not specialists. They preach, teach, visit hospitals, care for the dying and the grieving. They administer staff and deal with committees. William Tuck brings over fifty years of pastoral experience to bear on the multiple tasks that face pastors, and does so with a wisdom and grace, in this handbook on pastoral ministry.

—Robert Cornwall
Pastor, Central Woodward Christian Church,
Troy, Michigan

Smyth & Helwys Publishing, Inc.
6316 Peake Road
Macon, Georgia 31210-3960
1-800-747-3016

Library of Congress Cataloging-in-Publication Data

Names: Tuck, William Powell, 1934- author.
Title: Star thrower : a pastor's handbook / by William Powell Tuck.
Description: Macon : Smyth & Helwys, 2016. | Includes bibliographical
references.
Identifiers: LCCN 2016022682 | ISBN 9781573128896 (pbk. : alk. paper)
Subjects: LCSH: Pastoral theology.
Classification: LCC BV4011.3 .T83 2016 | DDC 253--dc23
LC record available at https://lccn.loc.gov/2016022682

Star Thrower

A PASTOR'S HANDBOOK

WILLIAM POWELL TUCK

Also by William Powell Tuck

With appreciation to fellow associate ministers,
who served faithfully with me in ministry.

Contents

Preface

The image of the minister as a "star thrower" was brought to my mind by the story that Loren Eiseley recounted in *The Unexpected Universe* about the man he watched along the beaches of Costabel who was seen throwing starfish back beyond the breaking surf that had been washed up on the shore. This image of the star thrower became for him a sort of parable about confronting the perplexities and struggles of life. Upon reading Eiseley's account of the "star thrower," I realized that this was a superb image for a pastor. Pastors are challenged to assist persons who feel like they have been washed up on many shorelines in life—sin, suffering, grief, depression, loneliness and countless other struggles and journeys. As pastors, we strive to "toss" them a helping hand in dealing with whatever life brings their way. We realize that a "star thrower" is a helpmate, a servant who follows the Greatest of all the Servants, Jesus Christ, our Lord. I expound more on the image of the "star thrower" in chapter 20.

These pages reflect my fifty-plus years of pastoral ministry. The suggestions I offer are not simply the "nuts and bolts" of doing ministry; they are a combination of practical, theoretical, philosophical, and theological insights. I make no claims to having the ultimate advice on doing the work of a pastor but simply share out of my own lengthy ministry. I have served as the only minister in a small rural church, as a pastor in a small community church with a secretary and a part-time minister of music, and as the pastor of several large congregations with staff members from about eight to two dozen people.

Pastors do not have nine-to-five jobs and often are called to work seven days a week or are called out late at night or at other inconvenient times. They are constantly challenged to figure out the right priorities.

Determining these priorities may be the most demanding task any pastor has. I believe one has to have a strong sense of call to engage in the heavy demands of ministry. My sense of call has sustained me during difficult and demanding times. But the rewards are measured in the gospel pastors proclaim, the lives that are changed, and the good we are able to render through faithful ministry. This book has in mind both the pastor who is at the beginning stage of ministry and the seasoned pastor who would appreciate a resource from someone who understands. Various sections will be useful for pastors at different chapters in their ministries. The book may be read straight through, read by sections as needed, or serve as a resource when appropriate.

There appears to be some duplication of thought in some sections, but I have allowed this repetition to remain because of special emphasis and the realization that some readers may not read all the sections. This book is not a collection of reflections by someone who has remained aloof from the day-by-day ministry in the local church; it is an offering of suggestions by someone who has spent most of his daily life involved with the local pastoral ministry. Even with the heavy demands of the pastorate, I have maintained through my years of ministry that there is nothing else to which I would rather dedicate my life. It has been such a rich blessing that I would have gladly done it without remuneration if I could have afforded to do so. I have been grateful to give my life to the pastoral calling, and I would gladly do it again.

I want to express a special word of appreciation to my fellow minister and friend, Rand Forder, for his thorough proofreading of the manuscript of this book and several others I have written. He has always been willing to do this cheerfully and with helpful suggestions. He served as associate pastor with me right out of seminary and did it with dignity and faithfulness. He later went on to serve effectively as a pastor in several churches and eventually returned to serve as pastor of the church in which he was an associate minister with me. The people of that church speak highly of him.

The Practice of Ministry

Earthen Pots, Empty Pots, Cracked Pots, Stew Pots, Crock-Pots, Flower Pots, and Serving Pots

A little boy tiptoed into his sister's room and began to shake her while she slept. No one else was awake in the house, and as the girl was aroused from her sleep, she looked at her brother and asked, "Why did you wake me up? You made me lose my place in my dream."

Like this little girl, some people have lost their place in their dream for parish ministry. Some are at a crossroads for their future in ministry and question whether they should be in ministry at all. The pressures, constant time demands, and sermon deadlines can become almost overwhelming. Will we continue to jog in place in our dilemma, or will we have a bold new vision that will enable us to recapture our dream or to see new possibilities for ministry?

In a half-whimsical approach, I've titled this chapter "The Practice of Ministry: Earthen Pots, Empty Pots, Cracked Pots, Stew Pots, Crock-Pots, Flower Pots, and Serving Pots." In many ways, I think these pots describe something of the nature of our ministry today. Examine them with me and see if you agree.

Earthen Pots

Typically ministers deny their humanity. We often suffer from a god complex, assuming that we are not supposed to get sick, express emotion, or have feelings about the conflicts and stress that surround us. We are often perfectionists, achievers, and performers. We pour ourselves into our jobs and spend a great deal of the time climbing the ecclesiastical ladder. Those of us who are leading others to Christ have often become castaways. We who are leading others to wholeness, fullness, completeness, and redemption often do not have this wholeness for ourselves. Instead, our lives are often filled with loneliness and pessimism. In his Beecher Lectures at Yale titled *Telling the Truth*, Frederick Buechner related an experience about Henry Ward Beecher, who traveled to Yale on January 31, 1872, to deliver the first of the Beecher Lectures. Beecher had not finished preparing his lecture. He had had a bad night's sleep. He went to his hotel, took a brief nap, got up to shave, and cut himself with his razor while shaving. While he was writing his notes for the lecture, the blood from his cut dripped on the pages. Whispers were everywhere about a relationship that he was having with one of his parishioners, and a public trial for adultery was not far off.[1] The blood falling on those pages was symbolic of his humanity.

Like Henry Ward Beecher, each of us bleeds a little in all that we do. As Paul has said, "All have sinned" (Rom 3:23). This is another way of saying that we are all human. We are indeed "earthen pots." We really cannot walk on water. Unfortunately, too many of us push ourselves as though we could. As committed, dedicated, serving people, we often pour ourselves into our work to such an extent that we burn ourselves out in doing it. This striving toward perfection and ministerial excellence pulls us in many directions. Sometimes we wonder who we truly are. We are always more than we think we are and yet less at the same time. Too many of us have identified ourselves with our role as a minister and have not seen our own humanity. Who are you and who am I when we are not ministers? Are we still authentic people? Have we accepted our acceptance by God and acknowledged that we too are human beings? We have often drawn the world's standards into the church and into our lives. We have duplicated the world's rat race, and we spend our lives scurrying, worrying, and huffing and puffing through the heavy burdens of our ministry. When we deny that we are earthen vessels, we do not take care of our bodies, enjoy our families, savor enough moments alone, or spend enough time playing, praying, reflecting, and just plain living.

Empty Pots

When we deny our humanity, we have become, as Flanders Dunbar has said, "compulsive strivers."[2] For ministers, the problem is usually not apathy but caring too much. Ministers pour themselves into their work to such an extent that they often suffer emptiness and burnout. When you are burned out, your emotional center is gone. There is nothing you really care about. There are no optimistic feelings, only negative ones. You begin to respond to people only in institutionalized, routinized, and dehumanized ways. Too many of us assume that we are like Albert Schweitzer. When someone asked him, "Don't you know you can't burn the candle at both ends?" he said, "You can if the candle's long enough." But sooner or later, like Elijah, you discover that you are sitting by a dry brook (1 Kgs 17:7). You can no longer pray. Your work does not excite you. Your nerves are on edge. You feel empty, lonely, and isolated. Your face is pressed against the window glass of life as you look for somebody to care about you. Your eyes are searching. Your spirit is groping. Your heart is yearning. Your hands are reaching out for someone to say, "You are important to me and I care about you." There is a loss of direction in life. Life seems to have come to a dead-end street. The game of self-pity soon begins to overwhelm you, and you play the repetitive record of "ain't it awful" or "poor me."

Our emptiness affects us in many ways. It makes us more vulnerable to temptation. Some ministers have turned to alcohol or drugs because of their sense of isolation and loneliness. These feelings of emptiness may cause us not to be able to come to grips with who, what, where, and why we are at a particular moment in our lives. John Milton wrote, "Loneliness was the first thing that the eye of God called not good." Sometimes a pastor experiences this emptiness in a lonely, isolated, rural church where there are no other ministers to share fellowship and mutual understanding. At other times, this lonely, empty feeling is experienced by pastors in large cities who are surrounded by many other ministers yet who experience no support, friendship, or encouragement from them. Few burdens in life can be as heavy to bear as emptiness, isolation, and loneliness. It is what Kierkegaard calls "the sickness unto death."

Stew Pots

Pastors today are under tremendous stress and pressure, and the current changes in church culture are only increasing the pressure they feel. Rather than seeing the minister as a pastor, many churches today want a coach or

CEO. When those pastors do not perform according to the expectations of certain members in their congregations, they are terminated. A study I read several years ago found that pastors were being terminated at a rate of 116 per month or 1 pastor every 6 hours. Thom Rainer, president and CEO of LifeWay Resources, in an article published in October 2011 in *The Christian Post*, stated that over the last seven years approximately 10.5 percent of senior pastors were forcefully terminated.[3] In his large pilot study project in 2013 that sampled Assemblies of God ministers, Marcus Tanner found that 41 percent had experienced a forced termination at least once in their ministry.[4] Charles H. Chandler states that in the United States, 1,600 Protestant ministers are forced out of their ministry positions every month, more than 19,000 a year.[5] Numerous ministers told Dean Hoge and Jacqueline Wenger, who did research in this area, that they left their church because of strain, weariness, burnout, and frustration.[6] Wherever I go I encounter pastors and other ministers who are unhappy, frustrated, and seeking to move, or are under fire from a group in their church. Ministers seem to live in a stew pot. Rather than facing the real issues that underlie the problems in a congregation, a select group often seeks a solution simply by removing the leader, assuming that will bring about whatever change is needed.

Conflict is inevitable in any kind of leadership, and if a pastor offers leadership, there will always be people who disagree with him or her. In some churches, a Sunday school class can become a church unto itself and bring pressure on the rest of the congregation to conform to what they want. If the pastor will not submit to them, then their solution is simple: get a new minister. Baby boomers, baby busters, Gen X, the millennials, the seekers, the young, and the old alike place frequently unrealistic demands and pressures on a pastor. No human being can be all things to all people. The pastor often becomes the target for congregational conflict. In many cases, the issue has nothing to do with poor performance or scandalous behavior by a minister. It is most often caused by internal conflicts, unrealistic expectations, or the unwillingness of a congregation to face the reality that they have "plateaued." There are various reasons for this: The membership has moved to another part of the city. The members are elderly, and there are no young people in that community. Businesses have relocated. The times simply have changed. The church is not the same as it was ten or twenty years ago. Regardless of the cause, ministers often experience a warlike zone in some churches. Rumors, accusations, or criticisms are directed toward the pastor. During this time, the minister feels anger, frustration, a loss of self-esteem, guilt, shock, depression, and sometimes even despair. (There are times, of course, when ministers *need* to be terminated. If they have sexually abused someone or have been engaging in sexual affairs with parishioners, have stolen money, or committed unethical practices, that is another matter altogether and is not my primary focus in this section.)

In an article in *The Christian Century* titled "Pastors Under Fire: A Personal Report," a pastor discusses his personal struggle with conflict in his church, his eventual termination, and his response.[7] Many denominations are beginning to realize that this is not a minor issue but a major concern for the church today. In my own denomination, this problem has a long history. I remember reading about it in the February 1994 issue of *Church Administration*, which was dedicated to the issue of "forced termination." I learned later that two years before the articles appeared in that publication, *The Deacon Magazine*, another Baptist publication, dealt with the same issue. In a more recent study in the *Journal of Religion and Health*, published in 2012, it was found that between 23 and 41 percent of pastors experienced "forced termination."[8] David Roach, writing in the *Baptist Press* on September 5, 2014, stated that as many as four in ten pastors will be forced to leave their church.[9] I personally believe that this issue has become a major crisis in many denominations. It is undermining the confidence of ministry and, unless corrected, will reap fiery havoc across the pastoral landscape.[10]

You may have seen the comic strip *Hägar the Horrible*. In one, Hägar says to a hooded doctor, "I have a stomachache, a sore thumb, a bruised knee, backache, chills, itchy scalp, ringing in my ears, fuzzy vision, night sweats, joint pains, and the blues." The doctor responds, "There is a lot of that going around." A lot of ministers today feel that they are caught in a stew pot. It is hard for one to verbalize the depth of frustration, loneliness, anger, depression, and fatigue that comes from such an experience. I spoke with a young pastor recently who had been at his new church only two months when a meeting was called by the deacons. He was excluded from this meeting and told afterwards that he needed to leave. He was called to that church by a vote of 96 to 7. Only seven people voted against him. What he discovered later, though, was that the seven who opposed him were members of the chairman of the deacons' family. This chairman happened to be the wealthiest man in the congregation. For some reason, he did not like this fine young minister, who had had a successful career in the past. He spoke in opposition to him, and the rest of the congregation was unwilling to oppose this wealthy man. And so the young man found his career wrecked and his family without a home and his income canceled. For some time he struggled to put his life back together.

Many of us cannot imagine how a congregation could do this to a pastor, but many are doing it. The pastors who have been terminated by churches, along with other ministers and congregations who are undergoing stress, need to know that there is some place where they can get help. The word "stress" comes from the Latin root *strictus*, meaning "to be drawn tight." Many of our common expressions state this truth. We sometimes say, "My stomach is tied up in knots," "Don't get your bowels in an uproar," "I feel like I am being pulled apart," "This job is breaking my back," "She gives me a headache," or "He gets on my nerves." These everyday sayings reveal a deeper truth about the impact of stress on our bodies. If you have ever walked any distance, you know what an aggravation it can be to have gravel in your shoe. Sooner or later you realize, "I will have to stop and remove that gravel." You know that if you do not, it will cause a blister or a worse irritation to your foot. We cannot go through life with a heavy load of tension and pressures upon us without seeking to lighten or remove that burden. Ministers, like any other person, cannot live with constant stress without it affecting their cardiovascular, digestive, skeletal-muscular, and immune systems.[11]

Cracked Pots

As ministers, we often deal with people during the time of their worst hurts and pain. Granted, we are also with them during some of the times of their greatest joys, such as weddings or the birth of a child. But many of us spend most of our time with people during times of hospitalization, illness, dying, or grief. Like other pastors, I have sat by many hospital beds, walked with parishioners to the cemetery, held the hands of those who were dying, and heard the confessions of those who were sinning. I wept with those who weep, and rejoiced with those who rejoice.

Several years ago my telephone rang late at night, and I was called to come to the home of a church member who had shot herself. Since it was midnight, I got up, dressed quickly, and drove over. When I arrived at the house, it was surrounded by vehicles, police cars, and television cameras. I wondered why so many people were present. I approached the door and a policeman asked who I was. I told him I was the pastor and the family had called me to come. He went inside, checked with them, and then let me in. After talking with the mother, I discovered that her daughter had indeed committed suicide, but first she had taken the life of her seven-year-old son. It was both a murder and a suicide. I then began the agonizing walk with the family through a dark valley of grief.

As a minister, you too have walked or will walk with your parishioners and others through their dark valleys. All of us will have this experience as a part of our ministry. But seeking to reach out to wounded and hurting people is not an easy load to bear. It also can affect our attitude, spirit, and sense of well-being. The wounded healer, I believe, is the most caring and responsive kind of healer. But sometimes the wounded healer feels unable to receive healing. The burden can be so heavy that he or she does not know where to turn. When we spend most of our time trying to mend pots, we find that our own can be damaged. There have been times when I have felt like a well beside a road. I have given all the water I could to quench the thirst of others, and then I have wondered if I had any left to quench myself.

Crock-Pots

My wife, Emily, often prepares stews or roast in a Crock-Pot. A Crock-Pot cooks slowly but thoroughly. I always find the meat tender or the soup delicious. I believe that most of our ministry is like a Crock-Pot. It is done slowly. We cannot expect quick results, overnight success, easy answers to complicated problems, and simple resolutions to the irresolvable. The best ministries are those in which a minister gives faithful service over a long period. One of the real indictments of the ministry and churches today is the short pastorate. There are too many short pastorates. This often comes about because of a conflict between the minister and the church. The congregation is unwilling to face the reality of the actual conflict and instead simply attaches it to the pastor. Careful sermon preparation, faithful visitation of the sick, caring response to the needy, and the love that comes from a lifetime of experience and responding to people are what make a ministry successful. Success should not be judged merely by numbers or statistics, but in faithfulness, love, and concern. If more churches could be taught and if more ministers understood that ministry is slow work that takes a lifetime, both churches and ministers would be more effective.

Flower Pots

Every single one of us has gifts and potential that we want to use in service for God. We hope that our gifts can bloom in a way that reflects the greatness of God's love and grace. The church affirms that all Christians have gifts. Some may be more gifted than others, but every Christian has some gift that he or she can use in ministry for Christ. My wife, Emily, is more outgoing than I am. She has a radiant, warm personality that attracts others to her. She has been a wonderful Sunday school teacher in various age groups—young couples, singles, older adult couples, elderly women, etc. They all affirmed her excellent teaching gifts and relational skills. Whatever class she taught, those in the class appreciated not only her teaching but also her love, concern, and special attention. The same could be stated about her ministry as a deacon or as chair of the Board of Christian Education. Emily has unique gifts. She serves Christ in her gifted way, and I serve him in my way. She has her gifts, and I have mine. The church must acknowledge the gifts that all of us have as ministers. As Romans 12:6 states, "Having gifts that differ according to the grace given us, let us use them." I believe that God has called me to bloom where I have been planted in the best way that I possibly can in service for God. When I stand before God one day, I do not believe God is going to ask me, "Bill Tuck, why were you not like Moses?" I believe God will simply ask me if I used my gifts in the best way I could in service for him.

Bill Staines has written a folk song titled "A Place in the Choir." "All God's critters got a place in the choir, some sing low, some sing higher, some sing out loud on the telephone wire, and some just clap their hands or paws . . . ." Indeed, all have a place in the choir. Staines is speaking about the place of everyone in God's creation. We all have a role in God's grand design. All of us have a part in God's great orchestra—the church. Karl Barth brought this into clear focus for me when he observed,

> There can be no talk of higher and lower orders of specific services. There is a differentiation of functions, but the preacher cannot really stand any higher than the other elders, nor the bell-ringer, any lower than the Professor of Theology. There can be no "clergy" and no "laity," no merely "teaching" and no merely "listening" church, because there is no member of this church who is not the whole thing in "his or her place."[12]

Serving Pots

Jesus has not called us to be successful as ministers but to be faithful. Could we say that our Lord, by the world's standards, was successful? What about Peter, James, John, or Paul? Many of the disciples ended up dying as martyrs for the cause of Christ. To serve in the name of Christ means that sometimes life gets difficult. Ministry is not always easy. When William Carey finally arrived in India after many years of trying to become a missionary, he labored for seven years before leading a Hindu convert to Christ. I read about missionaries in the Yukon who worked for fifteen years before they had a single convert. Too many have bought into the Madison Avenue notion of success and baptized it as the standard to judge what it means to be successful as a church. Jesus did not call us to be successful but to be faithful. We have been called to be like Christ, and Christ lived a life of servanthood.

As ministers of Christ, there are times when we will have to suffer inconvenience, endure hostility, and step into a dark, untried way. There are times when we will risk speaking to a person whom others might not care about or helping someone who might prove difficult or unappreciative. We may have to risk laughter, ridicule, mockery, or criticism. We may have to speak out for Christ even when it is not popular. We may have to go out of our way to help another. As we take up our cross and follow Christ, we will have to risk breaking new pathways, attempt new ministries, be open to new discoveries from God, and be willing to go without restrictions wherever God leads. As servant people, we will express compassion, care, understanding, empathy, and love. We will follow our Lord, who by his words, life, and death modeled the way of the Suffering Servant. The one who took up the towel and basin has called us to follow him. The one who said he had come to serve has called us also to serve.

Finding Resources

If you and I are going to follow our Lord in service, we soon discover that we need strength and support to do our ministry effectively. We will engage our responsibility as pastor more effectively if we do not try to do our ministry in isolation but link with others who are seeking to serve Christ. Ministers today are facing enormous challenges and crises. What are some ways parish clergy can confront these challenges today? Let me suggest some approaches.

Colleague Group

Strive to strengthen or begin new chapters or colleague groups with other ministers in your area. A colleague group of ministers from your own denomination might be one type of group you could form. I do not believe that we can survive long as ministers without the edification, inspiration, and education recourses we can draw from fellow ministers. These chapters or small groups provide opportunities to enrich our lives through study and contact with others. The real experts in parish ministry are those who practice it; we have much to learn from one another.

Ecumenical Group

Share our ministerial practice in an ecumenical environment. This kind of environment will enable us to be responsible and accountable to one another to encourage the best possible ministry. This, I believe, can be realized most effectively in what I would call "chapters" or small groups. The long-range approach to ministry is always difficult. The support and encouragement of other pastors are essential. The word "educate" comes from a Latin root that means "to make a plant grow." If we are going to be truly educated for ministry, we need the impact of others on our thinking, ideas, attitude, and struggles. Growth will not come without it. Our chapters or small groups offer us an opportunity to build relationships, share ministerial struggles, find guidance for doing ministry more effectively, discover new insights into ministry, and seek creative ways of serving where we are.

Support Group

Start or participate in a support group. Many ministers bury unresolved anger, guilt, anxiety, or depression buried deeply within themselves. They often unload this hostility on their congregations or families. Dr. Karen Horney, a psychoanalyst, has stated that "the biggest disturbing force is not repressed sexuality, but simple repressed hostility."[13] Rather than burying these feelings, ministers need a way to direct it. A support group can offer a safe place for sharing our feelings and building each other up.

I believe many of us need a place where we can "piously curse." Cursing has not come easy for me. I have always felt it was non-ministerial, but as Brer Rabbit has said, "Every person needs a cussing place." After suffering a heart attack, a minister friend of mine was facetiously told by his doctor that he needed a dog to kick. But he said, "If I had a dog, I wouldn't kick it." The doctor responded, "That may be why you have a heart condition." Of course, the doctor wasn't really advocating animal abuse, and regardless of whether my friend's repressed emotions led to his heart attack, it is certainly true that we need to find some way or some place to cope with anger, frustration, and hostility. Rather than sloshing our frustrations on our parishioners or family, a support group can help us resolve them. In

Carson McCullers's *The Member of the Wedding*, Frankie says, "All people belong to a *We* except me. Not to belong to a *We* makes you too lonesome." I'd agree that all of us need a "we." We all need some other person or people to touch our lives. One of the finest functions a chapter or small group could provide is a place for encouragement, understanding, acceptance, and love from other ministers. As with any group, some guidelines and objectives are helpful.

Mentors

The word "mentor" comes from the Greek word for the character of Mentor in Greek legend. Mentor was the loyal friend and wise advisor of Ulysses and the teacher and guardian of his son. A mentor is a wise and loyal advisor. I see a tremendous need for this ministry for pastors. Older ministers with many years of experience could share stories of wisdom with younger ministers who are just beginning. This practical guidance would arise from hands-on ministry over years of personal involvement in the life of the church. Educators know that learning does not take place merely with an appeal to the mind. Real learning comes only when a person is motivated to learn. The greatest teachers are not the ones who instill facts; they are the ones who know the power of inspiration. A good teacher is not content merely to instruct; instead, he or she seeks to light a spark in a student. A good mentor could awaken interest in a younger minister in the many possibilities that lie before him or her. Good teaching is not merely indoctrinating; it is bringing a person alive to the potential within himself or herself. Education is, to use Whitehead's phrase, "The continuing joy of discovery."[14]

As a college student, I was inspired by the preaching of J. P. Allen and Roy McClain. They made preaching come alive for me and challenged me to find creative ways to communicate ideas. I learned from them the marvelous gift of story in preaching. I also knew that if I wanted to be a minister, I had to give my life to the pursuit of truth and knowledge. Individuals along my educational path helped fan that spark. I can still see James Zambus, with his funny walk, boyish smile, and hair always in his face. He motivated and stimulated me to want to learn, to want to reach for the highest standards I could achieve. He challenged me to understand history, religion, science, and art. Mrs. Wilma Jackson's face still appears before me from my English class. She set the spark aglow within me so that I fell in love with words and their meaning. She motivated me to love literature and the classics. When I went on to seminary, Dr. Stewart Newman ignited my theological torch and inspired me to love "the study of God." He introduced me to ideas I never knew existed. He placed in my hand a light of discovery. Later, in graduate school, Bob Soileau taught me that none of us can look through God's glasses and see all of life. We know only partially. None can ever have an absolute grasp on truth, especially theological truth. These people were mentors for me.

When I was a junior in college, I began serving as a pastor of a small rural church. One of the church members died, and I led my first funeral with little knowledge about what I was supposed to do. I had been to few funerals in my life and could not remember what the minister did. Rather than seek help, I functioned out of ignorance. Somehow, someone had communicated to me the wrong idea—that seeking help was a sign of weakness. But the reverse is true. Refusing to seek help is a sign of ignorance. A mentor could offer to younger ministers guidance in developing their spiritual lives, preparing sermons, conducting the administrative functions of a church, dealing with conflict, meeting the pastoral needs of people through hospital visitation and home visitation, conducting funerals and weddings, counseling, and the other endless opportunities one has in ministry. Personal contact with one who has already experienced such a wide variety of ministry could inspire and encourage younger ministers as they begin ministry.[15]

Everyone Needs a Pastor

Every pastor and pastor's spouse needs a pastor. No one can be a pastor to himself or herself or to one's spouse. Every one of us needs someone else to be pastoral to us. I believe that the emptiness, isolation, loneliness, and frustration many ministers experience comes at least partially from the fact that pastors do not have a pastor to whom they can turn.

When I went to serve as pastor of St. Matthews Baptist Church, Louisville, Kentucky, the church had gone through a crisis. Its sanctuary and the major part of its educational unit had burned to the ground, and the church was meeting in the seminary chapel for worship and in the administration building for Sunday school. I came at this time to serve as pastor of the church, and we finished rebuilding the building and assumed a debt of four million dollars. I soon discovered that many of the church members had buried intense feelings of hostility, resentment, depression, and guilt. The Building Committee had guided the church to approve a building design with which many people were uncomfortable. The huge debt was more than the church needed or could bear. Being the new pastor, I soon found myself the target for the buried feelings the people had diverted. They could not get to certain other people, so they aimed their feelings toward me.

At times I often found this experience more than I could bear. Fortunately for me, Dr. Wayne Oates was a member of our congregation. Although I was serving as his pastor, he soon became pastor to me as well. Through my ten years there, he and I often talked. I had an opportunity to lay my burdens on his shoulder. We talked, prayed, thought, reflected, and cried together. He served as a pastor for me, my wife, and my children. I can honestly say that without his pastoral help, it is unlikely that I could have gotten through what I consider my ten hardest years of ministry. I believe that a "pastor-to-pastor" program would enable us to assist ministers in supportive ways that they have seldom been able to find. We could help train and equip individuals to know how to be pastoral to other pastors. We could draw from books, pamphlets, and the knowledge of other pastors and professors, training older ministers in how best to be pastors to others. All of us need someone to listen to us.

Wayne Oates told me a young man once said to him, "Church, church, church, that's all I ever hear." This young man was simply tired of going to church all the time. Dr. Oates said to the man, "I know exactly how you feel. Anybody who has never gotten tired of church has just never been to church much." As ministers, we can get tired of church and our work and complaints and burdens. We need somebody to support us, listen to us, encourage us, and pray for us. We need a pastor. Let us labor to make that a real possibility for our ministries.

Maybe our fragile, broken, often empty pots may be filled with the refreshing water that comes from the encouragement, support, guidance, and affirmation of our fellow ministers. M. Scott Peck in his book *The Different Drum* shares a myth that I have heard in other versions, titled "The Rabbi's Gift."[16] The story is about a monastery that has fallen upon hard times. Once it was a great order, but it reached the point where only five monks were left. It was clearly dying. In the deep woods near the monastery was a little hut that a rabbi, who lived in a nearby town, occasionally used as a hermitage. One day when the abbot realized that the rabbi was in his hut, he decided to visit him and ask his advice on what he might do to save the monastery. The rabbi was cordial to the abbot. When the abbot explained the purpose of his visit, the rabbi could only commiserate with him. "I know how it is, and the spirit has gone out of the people. It is the same in my town; almost no one comes to the synagogue anymore." The abbot and the old rabbi wept together and read parts of the Torah and quietly spoke about deep things.

As the abbot was leaving, they embraced each other and the abbot said, "It has been a wonderful thing that we should meet after all these years, but I have still failed in *my* purpose for coming here. Is there nothing you can tell me, no piece of advice that you can give me that would me save my dying order?" "No, I am sorry," the rabbi responded. "I have no advice to give. The only thing I can tell you is that the Messiah is one of you."

When the abbot returned to the monastery, his fellow monks wanted to know if the rabbi had given any advice. "Not really," he said, "but just as I was leaving he said something cryptic: that the Messiah is one of us. I don't know what he meant." In the following days and weeks, the old monks wondered what the rabbi's words meant.

The Messiah is one of us? Could he have possibly meant one of us here at the monastery, and if that's the case, which one? Do you suppose he meant the abbot? Yes, if he meant anyone, he probably meant the abbot. He has been our leader for more than a generation. On the other hand, he might have meant Brother Thomas. Certainly, Brother Thomas is a holy man. Everyone knows that Thomas is a man of light. Certainly, he could not have meant brother Elred! Elred gets crotchety at times. But come to think of it, even though he is a thorn in peoples' sides, when you look back on it, Elred is virtually always right. Maybe the rabbi did mean brother Elred, but surely not brother Philip. Philip is so passive, a real nobody. But then, almost mysteriously, he has a gift for always being there when you need him. He magically appears by your side. Maybe Philip is the Messiah. Of course, the rabbi didn't mean me. He couldn't possibly have meant me. I am just an ordinary person, but supposing he did? Supposing I am the Messiah? Oh God, not me. I couldn't be that much for you, could I?

As time went by and the monks contemplated this matter, they began to treat each other with extraordinary respect in case, just by chance, one of them might be the Messiah. The people in the village occasionally came to visit the beautiful forest and the monastery, and they had picnics on its lawn, walked along its paths, and sometimes went into the chapel and meditated. Without being conscious of it, visitors soon sensed the aura of extraordinary respect that began to surround the five monks and seemed to radiate out from them and permeate the atmosphere of the place. There was something strangely attractive, even compelling, about it. Hardly knowing why, guests began to come back more frequently to picnic, to play, to pray.

They brought their friends, and their friends brought their friends. Then it happened that some of the younger men came to visit the old monastery and started to talk more and more with the old monks. After a while, one asked if he could join them. Then another asked, and another asked. Within a few years, the monastery had once again becoming a thriving order and, thanks to the rabbi's gift, a vibrant center of light and spirituality in the realm.

Maybe, just maybe, if we respected one another in ministry more and believed in and supported our fellow ministers, then we too might attract others to our calling or "dream." So let it be.

Notes

1. Frederick Buechner, *Telling the Truth as Gospel, Comedy & Fairy Tale* (New York: Harper & Row, 1977) 1–2.

2. Flanders Dunbar, *Mind and Body: Psychosomatic Medicine* (New York: Random House, 1955).

3. Thom Rainer, "Pastors and Forced Termination," *The Christian Post*, 29 October 2011, available at http://sowhatfaith.com/2011/10/29/pastors-forced-termination/ (accessed 12 March 2016).

4. Marcus N. Tanner, "The Backside of the Storm: Clergy Families in Distress," *Family Focus*, Winter 2013, F15.

5. Charles H. Chandler, *Ministering to Ministers Foundation, Inc.*, brochure, 2.

6. Dean R. Hoge and Jacqueline E. Wenger, *Pastors in Transition: Why Clergy Leave Local Church Ministry* (Grand Rapids MI: William B. Eerdmans Publishing Company, 2005) 115.

7. "Pastors Under Fire: A Personal Report," *The Christian Century*, 23 February 1994.

8. Marcus N. Tanner, Jeffrey N. Wherry, and Anisa M. Zvonkovic, "Clergy Who Experienced Trauma as a Result of Forced Termination," *Journal of Religion and Health* (26 January 2012): 1282.

9. David Roach, "Pastoral Termination Common but Avoidable," *Baptist Press*, 5 September 2014, http://www.brnow.org/News/September-2014/Pastoral-termination-common-but-avoidable (accessed 11 April 2016).

10. Ministers who have been terminated or are in the midst of such conflict might want to contact Charles H. Chandler at *Ministering to Ministers*. Solid support and guidance is offered by his group. See Charles H. Chandler,

Executive Director, Ministering to Ministers Foundation, Inc., email: mtm@ mtmfoundation.org; phone: 804-594-2556; website: www.mtmfoundation.org.

11. See Edward B. Bratcher, *The Walk-on-Water Syndrome: Dealing with Professional Hazards in the Ministry* (Waco TX: Word Books, 1984).

12. Karl Barth, article for *The Universal Church in God's Design*, quoted in J. Robert Nelson, *The Realm of Redemption* (Greenwich: The Seabury Press, 1951) 145.

13. Karen Horney, *The Neurotic Personality of Our Time* (New York: W. W. Norton & Company, Inc., 1937) 76–77. See also Rollo May, *The Meaning of Anxiety*, rev. ed. (New York: W. W. Norton, & Company, Inc., 1977) 89.

14. Alfred North Whitehead, *Science and Philosophy* (New York: The Wisdom Library, 1948) 180–81.

15. In a recent issue of *The Christian Century*, there is an article from selected ministers on what mentors have meant to them. See "Mentors," *The Christian Century*, 22 January 2014, 22–29. See also Gil W. Stafford, *When Leadership and Spiritual Direction Meet* (Lanham MD: Rowman & Littlefield, 2014) 64ff. and throughout the book.

16. M. Scott Peck, *The Different Drum* (New York: Simon and Schuster, Inc., 1987) 13–15.

2

Personal Concerns

One of the most significant challenges in ministry for pastors is balancing their time with the endless demands of the church and their personal lives. Pastors can devote so much time to the church's responsibilities that they neglects their health and family. Neglecting your health and ignoring your family are not only personally bad but also spiritually unsound. If pastors cannot care properly for themselves and their families, how can they care for their congregations? If, as Paul states, "you are the temple of the living God" (2 Cor 6:16), neglecting our bodies and our families is indeed a sin. And Paul was bold to declare that the qualifications for a pastor included the question, "If someone does not know how to manage his own household, how can he take care of God's church?" (1 Tim 3: 5). The proper care of our health and families is a spiritual requirement that we dare not ignore.

We will not neglect our churches by caring properly for our own health, families, and other personal matters; we will serve it better. If we do not attend to these matters in our normal daily pursuits, this failure will soon overshadow our ministries. The neglect of physical health and family will soon be apparent even to others. These personal concerns must be placed at the top of our priority lists.

We should also dress appropriately. When I was in seminary, I knew a professor who was so rigid about the "proper" attire of a minister that he cut his grass in his white shirt and tie. That seemed extreme to me even in those days. I know that we live in a day where dress is often more casual even for pastors. I believe, however, that pastors should always dress in an appropriate way for the occasion and not be an embarrassment to their congregations.

Physical Health

We are gifted with one physical body and charged with the responsibility of taking care of it. I believe that we should strive to eat healthy foods. Eating more fruits and vegetables, avoiding fats, and consuming red meat only occasionally are wise approaches. I have been blessed with a wife who loves to prepare meals from scratch. In the summer we eat lots of fresh vegetables, and we often have a meal of only fresh vegetables like lima beans, green beans, corn, and new potatoes along with a salad. In the fall we like to make a meal of cabbage, sweet potatoes, and kale. Substituting fish for red meat is also a good course when possible. I like to snack on fruit and nuts. For dessert, most of the time I eat sugar-free ice cream. We also eat a lot of homemade soups and stews. At holiday times and on other special occasions, we eat more meats and desserts along with our supply of vegetables. This policy works for me and my family, but you need to determine the best approach for you and your family regarding healthy meals and snacks.

Along with eating healthy, I have tried to engage in plenty of physical exercise. When I was younger, I used to jog three miles three times a week. Now, being older and retired, my wife and I get up each morning around six o'clock and walk before breakfast for thirty minutes. I also go to the YMCA at least twice a week to jog on the treadmill for thirty minutes and exercise with the weight machines for another thirty minutes. In the summer I enjoy swimming in the pool, and I try to go about twenty laps. I do yard work like cutting my acre lot by walking behind my self-propelled lawn mower for the exercise rather than using a riding mower. I pull weeds, put down mulch, and do the other necessary responsibilities of caring for my yard. In the fall I rake and blow the leaves under my large oak trees and split logs for my fireplace. In the winter I shovel snow off my driveway and continue my walking and Y exercise programs. Rather than yard work, many ministers prefer golf, racquetball, tennis, basketball, volleyball, or some other sport or activity. Whatever your choice, select an activity that will keep you physically fit. When I was pastor in Bristol, Virginia, I enjoyed the special feature the YMCA added to a gym membership: the weekly massage. On late Friday afternoons, as often as I could, I went to the Y and got a massage. I have found almost nothing as soothing as a massage. I have missed those weekly occurrences. Now I get a massage only on rare opportunities. I certainly recommend them for one's health and peace of mind.

Be sure to get an annual physical exam and see your dentist and eye doctor on a regular basis. I have tried to do this faithfully, and doing so has alerted me to times when I needed to see a specialist for kidney stones or other problems. Several years ago, I discovered that I had type two diabetes and begin to take glipizide medication daily and to watch my diet more carefully. If your doctor prescribes certain medications, then use them faithfully and see your doctor at the appointed times. It is foolish not to take the appropriate medicine that can improve our health.

Spiritual Health

If pastors are to be the spiritual leaders of their congregations, then they must work hard to develop and enrich their personal spiritual growth. How can we lead others effectively in their spiritual growth if we neglect our own? For my "quiet time" or spiritual devotion time, I set aside an uninterrupted, focused period. In my years in the parish ministry, my time for quiet meditation usually came soon after I arrived at my church office. My secretary guarded that time for me and did not interrupt me except for emergencies. Some ministers have their devotion time when they get up in the morning. Others may like to do this before bed. Even when I cannot keep the same time each day, I make it a daily practice to have a personal spiritual time. Now, as a retired pastor, I have a special chair in my quiet, private library that I use for my place of meditation each day.

During my devotional time, I normally read a portion of a chapter in the Bible. My preference is to read through one book at the time instead of skipping around. I also read sections from several devotional books by writers like Leslie Weatherhead, Henri Nouwen, Joyce Rupp, or Richard Foster, along with books of prayers like the ones by John Baillie, William Barclay, John Killinger, or Walter Rauschenbusch. I engage in a brief time of praying, offering my adoration for God's grace, expressing my thanksgiving for all my blessings, offering my confession for my sins, and focusing on prayerful intercession for my family, friends, and church members who have special needs.

Sometimes I focus on "the breath prayer" or "Jesus prayer." For this, I inhale and then exhale and repeat several times a phrase like "Jesus is Lord," "Have mercy on me, Lord Jesus," or simply "Jesus is my peace." I also try to focus inwardly and say one word like "peace" or "grace," repeating it again and again as I strive to center my thoughts on God. Sometimes I practice what the mystics call "ingathering." I simply wait silently before

God without speaking, reading, or praying. I try to be silent before God and listen. In my book, *Lord, I Keep Getting a Busy Signal: Reaching for a Better Spiritual Connection*, I delineate a number of ways to practice our time of meditation with God. We need to practice opening the door and inviting God into the depths of our inner being so we can be warmed and nurtured by God's presence. We need to move out of the noise, the rush of daily activities, and the crowds around us into a quiet place and lay open our souls like freshly plowed soil for the "rain" of God's grace to fall on our lives. Develop your preferred method of spiritual enrichment and practice it faithfully with the confidence that your spiritual growth depends on it.

Family and Time Off

How a pastor treats his family reveals a great deal about his character and priorities. The love and care a pastor exhibits for his family can be a model for family life in the congregation. A minister is deeply blessed when his or her spouse is active and supportive of the pastor's ministry. I know I have been blessed by my wife's support of me and her devotion to serving in churches where I have been pastor. At various times, even with small children, she has sung in the choir, played the piano, and taught Sunday school classes of various ages. In the church we joined after I retired and where I am not the pastor, she has taught several Sunday school classes, served as a deacon and as chair of the Board of Christian Education and Spiritual Growth, and used her gifts in other ways. She has always found her place of personal ministry and been faithful in it.

As someone has observed, "It is hard for a wife to listen to her husband be the 'voice of God' on Sunday and live with him the rest of the week." This applies to husbands who listen to their preaching wives as well. The minister who is overheard yelling at his wife and demeaning her will not be respected by his congregation. Paul's admonition in Ephesians in 5:25, "Husbands, love your wives, just as Christ loved the church and gave himself up for her," is still appropriate for today's pastor. I am forever indebted to my wife, Emily, for her willingness to live in the minister's fishbowl, to be supportive of my ministry, and to share her special gifts through the churches I served as pastor. She shared in the work of ministry while caring for our children, tending to the demands of our household, and preparing healthy meals to keep me and the children strong. When our children were small, I tried to eat breakfast and dinner with them. Emily always served our evening meal at six o'clock, and if I discovered I was going to be late,

I would call and alert her. I rarely had to do that. I also tried to attend my children's school functions and sporting events. To miss them was to communicate that I did not think they were important.

I often was a "workaholic" and did not always take a day off. Looking back, I know that was a mistake, but at the time my ministry seemed to demand that much attention, or at least I thought it did. Some ministers today abuse their time off and take too much time away, soon gaining a reputation for being lazy and inconsiderate of the church. The pastor needs to avoid both extremes. I never gave up my vacation time with my family. Throughout most of my ministry, I usually took the month of August off, since I got that much vacation. We always did something together as a family—a beach or mountain trip, a visit with relatives, or a journey to a special place we all enjoyed. That lengthy period was necessary for me to recoup my strength and get energy to carry on, and it also kept our family bond strong. But I also never abused my vacation privileges. I made sure the church was well cared for in my absence and was available for emergencies.

Personal Finances

Too many ministers have a reputation for managing their financial affairs poorly. This is likely a reflection of the times when ministers were paid very small salaries. When I was in graduate school and Emily taught public school, our income was so small and our expenses so large that we were barely able to get by. During our early years in ministry, our income was still small, and we had to budget our spending carefully.

From the beginning, we always practiced tithing. I did not believe that I could challenge my congregation to give if I did not give. We also did not purchase furniture and other things we could not pay for or afford. We added our furniture slowly, bought from secondhand stores, and used furniture passed down from our family. One of my deacons at the Bristol church told me about a former pastor who had gone into debt in the city. Some of the merchants complained to several of the businessmen in the church. They went to the pastor, talked to him about the matter, helped him put a budget together to pay off his debts, and showed him how to live within it. He went on to be a great pastor and learned a valuable lesson from his laity. Every pastor needs to try to live within his budget. Pay your bills on time, and do not put more on a credit card than you can afford to pay back each month.

Retirement

In my early years of ministry, my churches put a small amount in my retirement fund, something like $500 a year. I did not add anything else. I first started adding a reasonable amount into my retirement account when I went to teach at the seminary and learned that they would match up to 10 percent of my income. Granted, my seminary salary was low, but we put in our 10 percent and the seminary put in their 10 percent. Later in my other churches where I served as pastor, I followed the same practice. There is no question of the real difference this has made in my retirement account. I encourage every pastor, as difficult as it may be at times, to start as early as you can and put 10 percent of your income into your retirement fund. Try to get your church to match it or come as close as they can to that percentage. Of course, this means living off only 80 percent of your salary. As hard as it may be, the effect on what you have in retirement later will be worth the present sacrifice.

In your retirement years, if you desire, you may have the opportunity to be an interim pastor. I have had the privilege of serving in about a half dozen interim pastorates since retirement. The extra income has helped, and it has also been a blessing to continue in a limited engagement of ministry. I have found all of the interims rewarding and fulfilling, and my wife again has been supportive of my engaging in this kind of ministry at this stage in our life. I still try to allot time for us to do all the other things we still want to do to find fulfillment. My children sometimes say I am "flunking retirement," but I see it as another chapter in my ongoing ministry. If you are healthy and still enjoying preaching and serving as a pastor, then find some place to continue using your gifts.

Friendships

Like everyone, pastors and their families need to have friends while they are part of a church family. Some church officials have discouraged pastors and their spouses from having friends in the church where one of them serves as pastor. There are, of course, dangers—like favoring your friends by placing them on strategic committees or boards—but if caution is taken, I believe life will be happier for the pastor who has solid friends in the church. In churches where I had a ministerial staff, fellow ministers were often among my closest friends. Several laypersons who were close to my age and my wife's age and had children near our children's age often took the initiative to become our close friends, and they have continued to be our friends years after we left the church. After evening worship in one of my churches, several families often shared pizza together and shared other times in fellowship with us. Pastors should never parade their friendships or use them to manipulate the political structure of the church to get their way. But, if discretion is used, I believe that pastors and their families can have healthy friendships with carefully selected persons in their congregations.

Morality

It would seem like a "no-brainer" to declare that a pastor should always exhibit the highest ethical and moral character possible. But too many headlines in newspapers and on TV have shown how spiritual leaders succumb to moral temptations. I believe pastors need to guard themselves carefully to avoid positions that might provide an occasion for temptation or misunderstanding. For example, do not go alone at night to counsel a person of the opposite sex without another person present. Avoid going to a home alone to visit with a person who is young or possibly confined to a bedroom without others present. Do not dress in a way that others might consider provocative or inappropriate for the occasion.

Billy Graham never went into a hotel room at night when he was away on a crusade without having staff check out the room to make certain that no one was present trying to create an unpleasant or controversial situation for him. Be ethical in your behavior, speech, finances, taxes, and in all of your living, and you will bring honor to the kingdom's work. I love the line from Chaucer's *Canterbury Tales* where he mentions a kindly parson who traveled on the journey. He described him as one "who was a scholar, wise and true. He lived himself the Golden Rule he taught." What better observation about a pastor could be made? As pastors, we are challenged to live and attest by our words and actions that we are indeed above reproach.

Sabbatical Leave

I would encourage pastors to try to negotiate a sabbatical leave with their churches. This, of course, is best done when you are called to the church, but it is not impossible to contract later. When I came as pastor of St. Matthews in Louisville, Kentucky, the church had a policy that staff members could receive a sabbatical leave of three months after seven years of service in the church. Salary was paid, and a small stipend was also given during this time. This three-month time was one of the most rewarding and spiritually and physically satisfying experiences I have ever had. I came back rejuvenated and refreshed and excited to continue my ministry.

I began my sabbatical with a brief retreat at the Abbey of Gethsemani, where I spent the time in a period of silent meditation and prayer. Following this, Emily and I spent a month at Oxford, England. We spent this time studying at Regent's Park (a Baptist college at Oxford); visiting various colleges, museums, and shops; and worshiping almost daily in Evensong at Christ's Church Cathedral and on Sundays at the New Road Baptist Church, the University Church, Magdalem College Chapel, and others. We took side trips to Cambridge, Bath, London, Stratford upon Avon, the Cotswolds, and the Lake District. From England we went by train through the lovely countrysides to St. Andrews, Scotland, where we spent a week at the Sumer School of Theology at St. Mary's College at St. Andrews University. Later we visited Edinburgh University, and I did research on the papers of John Baillie, who had been the principal and professor of theology for many years at New College, and on whom I had written my doctoral thesis about his concept of religious knowledge.

I concluded my sabbatical with a week at a conference of the Alban Institute in Richmond, Virginia, on clergy's self-assessment led by Roy Oswald. We completed the away time with all our family and grandchildren as we gathered for the celebration of my parents' sixtieth wedding anniversary in Lynchburg, Virginia. I have shared these various details to indicate the wide possibilities one might take in using allotted sabbatical time. You can obviously plan your own sabbatical. It can offer a pastor a great time of rest, recreation, renewal, and education.

Emotional Burnout

If pastors pours themselves into the ministry over a long haul, there is the danger of emotional burnout. After all, the job of pastor is not a nine-to-five occupation but can sometimes demand an eighteen-hour day that requires working seven days a week. The heavy demands and emotional struggles with church members during times of conflicts, illness, grief, and tragedy can exert a heavy toil on a pastor's mental and emotional state. For some, this can result in burnout, where pastors feel that they no longer have the energy or desire to function in their responsibilities. This causes some ministers to leave the ministry altogether.

Let me offer suggestions that have been helpful to me to avoid burnout. Remember that no pastor can fulfill every endless demand. Do the best you can to set your priorities, focusing on the essentials for your ministry and avoiding giving time and energy to matters of lesser importance. Challenge and equip your laity to assume their rightful place in the ministry of the congregation's tasks. Try to focus your efforts on the main reason you chose to be in ministry in the first place, like preaching and pastoral care. Take time for a break or to play. All work and no play or time off or vacation will make Jack or Jane a dull person—and also a worn-out and frustrated one. As much as one may love ministry, we all get weary. If anyone has never gotten tired of church work, then that person has never been very involved in church work.

Learn to focus the unresolved anger created by someone or some activity in your church. Don't push it inward and keep it buried; instead, find a person with whom you can share it or even curse about it freely. As I wrote earlier, "Brer Rabbit used to say, 'We all need a cussing place.'" I know a pastor who used to write the names of troublesome people in his church on his golf balls, and he took out some of his frustrations by hitting the balls as hard and as far as he could on the fairway. It was therapeutic for him. If you don't have a friend with whom you can share your struggles, then a support group might be another opportunity for relief. Use your own gifts to the best of your ability, and do not try to be Reverend Super Star or some pastor who may have gifts that are different from yours. The best gift you can offer your church is the gift of yourself dedicated to the service of Christ. Acknowledge your humanity and limitations and solicit the support and encouragement of the laity in your congregation. I believe they will want to offer you that support.

3

The Congregation at Worship

Worship is one of the central focuses of a pastor's ministry. Each worship service demands time, planning, preparation and, when there is a staff, working with others. The pastor often works closely with a minister of music or worship committee in planning the service of worship and deciding what roles other ministers on staff will have during the service. Some of this planning requires looking ahead at the calendar and the particular emphasis for each Sunday. If a church follows the Lectionary, the focus will already be clear in a general sense, but the particulars must still be determined. If a church does not follow the Lectionary, then the themes and Scriptures for the various Sundays must be chosen ahead of time to allow for preparation.

Archaeologists tell us that they find three basic things in every civilization discovered through ancient ruins: they find an altar, a prison, and a cemetery. People worship. People sin. And people die. In some way, all civilizations have found that worship is supposed to be central to their way of life. But it would seem that as generations pass, other things become more significant, more important, and more to the front of people's lives than worship.

A small girl came to her mother one day and said, "Mother, you know the vase that has been passed on from one generation to the other?" The mother said, "Oh yes, I know. It is one of my prized possessions." "Well, this new generation has dropped it." Where is worship in the lives of many folks? They seemed to have dropped it. Somehow God seems missing, unimportant, or unrelated to their lives. Ministers have the responsibility of affirming the importance of worship in the church's life and guiding the congregation in meaningful worship. "In worship we take in the outpouring of God's creative and redemptive love," Geoffrey Wainwright exclaims, "and we offer in return our thanks and supplications."[1]

Worship Planning

Most worship services involve several elements, such as the call to worship, invocation, offertory prayer, pastoral prayer, benediction, hymns, anthem and choral responses, prelude, postlude, offertory, Scripture passages, sermon, and sometimes baptisms or Communion. The sermon should provide the theme for the whole service, and the other parts should reflect that theme in some way. The pastor needs to work closely with the music minister or other worship planners. Numerous helps for worship planning are available in lectionaries, hymnals, worship resource books, and many online websites. Though church services certainly vary, a sample worship order might look like the following:

Welcome and Announcements
Prelude
Call to Worship
Invocation and Lord's Prayer
Hymn
Old Testament Reading
Pastoral Prayer
Passing of the Peace
Hymn
Offertory Prayer
Offertory
Doxology
Gospel Lesson
Anthem
Sermon
Hymn
Benediction
Postlude

Worship: A Vital Part of One's Life

Why do we worship? What is the reason for this weekly service where we gather together as believers? When we read the Bible, we discover that the writers did not spend much time trying to argue why people should worship. They simply assumed that those who loved God would worship God. They assumed that those who had a relationship with God would come, bow down, and worship before God, because they saw it as a part of their very being and existence.

Jesus Christ Is Our Pathway to God's Presence

The writer of the book of Hebrews reminds us that we gather to worship because of what Christ has done for us. In ancient Israel, when the people went to the temple to worship, a veil separated them from the holy of holies, the place that held the presence of God. The high priest was allowed to enter the holy of holies only once a year. The Scriptures tell us that when Jesus Christ died, the temple veil was rent, torn in two, so that people were able to have direct access to God. T. H. Robinson writes, "The path to the inner heart of God is now open."[2] Through Jesus Christ, we can enter directly and boldly into the presence of God. This is the strong declaration of the writer of Hebrews, especially in the tenth chapter.

He tells us that Jesus Christ is our high priest. We do not need other priests. He is not only the high priest but also the offering to God. He is both the sacrifice and the one who opens the way to God. He literally is the way. He has bridged the gap that separated men and women from God and brought us directly into the presence of God. He has overcome the between-ness. In ancient times, every sacrifice required the sprinkling of blood, but the writer tells us here that we are now cleansed through the blood of Jesus Christ. Now we can come directly and immediately into the presence of God and worship him. Every Sunday, then, is an Easter celebration. The early Christians made a bold and dramatic move from observing the Sabbath on Saturday to celebrating Sunday, the Resurrection Day of Christ, as the new day of worshiping God. The Christians came boldly into the very presence of God.

God Is the Central Focus of Our Worship

Pastor needs to teach their congregations that we seek to approach the presence of God, declaring that God is at the center of our worship. We adore God. God is the One who has great majesty and power. God is the One who is high and lifted up—the exalted One. We gather not so much to study God as to be dazzled by God's presence. We come in a sense of awe. Through Scripture, prayer, hymns, and preaching, we are confronted by the majesty and righteousness of God. Sometimes if we enter into a dark room and someone else is there, we say to them, "Switch on the light so I can see." Coming to worship is an attempt to switch on the light so that we can see the presence of God among us. The pastor strives to remind the congregation that God is the central focus of our worship.

The word "worship" comes from an ancient Anglo-Saxon word that means "worthship." Worship is ascribing worth to someone or something. We have ascribed great worth to God as the One who is worthy of our highest worship. The Hebrew word for worship means "to bow down or prostrate oneself before God." The Greek word for worship literally means "to kiss towards." It is bowing with a sense of reverence and affection.

Worship Is Something We Do for God

As we gather to worship in the name of God, the pastor guides the congregation to remember that worship is not so much something God does for us as something we do for God. We raise the wrong question if we ask somebody, "Did you get anything from the worship service?" We do not *get* something from worship. We are supposed to *give* something. We come to glorify God not to edify ourselves. We gather to give something to God—our praise and adoration. We come before God because of what God has done for us. We have to remind our people that we worship even when we do not feel like it. We do not worship only when we are in the mood for it.

We worship because it is something worthy of doing for the One to whom we direct our allegiance and our lives. We do not pay our rent only when we feel like it; we do not make our automobile payment only when we feel like it. We do not make our house payment or buy groceries only when we feel like it. We must do all these things because they are a part of life. We come to worship and we bow before God because God is the One worthy of our praise. So let us remind our people that we need to worship God and forget the roast in the oven for a while or the buffet line at our favorite place to eat out. Let us forget the bills, forget the business problems, forget the economic and political problems, and come worship God. Let us focus on God. In these moments, let us guide the congregation to give God our lives and attention. Let our worship pour forth with enthusiasm and radiance as we sense the power of God's presence among us.

Worship Is a Time of Remembering

The pastor is charged with the responsibility of helping the congregation remember that worship is also a recalling of memories. It is like looking through a scrapbook or a picture album and reminiscing. It takes us back to the place of remembrance where we first met God. Worship is a time of going back through the pages of our lives in the church. It is linking our lives with Abraham, Isaac, and Jacob. It is joining with the generations of Matthew, Mark, and Paul. It is a time of recalling memories where others have met God and where we have met God. It is remembering times when we have sung hymns and praised God.

Worship is not just entertainment. One of the great corruptions of the worship of our time has come from television evangelism, which often equates worship with entertainment. Worship from this perspective focuses primarily on whether it makes us feel good. To these folks, worship is sentimental, entertaining, or clever.

I recall watching a couple of young people singing. They sang about the love of God, but they spent the whole time looking adoringly into each other's eyes. The young man and woman seemed more interested in each other than they were in adoring God. Too many churches have brought the show-business approach to worship and confused entertainment with worship. Although Donald Hustad, renowned music and worship specialist, knows that churches need changes in worship because recent past practices have been inadequate, he nevertheless is "convinced that many contemporary approaches to change have been superficial at best and destructive at worst."[3] In her book *Reaching Out without Dumbing Down,* Marva Dawn has challenged churches to consider whether they "have thought thoroughly about worship and culture to function effectively in contemporary society without 'dumbing down' that essential character formation."[4] The church should be open to meaningful change that will enhance worship, but let us always approach worship with a sense of the awesomeness of the holy God of the universe and bow before that divine presence. Let us sense God's majesty and presence. Let us approach God with an awareness of the radiance and power of who God is, and whether we are entertained or not, let us remember that worship is something we do for God.

Order in Worship

As we approach God in worship, let us do it with order. Paul admonishes the Corinthians, "Let all things be done decently and in order" (1 Cor

14:40). I am a Baptist, and we are not always noted for our great order in worship. Sometimes we are sloppy in our congregational worship. I hope that, regardless of our denomination, we can go back to the ancient Scriptures and learn what authentic worship is. The pastor should direct us to be open to sense the breath of God blowing upon us. Even as we seek to follow structure and order, let us not be confined to rigid molds of worship. God's creativity can warm the coals of our spirits and bring new fire into our lives as our worship is ignited by the power of God's presence among us.

As pastors, we need to have order but not rigidity in our worship. Direction and care are important for corporate worship. Let us be experimental, probe new avenues and opportunities, and make minor changes here and there—all of which help us avoid the sentiment "But we've always done it this way." We may study to see how others have worshiped God so we might discover new ways to sense the power of God's presence as we worship. James White notes, "Apparently our Creator relishes diversity; we are created with an enormous variety of gifts. The whole point of Protestant worship is that these various gifts be used in the praise of their Creator."[5]

Much dialogue and many arguments have focused on contemporary worship. Some feel it is the only way we can worship today, while others believe it is a distortion of authentic worship. Some recommend a combination of traditional and contemporary styles in "blended" worship. Still others encourage each congregation to focus on the tradition that best represents its culture and tradition.[6] My advice is to think carefully and prayerfully about the approach that brings your congregation closest to God. Here are some elements to consider as you plan your worship service.

Prepare for Worship

Pastors should guide their congregations in preparation for worship. I know it is hard to prepare. We often stay out too late on Saturday night and do not get enough sleep. We then come rushing into the service. For Jewish people, the Sabbath begins on Friday night, and they use that time to prepare for the next day's worship. Maybe we could lean on their tradition and use our Saturday evenings to become more prepared.

Most of our people, however, walk into the service of worship without any preparation or prior thought. They expect the ministers, choir, or praise leaders to make worship happen for them. When it does not, they often say, "That was not a good service." Everyone who gathers to worship has a part in preparation. As they arrive to the service of worship, encourage them to prepare to put themselves in tune with God. It is good for the congregation to talk and converse with friends, but have a clear way to begin the service: instrumental music, a welcome from the pulpit, or something similar. Encourage everyone to begin a time of meditation. Help them use that time to focus their thoughts on God and prepare for God's presence among them.

Some of us think worship is similar to newspaper ads: "Lose 30 pounds in 30 days" or "Learn to speak French in 30 days." Do you really believe those? I hope you do not, because it takes more time, preparation, and discipline to learn a language or to lose weight. In the same way, we need to encourage our people to give some time and discipline to preparing themselves for worship.

Participate in Worship

Pastors should call their people to participate in worship through every element of the service, whether it is singing hymns, offering the call to worship, praying, reading litanies, repeating affirmations, or actively listening to the sermon. Every moment in worship should call for us to participate in what is happening. Danish theologian Søren Kierkegaard once said that people often think the preacher and the choir are the chief actors in worship who stage a performance for those in the congregation. But that is not true. All of us are involved in worship. God is the chief actor as God meets us in worship. The ministers, the choir, or the praise leaders are merely the prompters who point us toward God so that each of us can sense the power of God's presence among us.

In Hebrews 10:19-39, the writer reminds us to approach God and then go forth with a sense of our beliefs incorporated into our lives so that those beliefs can direct us in how to live. Our beliefs give direction and meaning for our lives. Our origin and destiny are in God, and we have a deep hunger within that pulls us back to the God who made us. When people cut themselves off from worship, they begin to sever the tie that enables them to have focus, direction, and meaning in life. As the pastor, encourage your congregation to climb the hill of worship so they can capture a greater glimpse of how to live once they are enriched by the presence and power of God.

Recognize the Holiness of God

Pastors should guide their congregations to gather for worship with a sense of awareness that we come before the holiness of God. Isaiah spoke about the God he worshiped in the temple, who was high and lifted up (Isa 6). We should never merely stumble into the presence of God on Sunday; instead, we should come with the awareness that we are approaching the presence of the holy God of the universe.

In his worship of God, Isaiah experienced a presence whose robe hem filled the great temple. Isaiah's sense of God's height and majesty were almost overwhelming. Isaiah's faith became alive for him in this experience of worship. He would have understood the small book written by J. B. Phillips with the title, *Your God Is Too Small.* God is the great God before whom we fall down and exclaim, "Holy, holy, holy is your name." God is the Lord of hosts. As pastors, we exclaim, "God is here in this place of worship. Do not miss God. God is here! Bow before God in worship." As Tom Long reminds us, "Worshiping God is not simply a good thing to do; it is a necessary thing to do to be human."[7]

Praise God

Pastors should remind worshipers that we gather also with a sense of praise on our lips. An instrument like an organ or piano calls us to praise God for what God has done and to affirm God's good gifts to us. We praise God when things have gone well and when things have gone poorly. We praise God with assurance, both in the time of birth and in the time of death: "Blessed be the name of the Lord." We lift up our voices and sing with a sense of enthusiasm and joy. Not to sing is to sin against the body of the congregation, because it is part of what we do in unity together to express our joy unto God. We can all make a joyful noise. "The significance of music in culture," Hustad has observed, "is a gift of God which both glorifies God and edifies human beings."[8] The Scriptures do not say that we all have to sing well, but at the great sound of the organ or piano or other musical instruments, we should let praise go forth among us as we lift our voices to God. "In healthy congregations worship is corporate and dynamic, stirring and inspiring, helpful and hopeful," Kennon Callahan declares. "It is joy and wonder, grace and peace. Through it people discover help, hope and home."[9]

C. S. Lewis once commented that he got tired of people always saying that we should praise God. He could not understand it. He wondered if God were the great egotist who had to have people always talking about him. Gradually he began to realize that it was not a question of egotism; if you loved somebody, you *wanted* to express that love to them.[10] Sports enthusiasts want to express their feelings when the team scores a touchdown or makes a basket. Artist must express their talent on the canvas. If we genuinely love God, praise will come forth. It is a part of our very being.

Pray and Confess

Pastors should guide their people to worship God with a sense of prayer and confession. Notice that when Isaiah came into the holy presence of God, he was immediately made aware of his sinfulness (Isa 6). We come before God as people saved by God's grace, aware that we are still sinners. We come to confess our sins. Isaiah experienced the purging and cleansing power that came from the presence of God through the symbol of the hot coal on his lips. Forgiveness of sins is not easy. Forgiveness itself is sometimes painful as well as cleansing. We come to God to confess our sins and experience God's forgiveness as we gather together.

I would encourage pastors to give their worshipers a time in which they can wrap themselves in the mantle of silence. Pastors can incorporate moments of silence into the service so the congregation has an opportunity to confess sins and to experience the power of God during worship together.

Proclaim

Pastors should remind the congregation that we worship God through proclamation. We gather in worship knowing that in this place, God's word will go forth through song, prayers, preaching, the reading of the Scriptures, and silence. God's word will also be proclaimed among us so that God's spirit can come among us, challenging our styles of living and our understanding of life and lifting us up to be more than we are. Jesus, the Word of God, walks through the written and proclaimed word to confront us with our sins and the need to respond to God's grace. God's word will be proclaimed, "Thus says the Lord," as we seek to direct our lives in God's way.

Give an Offering

Pastors should remind the congregation that we worship God with an offering. As the psalmist says, "Bring an offering and come into my courts" (Ps 96:8). Does God need our money? No. God does not need it. But we remind our people that our money and our possessions are symbolic of who and what we are. We bring these gifts into the presence of God because they are signs of our commitment. We give a bit of ourselves through our money and possessions and declare through our giving that materialism is not our chief end. As pastors, let us seek to help our people use their material possessions in ways to glorify God. And let us give as well.

Worship and Daily Living Linked Together

As pastor, I affirm that worship reminds us of the high values in life. It calls us to set our priorities right and to put first things first. As we worship together, we get a renewed focus on what should have first place in our lives. Worship reminds us of the most important values and ideals to which we should give our highest allegiance. God is worthy of my praise, and my ethical living follows this adoration. When we worship God, unworthy motives should be far from our desire.

When the *Titanic* was sinking, a wealthy woman chose not to take her diamonds with her into the lifeboat, but she took a bag of oranges instead. Isn't it strange that when a crisis comes, we begin to get our priorities right? Worship directs us to examine our spiritual luggage. Worship calls us together so that we can get our values and priorities in the best order. And then we go into the world to live the kind of life that reflects that we have been in the presence of God.

We need to remind our people that after we have worshiped, we should then encourage one another. "Let us take heart with one another, let us support one another" (cf. Gal 6:1-10). Worship is not an isolated event. Worship is not just for ourselves; we gather to share in each other's lives. Worship and daily living are tied together. Our living is bound up with our worship, and our worship is striving to link God with our daily walk. We leave the sacred place of worship to go into the world and express concern for all of life.

If it is real, our worship invades our business, home, and recreation—our entire lives. People must not see us gathering to worship on Sunday and then living an entirely different kind of life that denies that act the rest of the week. When we have worshiped God, that worship ought to break into all of our being, and we must encourage one another to live the kind of life that Christ would have us live as God's people in the world.

John Sherrill wrote about his experience when he decided to join his church choir. He had not been part of a choir for a long time, and, as he began to sing, he became aware that he was not producing pleasing tones. Some of us do not have to join the choir to realize that! In the choir, John was sitting next to Bill Brogan, a man with a tremendous bass voice. Singing beside Bill helped John's singing tremendously, and after choir practice he told Bill how much his singing had meant to him. Bill said, "If that helped, I'll show you something even better next week."

Next week when they gathered for choir practice, Bill whispered to John, "Lean into me." "What?" John said. "Put your weight on me," Bill said. John leaned back until his shoulder blade was resting against Bill's chest. He could feel the resonance of the music coming through Bill's body penetrating his own, and John was amazed by the difference that experience made in his own ability to sing.

Let us encourage our people to lean into each other. In a worshiping community, we do not try to go it alone; we lean on each other. We draw strength from each other and begin to understand what it means to be the body of Christ. We are Christ's people who draw strength and encouragement from one another. Individually and together, we lean into the strength we draw from God.

A great symbol for worship might be Jacob's ladder. It extended up into heaven and then the angels descended (Gen 28). This ladder, as it goes upward, might symbolize our message to God: our prayers, praise, and offerings. Horton Davies says that the descending angels might symbolize God's messages in worship.[11] Let us approach God through the power of what Jesus Christ has done for us. May our worship be so powerful and real that we can go forth into the world and live differently because we have worshiped together.

Notes

1. Geoffrey Wainwright, *Doxology: The Praise of God in Worship, Doctrine, and Life* (New York: Oxford University Press, 1980) 462.

2. Theodore H. Robinson, *The Epistle to the Hebrews,* The Moffatt New Testament Commentary (New York: Harper and Brothers, n.d.) 142.

3. Donald P. Hustad, *True Worship: Reclaiming the Wonder & Majesty* (Carol Stream IL: Hope Publishing Co., 1998) 219.

4. Marva J. Dawn, *Reaching Out without Dumbing Down* (Grand Rapids MI: William B. Eerdmans Publishing Co., 1995) 4.

5. James F. White, *Protestant Worship: Traditions in Transition* (Louisville KY: Westminster/John Knox Press, 1989) 216.

6. I offer a summary of Don Hustad's evaluation of worship, entertainment, and contemporary worship in my chapter on his contribution to our appreciation of worship without "dumbing it down." See William Powell Tuck, "Donald Paul Hustad: Music and Worship Celebrant," *Modern Shapers of Baptist Thought*

in America (Richmond VA: Center for Baptist Heritage & Studies, 2012) 285–87. Marva Dawn's book, *Reaching Out without Dumbing Down,* is also a helpful resource in this discussion.

7. Thomas G. Long, *Beyond the Worship Wars: Building Vital and Faithful Worship* (New York: The Alban Institute, 2001) 17.

8. Donald P. Hustad, *Jubilate II: Church Music in Worship and Renewal* (Carol Stream IL: Hope Publishing Co., 1993) 20.

9. Kennon L. Callahan, *Dynamic Worship: Mission, Grace, Praise, and Power* (San Francisco: HarperSanFrancisco, 1994) ix.

10. See C. S. Lewis, *Reflections on the Psalms* (New York: Harcourt, Bruce and Company, 1958) 90.

11. Horton Davies, *Christian Worship: Its History and Meaning* (New York: Abingdon Press, 1957) 86.

4

Following the Christian Calendar

Worship, I am convinced, is the most important act in which the church engages. All other ministries flow out of our worship of God. Our senses of mission, evangelism, spiritual growth, and service arise from our having first met God in worship. No one can share with others a God whom he or she has not experienced. Because of its permanent importance in the life of the church, I do not want to lead my congregation in an act of worship that is poorly or thoughtlessly planned. I am aware that some churches prefer an informal or unstructured pattern of worship, while others lean toward a more formal or structured order. Although there are occasions where I desire an informal setting, for the most part, and especially for the Sunday morning hour, I prefer the more orderly approach. The Christian calendar has provided guidelines for me in making worship more organized and meaningful.

Celebrating the Resurrection

When the church gathers each Sunday on the first day of the week, it is celebrating the resurrection of Christ. It was a radical move on the part of early Jewish Christians to change from worshiping on the Sabbath to worshiping on the "Lord's Day." The Christian calendar began with that remarkable change. Jewish Christians already had celebrative events like the Passover and Pentecost to help shape their memory about God's providence and presence. Drawing on these and other festive days, early Christians began to formulate their own calendar of special days to commemorate what God had done through Christ and his church. For them and other Christians down through the centuries, the Christian calendar became a group of something like birthday or anniversary celebrations. It was a vivid reminder of the special days in the church year based on the life and ministry of Christ.

The Pattern of the Christian Year

Christian churches that follow the Christian Year normally divide the calendar into Advent, Christmastide, Epiphany, Lent, Holy Week, Eastertide, and Pentecost. Some traditions have added Kingdomtide, which follows Pentecost. Christians, with only a few exceptions like the Seventh Day Baptists, observe Sunday as the "Lord's Day." The early church chose Sunday as the first day in the Christian Year. Most Baptists and other major denominations celebrate Christmas and Easter. Although many Baptists do not celebrate the other major festivals as a normal part of the church year, we would certainly affirm the basic doctrines they proclaim.

The Meanings of the Various Festivals

A brief explanation of the meanings of these festivals on the Christian calendar might be helpful.

Advent, Christmastide, and Epiphany

Advent is observed for the four Sundays prior to Christmas. The word *Advent* means "coming" or "arrival." The emphasis is on expectancy and preparation for the coming of Christ. Attention is directed both to the preparation for the first coming of Christ and for his final coming as Judge. Christmastide is a twelve-day celebration of the birth of Christ, beginning on Christmas Eve and lasting until January 5. It includes one or two Sundays, depending on which day of the week is Christmas. It is primarily a celebration of God's incarnation. *Epiphany*, which means "appearance" or "manifestation," begins with the day of Epiphany (January 6) and lasts until Ash Wednesday. Epiphany may include four to eight Sundays, depending on the date of Easter. This season notes the giving of God's revelation of God's self to all people. Celebrated during this time are the coming of the wise men, the baptism of Jesus, and the first miracle of Jesus at the wedding feast at Cana.

Lent

Lent is a period of forty weekdays and six Sundays; it begins on Ash Wednesday and concludes on the Saturday before Easter. During this season, the church proclaims and remembers the suffering and atoning death of Christ. The church began observing Lent probably in the second century in commemoration of the forty hours Jesus was in the grave. Later, the church included in this period references to the forty days Jesus spent in the wilderness, the forty days Moses was on the mountain in God's presence, and the forty years the children of Israel wandered in the wilderness. During the early part of Lent, the focus is on the Christian's need for sorrow and penitence as he or she reflects on personal sins and on the costly nature of Christ's death. Holy Week is the week from Palm Sunday through Easter Eve. Special attention is given in this week to Palm Sunday (the triumphal entry of Jesus into Jerusalem); Maundy Thursday (the last meal Jesus had with his disciples in the upper room before he was crucified on Friday; the word *Maundy* comes from a Latin word meaning "command"); and Good Friday (the day of Jesus' crucifixion).

Eastertide

Eastertide was the earliest period of celebration on the Christian calendar. The resurrection of Christ was the event that ushered in the church's true beginning. Therefore, it is the most important festival on the church calendar. In AD 325, the Council of Nicaea set the date of Easter to be on the Sunday that follows the first full moon on or after March 21. Beginning with Easter, this festival continues for a fifty-day period with seven Sundays. Ascension Day is celebrated forty days after Easter in order to affirm that the risen Christ is Lord of all times and places.

Pentecost and Kingdomtide

Pentecost is the festival that commemorates the coming of the Holy Spirit upon the church. The first Sunday of Pentecost is often called Whitsunday because of the white garments the catechumens often wore in the early church when they were baptized. This season begins on the seventh Sunday after Easter and continues until Advent. Only recently have some Protestant groups begun to celebrate Kingdomtide. If this season is observed, it begins on the last Sunday in August and concludes with the beginning of Advent. This season focuses on the continuous presence of Christ and the Christian's responsibility to serve in Christ's kingdom. Most of the churches that follow the Christian calendar continue to observe Pentecost, which may last for as long as twenty-nine Sundays. The Sunday after Pentecost is normally called Trinity Sunday, when the chief emphasis is on God's people living under the guidance of God's Spirit.

Some Christian churches celebrate several special days in addition to those already mentioned, but these vary greatly. Most people consider the Christian calendar to be primarily the special seasons mentioned above.

Flexibility with the Calendar

As a pastor, I never tried to lead any of my congregations to follow the entire Christian calendar all the time. The names of some festivals would have little meaning to many because of the unfamiliar tradition. On the most well-known and popular occasions, such as Advent, Easter, and Maundy Thursday, I have announced the festival and indicated why we followed that particular order. But I have often followed the Christian calendar in my congregation without directly referring to a festival. The calendar has served as a guide to assist me in my overall planning and has often remained in the background.

Benefits of Following the Christian Calendar

Worship and Preaching Planning

I have found that whether I follow the Christian calendar directly or indi-rectly, it offers a vast resource for worship planning. Following the Christian calendar has enabled me to deal with the whole gospel rather than only parts of it. The Christian calendar offers a "balanced diet" in its emphasis throughout the year and helps preachers avoid gaps in their preaching and worship themes. It moves from the birth of Christ through his life, teach-ings, death, and resurrection and to the gift of the Holy Spirit upon the church and its mission in the world. Too many preachers follow whatever suits their tastes or interests and not necessarily what is the "full gospel." I am convinced that by following the Christian calendar, I have been guided to declare more carefully the whole counsel of God.

If preachers are willing to follow the lectionary for the Christian year, they will be led to deal with biblical passages that they otherwise might avoid. The lectionary is simply a list of Scripture lessons that are assigned to be helpful on a particular Sunday within the Christian calendar. Most lectionaries provide a three-year cycle of readings. Old Testament and New Testament lessons are given. I have never followed this approach dogmatically, but it does offer a valuable guide for the preacher. Ministers should either follow a guide like this or develop their own carefully structured plan for sharing the central Christian seasons with their people. Otherwise we will preach mostly on our favorite themes or ride our special theological hobbyhorses. We will be like the preacher of whom it was said, "It didn't make any difference where he began preaching in the Bible—Genesis, Jeremiah, or Revelation—he always ended up talking about baptism."

I try to plan my worship and preaching emphasis months in advance with the central themes of the Christian calendar before me. This is not only a good discipline for me but also enables my minister of music, worship committee, and any other staff or layperson involved in worship to know well ahead of time the major goals for those services so that they, too, can do their planning. I believe that our worship of God demands careful thought and preparation. We are seeking to lead our people in worship before the Holy God of the universe, and I want to offer my best efforts.

A Teaching Tool

The use of the Christian calendar in worship is also a good teaching tool. The calendar focuses on the central doctrines of our faith: the birth, incarnation, life, teachings, death, resurrection, and ascension of Christ; the gift of the Holy Spirit; and the mission of the church in the world. Using the calendar as a guideline, one will have the opportunity to preach doctrinal sermons on the great Christian themes of our faith. It has provided me with a guide to teaching the great doctrines on which we stand. This emphasis in preaching will keep pastors on the foundational path that is closest to the heartbeat of the early Christian church. Through this kind of preaching, we can more readily share the good news of God's mighty acts of love, grace, redemption, and forgiveness and focus less on condemnation, trite moralism, civil religion, or personal preferences. The theological thrust of the Christian calendar calls us back to examine the roots of our faith. If our people are not taught the basics, they cannot grow.

An Alternative to the Civic Calendar

If we follow the Christian calendar and focus on the great Christian themes, we will not so easily fall into the trap of using a civic or promotional calendar as our basic worship guide. Mother's Day, Labor Day, the Fourth of July, and even some of the denominational emphases are important, but they are not necessarily religious holidays. On occasion, the preacher can preach on some of the holidays or special days with a meaningful sermon.[1] But I have often seen churches and pastors give more time and attention to planning a Mother's Day service than one for Christmas. Keeping the Christian calendar before me has constantly reminded me of my basic responsibility to declare the biblical message and not merely to parrot the major emphases of secular society, civic days, or personal or denominational interests. The other emphases find their place after the basic message is addressed.

Focus on the Central Themes of the Christian Faith

In this sense, I am convinced that following the Christian calendar guides me in being more biblical in my approach than if I follow some other guide. It constantly forces me to examine the content of my worship and preaching to see what motivates it. For example, I cannot imagine preaching only one Christmas sermon. For years I have followed the Advent tradition and have preached at least five sermons on this theme. I have noticed that our people have found Christmas much more meaningful and have prepared better for its celebration because our church put a more thorough emphasis on its importance. Christmas music was carefully planned and prepared for Advent Sundays and other special occasions. My sermon topics, beginning on the last Sunday in November (which was the first Sunday in Advent) and continuing until the Sunday after Christmas, were "The Advent of Hope," "Good News in a World of Bad News," "Unwrapping Presents and Ourselves," "Ready or Not, Here I Come," and "Holding on to Christmas." With a month-long emphasis, our people may be better prepared to celebrate Christmas and discover its real meaning.

A Series of Sermons

I usually did a series of sermons leading up to Easter. Sometimes I also did a series or at least several sermons on other major festivals of the church year. I have found this helpful for my people and me. Often during Holy Week, special services were held on Maundy Thursday (usually a Communion service) or Good Friday. Sometimes noonday services were held in our church or in cooperation with other area churches. I believe that the great events in the life of the church merit thorough attention.

The Christian calendar has already made this provision for us. We can follow its guidance in giving these events careful attention. The Christian calendar can be followed too slavishly, and preachers may forfeit originality or overlook the needs of the congregation. But, if followed wisely, I have found that the calendar can offer rich guidelines for effective worship and preaching. Every congregation celebrates certain special Sundays that form their unofficial church calendar. I enjoy following a church calendar that I know is part of the long tradition of the larger church family.

Note

1. See William Powell Tuck, *Holidays, Holy Days, & Special Days: Preaching through the Year* (Gonzalez FL: Energion Publications, 2015).

5

The Preaching Ministry

Since I preached my first sermon as a youth week pastor in my home church at seventeen years old, I have been fascinated and challenged by preaching. In my many years as a pastor, I always took preaching seriously and tried to give my best efforts to my preaching ministry, aware that my best was always a shallow attempt to proclaim the mystery of the Christian faith. In his chapter on Christian preaching, noted theologian Karl Barth asks, "Who dares, who can, preach, knowing what preaching is?"[1] Yet we must dare, striving to proclaim the mystery and wonder of God's grace and love. Reflecting on my beginning attempts to preach and my struggles to improve through the years affords some tough memories. If we only knew at the beginning of our ministries what we know after forty or fifty years of preaching, we would all be better spokespeople of the gospel. My agenda would carry a number of fresh pages.

Unfortunately, some ministers do not give the necessary time and attention that good preaching requires. When pastor search committees look for a new pastor for their churches, at the top of the list of expectations is effective preaching. Good preaching always demands sufficient time and a willingness to set sermon preparation as a major priority. In the next few pages, I offer a brief discussion about the preaching ministry.[2]

Sermon Preparation and Delivery

I encourage pastors to set a goal of spending at least twenty hours a week in sermon preparation. In my early years, this was hard to do. In addition to

Sunday morning sermons, I had to preach on Sunday nights and do a devotional or a Bible or book study on Wednesday nights. No preacher can give all three the highest priority. Sunday morning should demand our major attention, and I suggest finding ways to assure this by enlisting laypeople or others on occasions like Sunday nights or Wednesday nights. Another option would be to use those nights to focus on contemporary theological book studies or selected Bible studies. I have learned that my preaching is always of a much higher caliber when I give it the necessary twenty hours of preparation.

This preparation includes wide reading of background material, focusing on the biblical text, and laying out the movements of the sermon, including content and illustrations. I tried to block off several uninterrupted hours every morning to do my sermon preparation, informing my congregation of this study time and why I felt it was essential for effective preaching. I asked that they honor this time except for emergencies. I have found that my churches usually understood this requirement and were supportive of the necessary time to prepare sermons.

The following are elements I considered when I prepared and delivered my sermon each week.

Sermon Length

The length of the sermon is important. Some good sermons have been ruined because the preacher could not seem to find a good stopping place. He or she kept circling the field and could not or would not land. The sermon conclusion, of course, should be carefully planned to assist in reaching this destination. I try to limit my sermons to twenty minutes and no more than twenty-five minutes at the longest. After that time, I think we lose the attention of our listeners. Careful sermon preparation can help you honor a time restriction.

Writing Out the Sermon

In my early years of ministry, I usually wrote a three- or four-page broad outline. I did not write the sermon out in full until after I had preached it. I always stressed the major movements, indicating my transitions to the next movement and placing the illustrations at the appropriate places to clarify my thought. Looking back now, I believe that writing out the sermon before I preached it would have helped me focus more on the way I expressed sentences. It would have given me the opportunity to work on creating more attention-grabbing images and expressions that would linger in the hearers' mind or direct them more easily into the thrust of the biblical text. In the past, I attempted to do too much of this in the act of delivering the sermon. Careful preparation ahead of time, I believe, would make this effort a more realistic possibility instead of using phrases I may have recently used in previous sermons. I believe the preacher will enhance her preaching by carefully writing out the sermon ahead of time.

Wide Reading

Sermons that are thrown together at the last minute on Saturday night become Saturday night specials that are rarely "special" in any genuine sense. Last-minute preparation often finds the preacher "borrowing" most of the sermon thoughts from another preacher's sermon book or off a sermon website. Learn early to preach your own sermon and honor your commitment to proclaim the gospel message out of your own study and preparation. Secondhand sermons from secondary sources will hardly ever be an effective means of communicating the sacred word of God. "A preacher who does not prepare is not 'spiritual,'" Pope Francis admonishes. "He is dishonest and irresponsible with the gifts he has received."[3]

On the other hand, it is wise to craft your own sermon through careful preparation, and that involves wide reading. Patricia Farris has urged pastors to "build books" into their ministries. Studying and reading, she insists, is like food for the pastor. "Without it we [pastors] soon starve. Our preaching becomes repetitive and overly self-referential."[4]

Wide reading has always been a vital part of my ministry, and I would encourage every pastor to establish that practice with a focus on reading novels, autobiographies, or biographies. Especially in the reading of novels, I suggest trying to discern the author's special gift of imagery in his or her use of words. I have enjoyed reading a wide variety of fiction from authors such as John Grisham, Dean Koontz, Frederick Buechner, C. S. Lewis, Arthur Miller, Alan Paton, Ernest Hemingway, John Updike, Jill McCorkle, J. K. Rowling, Albert Camus, and countless others. From these writers, I would seek not only inspiration from the writing and the freshness it might communicate to me about contemporary life but also reflection on how the words were framed. This can enable me to be a better wordsmith myself. I taught a seminary course on preaching and contemporary literature, and the students said it was an enriching and provocative aid in their sermon preparation. A pastor should also read widely in the areas of theology, ethics, biblical studies, church history, etc. and read the latest books on preaching and sermon preparation and delivery. I would also encourage a pastor to enroll in or audit some literature or writing courses at a local college to improve important writing skills.

Probing the Biblical Text

Whether you begin with a text or several texts, select them early in the week to give yourself time to muse over them, internalize them, reflect on them, and live with them until they become a part of you. Even when you are not in your study, these texts should demand attention as you go about your other ministries or recreation. Before you use Bible commentaries, ponder what you think the text is addressing and make notes. Spend time trying to grasp the deep meaning of the biblical text; never settle too quickly for what appears to be the obvious meaning. If you are able to read either language, a careful study of the Greek text in a New Testament passage or the Hebrew may move you in a direction you didn't see at first. I attempt to do this most of the time in my sermon preparation, but sometimes the lack of time has forced me to settle too quickly for the surface meaning and maybe not the central truth of the passage. If we can spend more time struggling with the text, the extra effort might open our eyes to the essential movement that could guide our sermon preparation more carefully.

Your next step is to probe the text with an exegetical process in various Bible translations and search several commentaries for their interpretation to determine what the text said in its own day and how it addresses a current issue, whether by informing, confessing, encouraging, correcting, persuading, etc. Once you determine what the text is saying and doing, you need to address how it relates to your listeners today. Focusing merely on what it said in the past is not sufficient. If your listeners are to carry its meaning with them, your sermon must become a window that opens the relevance of the text for their world today. Tom Long expresses it this way: "When preachers go to the Scripture, then, they must take the people with them, since what will be heard there is a word for them."[5] You might address this application directly or seek to draw the listener into the sermon so he or she overhears the message and senses its meaning. Your real goal in preaching on a text is not simply to impart some information, proposition, or truth but to connect the listeners with how that text relates to their lives today.

Carefully select your sermon's main focus based on insights from your study of the text. You must know where you are going before you can guide your people to their response to the sermon. Sometimes the sermon focus may arise from a theological theme you want to address, and then you seek an appropriate biblical text. If you follow the lectionary, the text will be your point of departure as you determine your central focus. Sometimes the focus may come from a special time in the life of your congregation like the church's anniversary, mission Sunday, stewardship emphasis, or children or youth Sunday. In some way, the sermon focus will be directed to the theme of the particular day. Also try to have both variety and some kind of "surprise" in your messages. Your conclusions will be more effective if they follow up by leading the congregation toward a response or commitment.

One of the essential ways to connect the text with the lives of your listeners is through an image or illustration. People usually think better visually than they do logically. Search, read, observe, inquire, listen, and store all the stories, images, word pictures, and illustrations you can. They are the pathway into the minds of your listeners. The congregation will likely not remember your main point or movement if you do not paint some kind of word picture through a story or other illustrative means. The preacher Gardner Taylor was a master at this. In a sermon titled "A Storm-Proof Religion," he noted that Edgar Goodspeed had translated Jesus' words, "Peace, be still," as "Hush." Drawing on that translation, he proclaimed,

> "Hush." The lightning folded its flame and ran back to its hiding place. "Hush." The winds got still and fled to their homes in the hills. "Hush." And the sea stretched out like a pet before its master. "Hush." And the elements grew calm. The Lord can speak to our souls. He can say to us, "Hush." Do not be disturbed. Do not be troubled. It is I—be not afraid."[6]

This colorful language hangs in the mind and will linger long after the sermon is preached.

I have files of illustrations, markings in my books, and indexes on the back page with references to illustrative material or colorful thoughts from other writers. I have notebooks of clippings and cartoons from the newspapers and magazines. I have several binders of *Peanuts* comic strips. Build your own files in a cabinet and on your computer. Most great preachers become gifted proclaimers through their wide use of illustrations and stories in their preaching. All pastors need to work to perfect that art if they expect to preach effectively. I think it is also important to carry a small notebook with you at all times. You never know when an idea or illustration may come to you. And I have found that if I do not make a note of it when it comes, I often forget it. Sermon ideas may also come in a serendipitous way through a movie, TV show, e-mail, letter, play, conversation, and reading. Be prepared to jot down that thought when it comes so you will not miss it.

Sermon Delivery

There are five basic methods of sermon delivery. Some preachers may employ a combination of several in their delivery. One method is to *read the manuscript* that you have carefully prepared. This may be comfortable for the preacher, but most listeners say it is their least favorite form of hearing sermons. If you are going to take the manuscript with you into the pulpit, learn to preach it and not simply read it. Only a few preachers with rare gifts can truly read the sermon so people will want to listen.

Another method is to *memorize the sermon* and preach it. Again, only a preacher with a rare gift for memorizing can deliver an effective sermon this way. I have seen some preachers try this approach and have a memory block, forgetting where they are in the sermon and struggling to continue. Others have recited the sermon like a professional performer, and I wondered if I was supposed to applaud when they finished.

Some preachers do what I call *impromptu preaching.* They come before their congregation without any outline or plan other than to read the text and talk about it off the top of their heads. This is dangerous preaching that will always be trite, repetitious, boring, and un-illuminating for listeners. Few, if any, preachers can preach out of the "overflow" week after week and offer any real content or have a true grasp of the biblical text. No congregation will tolerate this lazy and disastrous approach for long.

The method most preachers use is to preach from *carefully prepared notes.* Even those who write out their sermons in full often make notes of the major and minor movements and highlight key thoughts and illustrations to guide them. These brief notes keep preachers from forgetting and do not require them to keep their heads down in the manuscript. They can refer to the notes and still make frequent eye contact with the listeners.

The method I followed for most of my preaching ministry is called the *extemporaneous* or the *free preaching approach.* I carefully prepared the sermon with lengthy pages of notes or even a full manuscript. I memorized the major and minor movements, the transitions, and the quotes. I focused on the illustrations and used the movements as steps to guide my thought in not forgetting. I would normally spend at least thirty minutes before I preached the sermon reading through it again and again and then "rehearsing" it in my mind before I delivered it. This required preparation in writing the sermon and then getting it into my head. This style of delivery allowed me to keep my eyes focused on the congregation and not on my notes, and I always felt freer and more forceful. In my later years, I have sometimes carried a full manuscript in a book-size format into the pulpit and used it like an outline to deliver the sermon with my eyes focused as much as possible on the congregation.

Every preacher should try several methods and then determine which one makes you most comfortable. Remember, no matter how well you may have written the sermon on paper, the real test comes in the delivery of that sermon. At the pulpit, we succeed or fail in communicating the gospel message. Work hard to find the best way for you to share the good news.

Sermon Planning

Again, if the preacher follows the lectionary, then the direction of the sermon is clear except for selecting the particular texts for Sunday. My sermon planning usually carried me for at least three to six months. I believe that it would be better to plan your preaching for the whole year instead of the shorter period. This would help in the planning of your reading, study, and focus. I have not always followed the lectionary, and I often offered sermon series. When I was not following the lectionary, advance planning enabled me to decide what kinds of series I would do, when I would present them, and how many sermons I would need. I could more easily plan my study, acquire the necessary books, and seek other resources. My careful preparation also assisted in the overall worship planning because the central theme was known far in advance, so the minister of music and/or worship committee and I could focus earlier on the other important dimensions of the worship service.

As I mentioned earlier, preaching can be planned around the Christian year of Advent, Christmas, Epiphany, Lent, and Easter. Or you might follow the calendar with emphasis on the New Year, Mother's Day, Memorial Day, Father's Day, Independence Day, Labor Day, Thanksgiving, Christmas, and Easter.[7] You would approach these sermons with a topical theme and find Scripture appropriate for each occasion. Some preachers like to preach through the Bible or to preach on Bible personalities, the Ten Commandments, the Beatitudes, the miracles of Jesus, the difficult sayings of Jesus, major biblical doctrines, selected psalms, the disciples, the parables, or women in the Bible. You might focus on denominational emphases like Baptist's Men's Day, Home or Foreign Missions Sunday, Christian

Unity Sunday, Race Relations Sunday, Youth Sunday, etc. The list can be endless, but variety is essential.

Ways to Vary Your Sermons

To me, one of the difficulties with preaching is maintaining a wide variety of sermons. I would strive to vary between doctrinal, ethical, expository, pastoral, and other kinds of sermons to communicate the gospel more effectively. This could be done on occasion through a series of sermons on various doctrines, ethical issues, or biblical themes. It could also be accomplished, for example, by preaching a doctrinal sermon in the Advent season on the meaning of the incarnation or one in the Lenten season about the cross or the resurrection. I often found myself preaching on pastoral care or human needs issues because of the problems or special needs in the congregation. This could still be accomplished by drawing on the lectionary biblical text for that Sunday and, when applicable, directing its ultimate meaning to the personal struggles of the listeners. In my opinion, no sermon should remain in the text or the ancient past without directing its meaning to the needs of one's congregation today. I would also suggest that you try doing dramatic monologues from biblical characters and attempt more experimental types of sermons, like dialogues or another creative form. Several of the sermon series I have done are listed below.

Series: Facing Life's Ups and Downs[7]
The Need to Wait
When You Are Tied Up in Knots
From Frustration to Thanksgiving
Judging May Boomerang
Are Failures Final?
Facing Your Fears
When You're Lonely
Breaking the Hold of Pessimism
Learning the Art of Patience
The Sin of Small People: Jealousy
Enough of this Self-Pity
When You're Depressed
On Taking a Detour

Series: The Beatitudes of Jesus[9]
Spiritual Poverty
The Strange Happiness of Grief
Disciplined Strength
The Challenge of Goodness
The Price of Mercy
An Undivided Aim
Waging Peace
Standing to Be Counted
Disciplined Strength

Series: Through the Eyes of a Child[10]
To Become Like Children
Rediscovering a Sense of Wonder
Let's Come Alive to Life
In Praise of Play
Thank You for Listening
The Gift of Touch
Prescription for Joy
A Theology of Sleep

Series: Who Is This Jesus Christ?[11]
Who Is This Jesus Christ?
The Incarnate Christ
The Healing Christ
The Teaching Christ
The Rejected Christ
The Crucified Christ
The Risen Christ
What about Christ Today?

Dialogue about the Sermon

Invite your congregation to engage in dialogue with you on Wednesday or Sunday nights about the sermon you preached the Sunday before. When I did this, I provided an outline of the sermon and tried to be open to questions, challenges, and a variety of interpretations of the text and its application to life. I found this was an effective way to involve the congregation and to deepen the sermon I had preached in the minds of my listeners.

Another helpful activity is to invite a small group of laypeople in your congregation to dialogue with you not only about the sermon but also about sermon needs or expectations of the congregation. This group could be a vital listening or feedback component to help you determine the church's needs or to provide a critique of a sermon you have preached to determine its effectiveness or whether you missed the mark altogether. This group could be composed of three or four volunteers who would rotate off, perhaps monthly. Hopefully, you could build a trusting relationship with a number of those in your congregation who might offer you genuine criticism of your preaching and express how you might communicate more clearly with them. You would need to indicate clearly that they could be honest, and you would have to receive the feedback graciously and without making the group feel ill at ease. This could be a daring adventure of learning both for the preacher and those in the congregation who participated.

Use a Mentor

I encourage pastors to find a mentor who will listen to or read their sermons and offer a critique. Get copies of your sermons to this mentor several weeks in advance. You might plan to meet once a month, and the mentor could share with you your strengths or weaknesses along with ways to improve. You could agree on a proper stipend for the sessions. This would put your sessions on a serious level and compensate the mentor for the time and expertise given. You could also find a seminary professor or a gifted pastor who would be willing to offer such guidance. Another suggestion is to take a speech course at a local college to work on problems that linger. Every week, listen to tapes of your sermons to see how you might improve content, style, language, and overall preaching. John Killinger reminds us that "we preachers are mere fragile vessels of the heavenly treasure. We will be worn and broken and eventually left behind when the next generation comes along. But for now we have the treasure, the message, and we must learn how to preach it."[12]

Read and Listen to Great Sermons

As a good musician improves his or her playing by listening to good music as well as by practicing, I would encourage you to listen to and read sermons by outstanding preachers. Try to discover what makes their preaching so effective and invites others to want to listen to them. Look for how they develop the sermon, use illustrations, involve themselves in the sermon, and make their words dance across the page or in your head and compel you to listen or read on. Select preachers from a variety of denominations, ethnicities, and identities. Be willing to travel to hear them preach or lecture on preaching, and acquire audio recordings of their preaching. Consider the following excellent preachers: Fred Craddock, John Killinger, Tom Long, William Willimon, James Howell, Barbara Brown Taylor, Amy Butler, Ginger Gaines-Cirelli, Shannon Johnson Kershner, T. D. Jakes, and Gardner C. Taylor. Read and listen to their sermons. Also reach into the past and read or listen to sermons by Harry Emerson Fosdick, Leslie Weatherhead, James Stewart, Wallace Hamilton, and George Buttrick. These models of preaching will enrich your mind with the various styles, content, and depth of their preaching.[13]

Continuing Education

I believe that constant renewal at seminary and divinity school conferences or national preaching conferences can keep pastors aware of new trends and preaching developments. Consider taking advantage of these conferences by attending them annually. This kind of study can help us stay fresh and up-to-date on the best in preaching literature and on gifted preachers and teachers of preaching.

Preach for a Response

Søren Kierkegaard, a noted Danish philosopher of the nineteenth century, shared an interesting parable about a preaching goose. The goose is flying over a barnyard one day and notices that the dirty lot is filled with geese. He stops, gathers a crowd in the barnyard, and begins to preach to them. He reminds the geese of the adventures of their forefathers who flew the trackless skies in years past. He challenges them not to be content with their confined earthbound existence behind the wooden fence. He tells them about the Creator who made their life and gave them wings so they could migrate great distances. All of this pleases the geese, and they nod their heads in approval. When the goose finishes his sermon, the others applaud and speak about the wonderful eloquence of the preaching goose. But they do not leave the barnyard. They return to their corn and their security.

Genuine preaching must demand more than applause and approval. In my opinion, a sermon has not succeeded unless there is a moment of response that challenges listeners to want to live, think, act, or desire a higher vision or way of living. This may be what Fred Craddock meant when he said, "Effective preaching carries within it and generates in the listener a shock of recognition. We all wish to create the shock in preaching, for people to be startled and see something afresh and anew."[14] God, I believe, has called us as individuals to lift our vision beyond the immediate and look to what we can become as God's people. This is part of the challenge of preaching. There are always those who want to build fences around our visions and look down or look back. But God is calling us to look ahead—to look forward at what we can be. The gospel we received from Jesus is always fresh, new, and vital. The preacher is charged with reminding his or her listeners that Jesus challenges us to lift our wings and fly into new realms of service and creativity.

The preaching of the word should summon a response. By this, I don't mean the old-fashioned revival type of response where the sinner comes down to the kneeling bench and confesses his sins, though that may be appropriate at times. But our preaching should always call or summon the listener to respond. Sometimes it may be a conversion from an old way of life to a new beginning, from apathy to a renewed faith, from unbelief to belief, from immoral practices to a moral life, from prejudice to acceptance of others who differ, from close-mindedness to openness, from hatred to love, from selfishness to service, from wagers of war to peacemakers, from those who push down the fallen to those who lift them up, from endless ways that belittle us and destroy us to refreshing avenues that lead us to sacrificial living or learning about the countless means of God's grace in our lives.

Let your preaching sing with hope, communicate with love, resound with grace, be assured with redemption, be shared with confidence, and be expressed in humility through Christ's servant. "Even the best sermon," James Howell noted, "fails to capture the mystery, the grandeur, and sheer humility and mind-boggling grace of God."[15] We know indeed that we can never fully describe the wonder and mystery of God's grace and love, but we should seek to use the best resources available in our attempt to share that powerful word. May the listener never have to question whether the preacher is in the sermon as we boldly proclaim the eternal message of God's grace. May we never lose the thrill of the power of the gospel and the wonder of the redeeming message we proclaim.

Notes

1. Karl Barth, *The Word of God and the Word of Man* (New York: Harper & Brothers, 1957) 126.

2. For more detailed study, I suggest that you examine my two books on preaching and sermon preparation, *The Pastor Preaching: Toward a Theology of the Proclaimed Word* (Macon GA: Nurturing Faith, Inc., 2012) and *Overcoming Sermon Block: The Preacher's Workshop* (Gonzalez FL: Energion Publications, 2014).

3. Pope Francis, *The Joy of the Gospel: Evangelii Gaudium* (New York: Image, 2013) 104.

4. Patricia Farris, *Five Faces of Ministry: Pastor, Parson, Healer, Prophet, Pilgrim* (Nashville: Abingdon, 2015) 24.

5. Thomas G. Long, *The Witness of Preaching*, 2nd ed. (Louisville KY: Westminster John Knox Press, 2005) 64.

6. Gardner Taylor quoted in my book *Modern Shapers of Baptist Thought in America* (Richmond VA: Center for Baptist Heritage & Studies, 2012) 239–40.

7. See my book, *Holidays, Holy Days and Special Days* (Gonzalez FL: Energion Publications, 2015) for examples of these kinds of sermons.

8. See my book, *Facing Life's Ups and Downs* (Macon GA: Smyth & Helwys, 2010).

9. See my book *The Way for All Seasons: Reflecting on the Beatitudes for the 21st Century* (Cleveland TN: Parson's Porch Books, 2013).

10. See my book *Through the Eyes of a Child* (New York: Writer's Club Press, 2003).

11. See my book *The Compelling Faces of Jesus* (Macon GA: Mercer University Press, 2008).

12. John Killinger, *Fundamentals of Preaching* (Minneapolis: Fortress Press, 1996) 12.

13. Good resources include *20 Centuries of Great Preaching* and *The Library of Distinctive Sermons*.

14. Fred Craddock, *Craddock on the Craft of Preaching* (St. Louis MO: Chalice Press, 2011) 128.

15. James C. Howell, *The Beauty of the Word: The Challenge and Wonder of Preaching* (Louisville KY: Westminster John Knox Press, 2011) 113.

6

Addressing Change through Preaching

One day a man observed a small boy trying to get a kite to rise up in the sky. The young boy ran back and forth as fast as he could, up and down the field, to get his kite to fly. The kite would rise a few feet and then tumble to the ground. Finally the man said to the boy, "Son, you've got to wait for the wind. You can't make your kite go up in the air on your own. You've got to wait for the wind." "Well, Mister, I know," responded the small boy, "but it's hard to wait."

As ministers, we know that it is hard to wait before we speak about an issue that we believe needs a prophetic word. But sometimes we must wait for the right wind of timing, occasion, opportunity, place, or manner. Otherwise our words fall to the ground, return to us void, or, worse, return as arrows to destroy us. Many preachers have offered advice on the timing of addressing new issues. Some say to wait at least a year at a new church before taking such an approach, while others encourage the preacher to launch into the deep immediately. Which is the best, safest, most positive, or successful approach? I am not certain, for I can only tell you what I have done.

I do not have a new or innovative word about addressing change through preaching. But perhaps my thoughts and the reaction to them will be useful. Words are sometimes heard and perceived differently by the listener. Jesus said, "He that hath ears to hear, let him hear" (Matt 11:15). James 1:22 asserts, "Be ye doers of the word and not hearers only." We must speak. "Woe unto me," said Paul, "if I preach not the gospel" (1 Cor 9:16). But speaking is not enough. We must both speak and do. Our words are insipid without structures to implement them into ministry. Our words should be vehicles to enable the listener to encounter the living Word and then to flesh out his work into living epistles among us today. The incarnate Word seeks new temples and instruments to hear him in the world today. God is personal; God's relationship has always been personal rather than abstract, theoretical, or propositional. His presence is revealed in the present. We wait for the wind of his spirit to guide us into all truth.

When that wind begins to blow and we sense the need to preach about change, we must proceed carefully. I have condensed my experiences into four steps we can take as we prepare to share difficult messages: initiate, involve, identify, and illumine.

Initiate

Before we address new issues, we must open a door so our congregations can get a glimpse of them. I have taken steps to initiate people to new ideas or issues by preaching sermons on "The Difficulty of Change." In this way, I acknowledge that I, like others, want to cling to the old and familiar. I note that we often prefer the known pathways and comfortable haunts. We enjoy a merry-go-round life that moves around in familiar, secure circles. We like schedules and routines. We hang on to security blankets of orthodoxy, customs, or traditions. We hug the shore of familiarity and cling to the known and permanent. We search for a safe, snug harbor where we can put down our anchors. Part of being human is to be frightened by change.

But the Christian faith centers on change. The New Testament speaks about new birth, new beginnings, a new song, a new commandment, a new covenant, and a new life. Salvation is about a fresh, new life. The new birth is about becoming a new creation of God. Following Christ results in a call to a life of growth and openness to the freshness and newness God brings before us. A Christian is always on a journey to be more mature today than yesterday. This life is about change.

I have always tried to mark the trail for my congregation so they could see clearly the direction I planned to go. After much study and prayer, I firmly took a position on an issue. I avoided fog talk and theological evasiveness and instead stated my position plainly. I have found that my people usually appreciated my honesty and forthrightness, even when they disagreed. People have said, "Pastor, we now know where you are on that issue. Thanks." Most people like to know where we stand theologically on important issues, and this knowledge may offer them guidance and sometimes give them the courage to stand with us.

People cannot follow our leadership if they do not know where we are trying to lead them. Only light on a dark path can show the way clearly. I heard Bill Mueller, my former seminary professor, say, "When you try to walk down the yellow median strip in the road, you are likely to get hit from both sides." So I have taken my stand and given my directions. If our members did not know exactly what I was saying about an issue, they were not likely to help bring about change. I sought to clarify the issue for myself and then for my people.

When a minister takes a position, he or she should not be surprised by some negative reaction. Who among us gets 100 percent positive response to everything we say? We should expect negative responses to an important issue and, frankly, be disappointed when there is not any. Learning not to react negatively toward negatives is hard, but it's an important life skill.

A friend told me about a big old dog that walked down the middle of Main Street in a small city. As he passed down the street, every small dog along the way barked at him, but he never stopped to respond. He walked straight toward his goal. If he had turned to respond to every barking dog, he never would have reached his destination. We need to have sight of our goal and move toward it with faith and confidence.

Involve

Before addressing some issues outright, I sometimes involved certain members of my congregation in brainstorming sessions. I selected a small group or committee or even used a Wednesday night prayer meeting to discuss an important issue and get the impact of that particular group. On other occasions, I asked this group to suggest major issues or subjects for me to address in upcoming months. This group suggested I look at such topics as race, famine, peace, war, pollution, sexism, AIDS, homosexuality, inerrancy, the will of God, suffering, death, and many others. When you talk with laypeople first, you will find that they benefit by having input into the preaching process. They may acknowledge a positive feeling when they suggest a theme that you later address in a sermon. Sometimes the group can even clarify where the congregation is on a certain issue.

Working through leadership organizations we already have in our churches is helpful when dealing with some of these issues. A social action committee, the worship committee, special committees of deacons, or others may serve as a sounding board for new ideas. If we work through established organizations, they may feel more ownership of the idea and therefore be more open to it in the future. If the congregation feels that the issue is important to the preacher but not to them, positive response is less likely.

One important way to involve our congregations is to use dialogue. Every sermon should be a cooperative venture with our people. We should let them know we have heard and continue to hear them. We need to challenge our congregations to be active listeners. Preaching is not a monologue but a dialogue. Let us listen to the concerns, aches, needs, issues, questions, and hopes of our people. Encourage them to jot down concerns on a piece of paper and give them to you. Assure them that you will take them seriously, and then do so.

On other occasions, I had times of dialogue on Sunday nights or Wednesday nights following a special series of sermons on issues like science and creation, grief and death, the will of God, or the new morality. These "talk-back" times provided the people with an opportunity to ask questions or to voice their opinions or interpretations. I tried to be open, listen attentively, and respond honestly to their questions. These sessions usually helped pave the way for new understandings and openness on the part of my congregation. I usually enjoyed these sessions and was often informed by them. Many laypeople are far more open and creative than we give them credit. It's important, though, to give them freedom to disagree with you and state another approach to the issue. I have found that even when this happens, and sometimes it does, the person usually offers the idea with grace and fairness. But pastors set the tone by our openness for mutual trust.

Carlyle Marney has an interesting dedication in *Faith in Conflict*: "To VICTOR who agreed with me in nothing and was my friend in everything."[1] What a marvelous understanding of what it means to be Christian! Here is one who is able to differ with others and continue in dialogue and relationship with them. Though they disagree, they are still friends, knowing that they do not have to agree on everything. They recognize that they are brothers and sisters in Christ and still allow another person to have an opinion that differs from their own.

Identify

One of the most effective ways of preaching on issues and getting a positive response is learning to address the transconscious level of our people. Our preaching should say to listeners, "I have sat where you sit and know your struggles and problems." When we have felt the pulse of their daily needs, our preaching will touch a chord and set loose a response within them. Our words will scratch where they itch and address them at the point of their real needs: the intuitive self, the unconscious self, or the existential self. The listener will sense that the preacher feels with him or her and really understands the struggle. This sense of empathy creates openness, trust, and understanding. We participate in "priestly listening," to use Leander Keck's words, when we listen to the words of the biblical text like one of the members of the church's congregation would listen to them.[2]

Many, like the prophet Jeremiah, have sat alone and wondered if anyone knew of their sense of ridicule, despondency, despair, dejection, anger, aloneness, hatred, fear, loneliness, hostility, or rejection. If the listener feels that the preacher understands, then communication will likely take place. The listener needs to feel that the preacher is identifying with his or her struggles. This type of preaching looks inside the listener's head and heart. The problems of people' lives or in the world are seen from within when they are addressed in a clear way rather than in abstract or in theory. The hearer will see how the Scripture relates to his or her own life, including the problems.

This kind of preaching opens a door through which a listener can enter. It overcomes the distance between the preacher and the people and pulls them into communication. The preacher stands in the pulpit as a fellow human being who identifies with his congregation in their struggles to follow our Lord. He does not have all the answers, but, like them, he is on pilgrimage to become more like his Lord. I openly confess that there are areas in my life where I have not arrived spiritually. I still struggle to overcome prejudice, pride, hatred, anger, selfishness, and other weaknesses. I am human like those to whom I speak. And so are you.

All authentic preaching is autobiographical. Where I have felt God's hand most keenly on my life, I can most clearly share with another. I cannot share what I do not know or have not experienced. As a "wounded healer,"[3] I preach out of my experience of God's presence and the awareness I have sensed in the lives of the biblical writers. I attempt to use words that drip with color, reverberate with sound, evoke sleeping memories, straighten sagging ideals, and refocus on the higher way of Christ.

I believe that every preacher must earn the right to be a prophetic voice. Too often and too long, many preachers have heaped guilt on their congregations, scolded them, and belittled them without offering any real guidance in how to meet the challenge they have presented. The preacher has too long denounced his congregation for not responding to a particular social evil and considered himself a martyr when they either rejected him or his message or simply ignored him. People do not respond to change by being scolded or berated.

Only a preacher whose life and ministry have earned respect will be heard by the congregation. When we have sat with the people in their sickness, grief, and pain and rejoiced with them at their weddings, births, and parties, they will listen seriously to what we say. "If we have spent twenty hours listening to our people during the week," Carlyle Marney once said, "then we can expect them to listen to us for twenty minutes on Sunday." The priestly and prophetic ministries are bound together in a yoke of love and compassion. Out of the background of this caring ministry, our people will know that we are addressing a new issue so that they will be enriched in their Christian lives. Because we have loved them, and they have loved us, they know we want the best spiritual growth possible from them.

Sometimes we address new issues indirectly in our preaching. To use Craddock's phrase, we let our members "overhear the gospel."[4] For example, we do not have to point out on every occasion the way the parable of the good Samaritan applies to today's issues of race. Listeners can overhear the story and think it is addressing someone in the past who is anonymous and distant, and then suddenly realize that they are drawn into the picture and their prejudice is challenged. Many passages of Scripture that deal with issues of war and peace, justice and righteousness, tradition and change, and other themes can be presented in ways that draw the hearer into the story. Preaching "is not designed to convey information but by its very form arrests the attention, draws the listener into personal involvement, and leaves the final resolution of the issue to the hearer's own judgment."[5] We tell "the story" and trust God's Spirit to work within the people's lives. Like Kierkegaard, who overheard a grandfather telling his grandson about life after death and found his own belief in life eternal affirmed, our listeners overhear the gospel message and find affirmation for their own faith.[6] Sometimes the shortest distance between two points in preaching is not a straight line but an indirect one.

Illumine

If our people are to respond when we address new issues, they need to see that our preaching is strongly biblical. All authentic preaching is biblical. Our people want more than your opinion and my opinion. They want to know how the Scriptures speak to the issues at hand. As we take seriously the concrete situation that the biblical text originally addressed, we show how the text is released to confront a similar issue today. We can avoid taking an isolated passage of Scripture and assuming that it has the whole of God's revelation within it. We can study the Scripture and seek to find the truth within a particular passage that needs to be incorporated into the greater truth of the whole of Scripture. We can also remember that sometimes a Scripture passage may be concerned with a particular situation or problem of its own day and may not be a universal teaching that is meant for our day. A case in point is Paul's discussion of the dress of women in 1 Corinthians 11:2-16. In my judgment, this was a local problem that was not meant as an example for modern dress codes or hairstyles.

Good, consistent biblical exposition can address many contemporary issues confronting society today without naming them one by one. For example, if a church has divisions, you might turn to Paul's discussion of the quarrels in the Corinthian church (see 1 Cor 1:10-18) as a guide for dealing with this problem. You do not have to touch on your congregation's issue today but simply expound Paul's message to the Corinthians. The listeners can "overhear" the message for the church right now. I have found, too, that humorous stories sometimes enable me to communicate a point that would be awkward otherwise. I love the story about the young preacher who in his first sermon at a small country church preached against tobacco. After the service, one of the deacons pulled him aside and reminded him that most of the farmers raised tobacco and paid his salary from their sales. The next Sunday he preached against drinking. He was pulled aside and informed that some of the members worked at the local distillery and paid his salary from what they made there. The next Sunday he preached against horse racing. Again he was pulled aside and told that a number of the congregation raised horses and paid his salary from what they made. By now the young preacher was frustrated and asked, "What, then, can I preach against?" "Preach against them heathen witch doctors in Africa," the deacon responded. "There's not one of them within a thousand miles!"

I have often used this story to introduce a sermon on the importance of speaking to issues close at home. Good illustrations from Charlie Brown, the Wizard of Id, and many other comic strip characters provide a fresh door into the listener's ear. Many of us fail to address new issues effectively because we do not nail down the truth clearly in the minds of listeners. Jesus used parabolic illustrations that are unforgettable, even centuries later. Dullness is a sin that the pulpit can avoid with fresh illustrations and language. Illustrations are more than ornaments in a sermon. They should enable the hearer to remember the message. Henry Mitchell in *The Recovery of Preaching* stated that unless the preacher can illustrate his point, he might as well not make it because the listener will not likely recall it."[7] Illustrations about the issue at hand can enable those to whom we preach to get a handle on the truth we are preaching.

Sometimes I have found that a series of sermons on a particular issue or issues has helped me communicate my emphasis better than just one sermon. I have preached series on grief and death, contemporary social issues, science and creation, the church in a changing society, and others. I have preached these on Sunday mornings, Sunday nights, or Wednesday nights. Often dialogue would follow. On some occasions I have coordinated my preaching series with a special study in Sunday school. This helped reinforce the emphasis even more. I have also used my pastor's paragraph in the church newsletter to support, clarify, expand, digest, or undergird my preaching emphasis on new issues.

Sometimes I have found that I could address new issues best in a more innovative sermon format. This might take the form of a pantomime, monologue, or dialogue; drama; multimedia presentation with musical sounds, slides, lights, and other props; contemporary parable; letter; musical; or other experimental forms. In the book *Experimental Preaching*, Jerry L. Barnes has a powerful sermon titled "A Christmas Eve Letter," which deals with war.[8] These experimental sermon forms can be effective if planned with care and good taste. Another advantage of this type of sermon is the opportunity to include other people. Having others share in the presentation gives them ownership of the process and often a resulting ownership in the new idea.

As ministers, we are challenged to enable our people to become "seers"— to look into the future, to dream dreams and see visions. We are all novices in religion. We are always beginners, constantly in the process of becoming. We never arrive. We are less than we think we are and yet more. We know that we do not know all or even much about God. We are changing and working as change agents. Change produces pain. In fact, almost any real growth in our lives is accompanied by pain. In the parable of old and new wine skins, Jesus reminded us that God is constantly bursting old wine skins with the freshness and vitality of his presence (see Matt 9:17). We do not attempt to confine his gospel in old skins of custom, tradition, or provincial religion. Let us lift up our hearts and let the wind of God's Spirit guide us into the freshness and vitality of living in his presence.

Notes

1. Carlyle Marney, *Faith in Conflict* (New York: Abingdon Press, 1957), dedication page.

2. Leander E. Keck, *The Bible in the Pulpit* (Nashville: Abingdon. Press. 1978) 62ff.

3. Henri J. M. Nouwen, *The Wounded Healer* (New York: Doubleday, 1942).

4. Fred B. Craddock, *Overhearing the Gospel* (Nashville: Abingdon Press, 1978).

5. lbid., 77.

6. Ibid., 105–106.

7. Henry H. Mitchell, *The Recovery of Preaching* (New York: Harper & Row, 1977) 45ff.

8. In John Killinger, ed., *Experimental Preaching* (Nashville: Abingdon Press, 1973) 111–15.

Pastoral Care

Pastoral care is rooted in the concept of the pastor as the shepherd of the congregation, which is drawn from Jesus' view of the Good Shepherd (John 10:14). In the concept of the shepherd in the times Jesus lived, a shepherd was one who literally cared for, watched over, fed, guarded, guided, healed, rescued, and genuinely loved his flock of sheep. In a similar way, the pastor has responsibilities like the ancient shepherd in caring for a congregation. Like shepherd, the word "pastor" is a reminder that the leader of the congregation also has a duty, responsibility or obligation for those in his congregation or "flock." Jesus also made it clear in his declaration to his disciples about their care for one another: "This is my commandment, that you love one another as I have loved you" (John 15:12). Pastor are charged to love their congregations as Jesus loved his disciples—the beginning components of the church.

What Is Pastoral Care?

Pastoral care is love, compassion, and concern for the congregation a pastor serves. Pastoral care to me has always covered all the other aspects of my ministry aside from preaching, teaching, and church administration. It touches the congregation in the times of their joy and sadness, health and illness, birth and death, youth and aging, marriage and funerals, rejoicing and grief, celebration and depression, faith and doubt, and assurance and questions. In other words, it seeks to address the life of a pastor's congregation during most of the routines of the ups and downs of normal living. Pastoral care has sometimes been divided into pastoral calling and pastoral counseling. Wayne Oates has depicted pastoral care on at least four levels—the level of friendship, the level of comfort, the level of confession, and the level of teaching.[1]

Some pastors seem to have a difficult time getting involved in the pastoral care of their congregations. They allow sermon preparation, administrative matters, committee meetings, and financial concerns to take so much of their time that they ignore their people. I remind you of what I noted that Carlyle Marney said in the last chapter: "a minister who spends twenty hours a week among his people then had the right to speak for twenty minutes on Sunday morning." As much as our people want and deserve good preaching, pastors will ignore the congregation at their peril. I had a church member beg me one time to plead with her pastor to visit his congregation. He simply did not, and I was not surprised to learn that he was soon asked to leave. On the other hand, I knew of one pastor who was not a good preacher at all, but his congregation loved him because he was so attentive as their pastor. As pastors, we should not disregard either component. Both are essential for effective ministry.

Pastors engaged in sermon preparation, I believe, will likely have a constant tug on their hearts to be out among their people, ministering to them. And when a pastor is out visiting, he or she may feel the pull to be working on the sermon. We will always have this inner struggle because both aspects of ministry are so important. And we should not neglect either. The size of the congregation affects how pastors are able to engage in pastoral care. A pastor of a congregation with one hundred members will certainly have more time to minister to them than a pastor of a church with five hundred or fifteen hundred members. Nevertheless, pastors must determine the most constructive way to use their time in offering pastoral care to their people.

Remember that you are the spiritual representative of your church. You represent the love of God to the person in need. I will never forget hearing from a church member that her small child saw me, his pastor, downtown one time and exclaimed to his mother, "There goes God!" Well, you and I are certainly not God, but we are God's representatives, and we have to act like it in our love and concern for our church members. You will do your pastoral calling in both the home and the hospital. I certainly cannot address every situation in a few pages, but let me offer a few suggestions that have been helpful to me. Let's begin with pastoral calls in the hospital.

Pastoral Care in the Hospital

Be sure to inform your people that you want to minister to them in times of need or crisis, especially when they go to the hospital. Urge them to call you or the church office and let you know when they or a family member is in the hospital or has a special need. Remind them that as their pastor, you cannot respond if you do not know of a need. The church members have the responsibility of informing you. Some hospitals provide ministers a list of their church members who are in the hospital. If that is the case, you should check the list when you go there. You may discover the name of a church member who failed to let you know that he or she was there. If you register with most hospitals as a minister, they will furnish you with a badge that identifies you as a "chaplain." Wearing this badge will indicate to hospital staff that you are a minister who is verified by the hospital chaplaincy.

People, of course, go to the hospital for many reasons—tests, emergencies, accidents, surgeries, strokes, childbirths, or some other reason. Your call will likely be different depending on the particular situation. If the door to the room you want to visit is closed, always knock before entering. If the doctor or nurses are attending to the patient, excuse yourself and indicate that you will return later. Visit another church member and call back in a few minutes. Remember that the patient's medical care comes first, and you want to work with the medical staff and not try to interfere with it. A light over the patient's door may indicate that the patient has asked for a nurse's assistance, and you will need to allow for that action to be administered. If the door has a "no visiting" or an "isolation" sign, you may need to check with the nurse to see if it is okay to visit or whether you need to put on a gown and mask. The patient may have indicated that it is all right for the pastor to visit.

When you enter the room, greet the patient cheerfully but not in a boisterous manner. Do not come into the room as Reverend Doom and Gloom or as a clown. Be friendly and relaxed. Don't communicate to the patient that you are in a hurry or tense about calling on them. I generally stand by the bed or take a seat in a chair near the bed rather than sitting on the bed. I allow the patient to indicate whether she wants to shake hands or not. Some genuinely want to feel the supportive touch of the pastor, and others remain aloof. Don't try to force the patient to tell you why he is there, but allow him to take the initiative in talking or not talking about his illness or accident. If he shares about his illness, listen and do not try to tell him about everybody else who has had a similar problem. You can often determine the extent of the patient's illness by the various intravenous tubes, glucose, etc. that he is receiving. Sometimes the patient may say that she knows how busy you are and you didn't really need to come. Assure her that you wanted to come and that you are genuinely concerned about her. In no way communicate to the patient that it is a burden on you to take the time to come and see him. You might unintentionally communicate this by talking about everything you have to do, the many others you need to call on, or the heavy traffic in the late afternoon as you go home.

As a rule, I try to make my visit brief but will remain longer if the church member indicates a need to talk further. If the person does not feel like seeing you when you enter the room, excuse yourself and indicate that you will return another time when he feels better. If I am able to visit with the person, I try to assure her of the concern of our church family and that our congregation is praying for her. When it is appropriate, I usually have a brief prayer with the patient. But if the hospital staff or other visitors are present and might make it uncomfortable for the person, I usually refrain from offering a prayer.

Sometimes I have sat with family members in the hospital waiting area while a family member has undergone serious surgery. During this time, I usually pray with them and with the patient before she undergoes surgery, and then I wait with them until the patient's surgery is complete and the doctor reports the outcome. During the waiting time, I try to listen to the family, encourage them, and simply share my presence with them. If it happens around a mealtime, I encourage them to get something to eat, and I go with them for the meal. I have been with a family when the loved one was dying and offered my presence to pray with them, listen to them, cry with them, and comfort them when the person died. Before the person died, I discouraged the family from talking in whispers. I continued to address the dying person as though he could hear me because we simply do not know whether they can or not. I continued to treat the person as if he could. That seemed the proper way respect a dying person. I would always tell the family that I would talk with them later about the funeral service.

When there were emergencies, I would go to the hospital when I was called. One Friday night when we were entertaining friends for a meal in our home, I received a phone call from one of my church members who said, "Pastor, this is Jean. We are at the hospital, and our daughter has had a stroke. We need you." I didn't tell Jean we had guests. Instead, I told my wife and guests the situation, excused myself, and left immediately for the hospital. On another occasion, I received a call about one of our college students who had fallen beneath a train and been run over. I, of course, left immediately to be with the family. In the case of emergencies, I knew that it was essential to be with the family as quickly as possible. One night my sleep was interrupted by a phone call at two o'clock in the morning. The person told me there had been a death and asked if I could come. I arrived at the home to discover that a young man had killed himself, and, as one could imagine, the family was deeply distraught. I tried to minister to his parents and the other members of the family. I remember being called on another occasion to help a wife get her husband admitted to a mental hospital after he attempted some violent act. These types of situations require immediate attention.

I would always try to visit the person several times a week if he was in the hospital for an extended period. On a normal basis, I visited the hospital at least three times a week when I was pastor of large churches. In smaller churches, I went as needed. Ignoring a church member who is in the hospital communicates an uncaring and, in my opinion, unchristian attitude. This lack of attention will also open the door for legitimate criticism and cause serious conflict not only with the family she ignores but also with the other church family members. Be reachable, be available, and be present when your people need you. That is part of being a good shepherd to your flock.

Calling on Those in the Home
Home Contacts

In many small churches, there is still a traditional expectation that the pastor will try to visit each family in the congregation. With the busyness of family life today, this has become difficult to do. Any pastor who attempts to perform this ministry today in order to get acquainted with his church family will need to call and set up a convenient time for the visit. Otherwise, he will waste time when the family is not at home, or they may not appreciate him arriving unannounced. In large congregations, this is a task that I believe is impossible to accomplish today with all the other pastoral responsibilities. There may be other, better methods in that case.

Evangelism

Some of the calls a pastor makes to a home provide an opportunity to lead someone in the family to make a commitment to Christ as Lord. This would be an evangelistic call.[2] The pastor may be aware of this person's desire through information received from a card in the offering plate, a call to the office, a family member, or the person himself. A call may also be made to a family interested in joining the church. In that situation, pastors need to talk with them about the procedure for doing that. A pastor might also call on an inactive member and try to encourage her to become involved in the life of the church again.

Deaths

Sometimes pastors may be called to the home of a family where a church member is dying. On a number of occasions, I was summoned to come and be with a member of my congregation in his last moments of dying and offer him and the family comfort. If the person was still conscious, I tried to assure him of our church's love for him and of God's love and presence with him. If he desired, I read a passage or two of Scripture and said a prayer with him. I stayed with him as long as he wanted me to. On occasions, I have held the hand of the dying person and the hand of his or her loved one during the final moments of life. By simply being present, the pastor can often bring assurance to a dying person and his family.[3]

On other occasions, a pastor may visit the home of a family who has experienced a loss with the intent to comfort them. Later, the pastor will return to help them plan the funeral service by determining the date and time (with the funeral director), choosing appropriate Scripture and music, and encouraging them to share personal information about the deceased that will enable the pastor to make the service more personal. I usually ask families to share words that best describe the loved one or stories that best depict who she was. This is usually helpful not only for me but also for the family, who is able to release some emotions—from tears to laughter—through the telling.

Nursing Homes or Extended Care Facilities

Many church members today spend their last few years in some kind of retirement home or nursing care facility. These individuals may be in various stages of health: some barely living; others with dementia or Alzheimer's; some with advanced stages of cancer or stroke symptoms; others advanced in age; and others in fairly good health for their age. A pastor will be called on to visit these members on a regular basis. I know one pastor who had ninety-eight members in eleven retirement homes. In cases like that, I would advise setting up a schedule for pastoral visits and also equipping lay members, especially deacons, to visit them. One way to involve laypeople is through a program called the Stephen Ministry. Laypeople receive fifty hours of training and continuing supervision in how to listen attentively, guide a person through difficult times, and keep confidentialities. These church members will not take a pastor's role but can render significant assistance to him or her. Some of these visits might be similar to hospital visits, depending on the state of the person. Other visits may be like calling on someone in their apartment or home.

Homebound or Shut-ins

One of a pastor's essential ministries is calling on church members who are confined to their homes because of illness or age. These people, like those in care centers, are in various stages of health: some lingering with grave illnesses; others with advanced dementia, hardly aware of your visit; others confined to home because of limited mobility due to strokes, arthritis, or accidents; and others facing some other health or mobility problem. I frankly enjoyed these visits and missed them when I was pastor of a church too large for me to visit all who were homebound. Those who were still alert often taught me valuable lessons. I remember calling on one of my members who was in her nineties and still very aware. She always shared with me a psalm she had memorized. A medical doctor who had to retire early because of crippling arthritis and was confined to bed always shared his latest Bible studies and devotional research. Another woman, confined to a wheelchair, welcomed me and shared with me all the letters, cards, phone calls, etc. she had enjoyed with others who were away at college or in the military service or who were shut in as she was. She was still doing what she could to cheer other people, even while she was homebound herself.

During the Advent-Christmas season, I called on every one of my shut-ins and had Communion with them. Some even had a table carefully prepared to observe Communion. They always told me how much this meant to them. Many shared a small cake, loaf of bread, or cookies they had prepared for me. Sometimes when I made a visit, the church member was confined to bed and not aware I was there. In those cases, the visit was mainly with other family members, to encourage and comfort them and especially to listen to their concerns and needs. I always tried to give the people I visited a chance to share their struggles, needs, and hopes and assured them of my love and concern for them. I closed each visit with prayer. My goal was to visit shut-ins at least once a quarter and more often when their health declined. In larger churches where I was pastor, we had a full-time staff member who called on the homebound. In these churches, I still continued to visit faithfully in the hospitals but no longer had the time to engage in the homebound ministry. The loss was mine.

Ministering through Technology

A whole new world has opened up for ministering to people through Facebook, Twitter, websites, e-mails, texting, etc. These virtual technologies have serious flaws and abuses; nevertheless, they can at times be helpful avenues for administering pastoral care. Technology offers a new dimension for communication in our culture today. Some people can be reached through a digital avenue when they cannot be reached in person. Sometimes they will ask for prayers, clarify their health issue, or note personal grief or some other special need or concern through these mediums. They may indicate a particular need that they have not addressed in a group or at church. People who may have experienced a similar problem often respond digitally to the hurting person to offer comfort and support. In her new book, *The Virtual Body of Christ in a Suffering World,* Deanna Thompson offers guidelines for how one might use technology to expand the ministry of Christ and his church to those who are hurting.[4] Another technological avenue, *www.caringbridge.org,* is a website used to communicate the status of a person who has had surgery or is undergoing cancer or other treatments and express love and concern for them.[5]

Pastoral Counseling

Every pastor will be called on to engage in some kind of pastoral counseling. The parade of problems and needs is almost endless—premarital counseling, struggles with marital problems, divorce, alcoholism or drugs, problems with teenagers, illnesses, HIV/AIDS, grief, depression, anxiety, teenage pregnancy, aging, loss of jobs, retirement, doubt, searching for God or faith, and many others. Pastoral counseling takes place as a pastor engages in conversation with a person about his particular problem and seeks to help him work it. Wayne Oates sees the pastor's conversation with the counselee as a series of covenants under the guidance of the Holy Spirit composed of confrontation, confession, forgiveness, restitution, and concern.[6] People come to the pastor for counseling because they recognize that she is unapologetically giving a Christian perspective on the problem or issue at hand. The pastor should not reject or minimize that expectation.

Some pastors have had clinical pastoral training and are better equipped than others to counsel their church members. Seminaries offer various courses to help train and update pastors in the art of counseling, and they should take advantage of these classes.

As I reflect on the years of my pastoral ministry, many faces come back into focus. I remember the young man who had AIDS and was concerned that he had committed an unpardonable sin, and I listened to his fears and assured him of God's forgiveness and unconditional love. I can still see the faces of those torn with fears, doubts, anxiety, confusion, anger, loneliness, and depression who came for a listening ear, hope, and sometimes forgiveness and a quest for redemption.

Sometimes our schedules can become so crowded with counseling that we cannot do our other ministries. Pastors will have to carefully allot the appropriate time to counseling so that it does not impede their other important ministries. I chose not to do long-term counseling, instead limiting my counseling sessions to about three and then referring the person to a professional counselor or appropriate agency. In my last two churches, we had counseling centers that were a part of our church or established by our church, and I could refer church members to those.

Although every counseling situation has its particular approach, there are some standard procedures one can usually follow. The first responsibility is to listen carefully and strive to reflect the thoughts and feelings of the counselee. I try to raise questions for clarification and understanding that will enable me to grasp the problem or issue clearly. I try to assure the person of my concern, support, and willingness to assist her. I try to affirm my confidence in God's love for the person and explain that we will strive to work together to find the appropriate resources to aid him. Sometimes I make another appointment with suggestions for consideration, or I offer to refer the person to a counseling center, a pastoral counselor, a psychiatrist, a medical doctor, or another appropriate agency. I always assure the individual of complete confidentiality, which is essential to any meaningful counseling situation. I often conclude with prayer when it is suitable.

General techniques are certainly not always the same in every counseling situation, but a pastor needs some kind of guidelines in the approach to the person being counseled. Quoting a French proverb, Wayne Oates declares that the counselor's task is "to heal sometimes, to remedy often, to comfort always."[7] As pastors, we should strive to follow that advice.

Notes

1. Wayne E. Oates, *The Christian Pastor*, 3rd ed., rev. (Philadelphia: The Westminster Press, 1982) 190–218.

2. See William Powell Tuck, *Authentic Evangelism: Sharing the Good News with Sense and Sensitivity* (Valley Forge PA: Judson Press, 2002).

3. For other suggestions in this area, see my book, *Facing Grief and Death: Living with Dying* (Cleveland TN: Parson's Porch Books, 2013) 53ff.

4. Deanna Thompson, *The Virtual Body of Christ in a Suffering World* (Nashville: Abingdon Press, 2016).

5. CaringBridge is a charitable 501(c)(3) nonprofit organization, established in 1997, that offers free, personalized websites to people facing various medical conditions.

6. Wayne E. Oates, *Pastoral Counseling* (Philadelphia: The Westminster Press, 1974) 154–58.

7. Ibid., 9.

8

The Pastor as Administrator and Leader

When I committed to go into the ministry, no one informed me that I would need the administration skills of someone trained in the Harvard School of Business. I did take the required seminary course in Church Administration. In fact, I still have the two texts we used in the course, *Building Better Churches* and *The Churchbook*, both written by Gaines Dobbins, which I read carefully and marked up. But I do not remember them being very helpful over my years in ministry. The fault is likely mine because, when I was in seminary, I was more interested in courses on theology and the biblical studies. When I was thrown into the administrative "lion's den" of a local church and had to offer concrete guidance in leadership and church administration, however, I felt inadequate. Although I have continued to read many books and attend special conferences about these areas, I have learned the most through my fifty-some years of having to do it. Few ministers are trained thoroughly in the area of business and administration, but we learn quickly that these areas dominate a great deal of our time. The following suggestions are drawn from what was helpful to me in these areas.

The Necessity of Leadership

The linguistic root of the word "administration" is drawn from the idea of "the steering of a ship." The pastor is to be the one guiding or steering the "ship" of the congregation. Whether the pastor wants to or not, the congregation expects her to offer direction in how the church should conduct not only worship but also administrative matters. When a congregation seeks a new pastor, they often indicate that they want someone who will be a good preacher, a caring pastor, and a good administrator. A pastor must learn quickly that he cannot lead from the middle. He must offer a vision, plan, dream, or goal for the congregation he is called to serve. This does not mean a new pastor will know this path clearly on arrival, but through listening sessions, surveys, retreats, committee meetings, and personal contacts, she will soon see the direction her congregation needs to go. "We as ministers," Cecil Sherman declared, "must strive to go beyond merely maintaining the current level of our churches. We must guide our people into greater service and more powerful worship."[1]

Pastors should seek to offer leadership and direction through mutual congregational assessment rather than a dictatorial, know-it-all fashion. Through listening sessions and contacts, pastors can seek to get commitment from others for the goals they have in mind. Careful planning and evaluation are important. Identify your goal for the church. You cannot hit your target if you have not clearly identified your goal. It may be to reach fifty new members in a congregation with declining membership, to bring in more staff to carry out a more effective ministry, to pay off the church's building debt, to do certain mission activities in the community around your church, to train lay leaders for their responsibilities, or some other ministry. The point is to define a goal and then determine what it will take to reach it.

Gil W. Stafford offers the "spiritual director" model as an approach to pastoral leadership. The four roles of the spiritual director are to serve as the steward of sacred safety, as a holy listener, as the advocate of silence, and as a wisdom teacher. Stafford's book, *When Leadership and Spiritual Direction Meet*, offers ways to use a spiritual model rather than a business one.[2] Stafford believes that the key for leading by spiritual direction involves the leader's ability to be in a meaningful, significant, give-give relationship with his or her people. He quotes Richard Rohr to describe what he means by spiritual direction: "Good leaders must have a certain capacity for non-polarity thinking and full-access knowing (prayer), a tolerance for ambiguity (faith), an ability to hold creative tensions (hope), and an ability to care (love) beyond their personal advantage."[3]

Another approach is that of applying systems thinking for effective leadership, which Israel Galindo describes in his book *Perspectives on*

Congregational Leadership. He delineates how to use the Bowen Family Systems Theory (BFST) in the practical realities of everyday ministry and in leadership in particular.[4]

In a crisis, Ronald Heifetz observes that we often look for someone with the wrong kind of leadership. We want someone with easy answers, decisions, and strength. What we should want instead, he suggests, is "leadership that will challenge us to face problems for which there are no simple, painless solutions—problems that require us to learn new ways."[5] A real leader may induce pain that the organization has been avoiding, but, if they respond appropriately, such a leader has the resources to help them shape the future. William Willimon asserts that real pastoral leadership may often inflict "pain" in order to force the congregation to engage in difficult conversations about problems or issues they have ignored.[6]

Servant Leadership

The goal of offering pastoral leadership is not to call attention to one's gifts or abilities but to follow the "servant" model of Jesus. Jesus declared, "The greatest of all is the servant of all" (Matt 23:11). In the upper room on the night Jesus had his last Passover feast with his disciples, he took a towel and basin and washed their feet (John 13:4-5). In this act, he modeled for us the servant role he calls us to follow. "For the Son of man also came not to be served but to serve," Jesus said, "and to give his life a ransom for many" (Mark 10:45). In writing about the incarnated Christ, Paul observed that he "emptied himself, taking the form of a servant" (Phil 2:7). As a pastor, always remember that you and I are called to be servant leaders. Therefore, we should serve Christ and his church in a humble manner.

Lay Leadership

Laity may be challenged to find ways of serving and visioning for their church in various ways. Established committees like the Mission Committee or the Board of Christian Education and Spiritual Formation may continuously seek new, creative avenues of ministry. A special Dreaming or Visioning Committee may be formed to undertake this task. In one of my churches, this special committee was called "Rekindle the Vision." I have challenged various committees and individuals to dream about new or different ways our church might minister in our community and within our own fellowship. Often laypeople recognize needs and respond with the method and volunteers to help a church implement a way to help in that area. I have preached sermons in which I have shared some of my "dreams" or "visions" for our church and have had dialogue in group sessions about these visions. I have written articles in our church newsletter about these dreams as well.

Some Lay Leadership Goals

Challenging and guiding the laity into undertaking essential projects and setting goals can be a positive approach. This might entail working through the deacons, church council, the board of administration, or by forming a special committee or task force. Care should be taken to allow enough time and thought to determine the best approaches.

Determine the Identity of Your Church

Every church has a distinctive personality and identity. Pastors must determine and understand that special identity if they are to enable the congregation to minister creatively in the community. "Unless pastors understand that they carry out ministry within the contextual culture of the congregation," Israel Galindo notes, "I suspect they will never be able to effect developmental change in that system."[7] The size, surroundings, and age of a congregation will be a factor. Whether a congregation is filled with conflict or unrest will also affect its mission. If a congregation is rigid and closed minded, the pastor should address that issue first. Some congregations are so inwardly focused that the pastor has to spend time addressing that perspective. Some congregations are made up of highly educated and mission-minded people and are thus more open to dreaming and visioning than others. Before the congregation can focus on ways to serve, the pastor must put a finger on the pulse of that congregation and seek to determine how it sees itself and how the community sees it. Determining the church's identity will enable the leadership to minister in a suitable way for its own body and for the community around it. "Leadership always has a where and when—a context. Without a clear understanding of leadership's times and contexts," Robert Dale observes, "leaders may mistakenly provide leadership for another place and time."[8]

Set Goals

The pastor is charged with the responsibility of guiding the congregation in setting some goals or a vision for the future. In an appropriate group in your church, talk about the dreams, goals, or plans for the future. Brainstorm together with your group about these goals and how the church might achieve them. Spend time in prayer about these goals to determine if you feel they are in keeping with what God wants for your church at this time in its ministry. Ask for a commitment to meet at definite times in the future for further planning sessions. No worthy goal can be reached without careful planning and prayer. Try to set realistic goals for your congregation and devise a definite action plan to reach them. Prioritize your plan by setting deadlines, listing the steps to reach your goal, gathering the necessary financial support, designating people to carry out various steps in the project, and choosing a means of evaluating the progress and verifying the efficiency of the plan. As pastor, remain on top of the work of the group and offer your support and evaluation.

Be the Motivator for Reaching Goals

It is not enough simply to talk about your dreams or goals; you need to strive to motivate your congregation to reach them. How do you achieve that? You may need to form special committees, such as a long-range planning committee, to implement the goal, or get the support and assistance of your deacons, board of administration, church council, or some other official body. A weekend retreat or several evening sessions to plan and discuss the steps would be helpful. Depending on your goal, preaching and teaching about the vision, dreams, or goals is an effective and necessary part in motivating your people to get involved and support the efforts. Finally, guidance in getting the necessary support in your church budget is essential. Some financial support for big goals is almost always necessary.

Involve Others

As I have already indicated, the pastor should not seek to be "the lone ranger" in this project. A good leader not only listens to others but also involves them in the process, trains and equips them to do the job, delegates responsibility for getting the job done to others, and continues to encourage people as they work. Spiritual gift studies can help pastors recognize and enlist people in the congregation who can assist in certain projects. At proper times, the committee and pastor should evaluate the progress, means, and efforts of those involved in the project. Be willing to make necessary changes, revise the goal, or even determine whether to abandon the present undertaking and go in another direction altogether.

The Basic Tasks of Pastoral Administration

I believe that there are several basic tasks in effective pastoral administration or leadership. *First, the pastor should work to build trust.* The congregation will not follow a pastor they do not trust or whom they feel does not have their best interests at heart. Establishing trust with our laypeople takes time that is earned through caring pastoral care, establishing relationships with individuals in the congregation, living with character that matches what we say, communicating graciously with those who differ with us, and preaching sermons that relate to the genuine needs of the congregation. Trust is established over a lengthy period within a congregation where a pastor has responded lovingly to them in times of illnesses, death, and grief as well as in happy times of weddings or the births of children. For this reason, I encourage pastors not to make any major changes in the life of a congregation until they have been there a while and earned the people's trust.

Second, the pastor should lead the congregation to manage its organizational structures and activities well. This entails guiding deacons, committees, and boards; overseeing the education organization like the Sunday school; supervising the staff, if applicable; setting goals or plans; enlisting and training people to serve in various capacities; and offering some form of supervision and evaluation of the ministries.

Third, the pastor should help the congregation be true to its declared mission statement. Many congregations adopt a mission statement but function in a way that differs radically from their stated purpose. At times, the pastor may need to help the church clarify or modify the mission purpose and ask, "Is what we are doing administratively consistent with our mission statement?"

Fourth, the pastor should guide the congregation to perform administrative functions in light of the people's spiritual commitment to Christ as Lord of the church. The spiritual authenticity of what a church does through its budget, programs, ministries, and all administrative activities should be solidly based on the people's commitment to serve Jesus Christ as Lord. The pastor has a responsibility to be the "voice of God," guiding the congregation not to forget, misstate, abuse, or fail to remember its basic mission responsibility to share the good news. Sometimes in budget discussions, I have seen committees totally forget the main purpose of the church. Instead, they surrender to taking care of the church building and its costs first, without regard for the call to serve Christ and others.

Fifth, the pastor should be an effective administrator who inspires and encourages the congregation and strives to offer a vision for service. A negative, fussing, defeatist approach will not inspire or encourage church people to want to engage in the life and ministry of a congregation. Genuine pastoral charisma will draw people in and encourage them to be involved. The engaging, charismatic approach of a pastor will inspire parishioners to use their spiritual gifts in ministry. As Ronald Heifetz asserts, a leader has to mobilize the organization to "address the conflicts in the values people hold or to diminish the gap between the values people stand for and the reality they face."[9] Like a good coach inspires his team to rise from losing a game to achieving victory, so an inspiring pastor will motivate her congregation to rise up and serve Christ who has redeemed us.

Administration Helps in Planning

Sometimes the various programs and activities of a church seem to collide like two trains meeting on a track without being aware of each other. This is often the result of poor planning or ignorance of what else is happening in the life of a congregation. Careful planning through staff meetings, church council, board of deacons, or board of administration can keep the whole church aware of various programs, meetings, funerals, weddings, and day-by-day ministries of the congregation. This will help avoid the over-lapping of programs and the confusion of what meets when and where in the church facility. Planning allows each person with a committee or board meeting, a special or normal activity, to get on the calendar. Planning ahead allows time for all to have input into the schedule without basing it on one person's decision. The church should publish the times and dates of these activities and programs so everyone is aware of them and will not seek to schedule something in the time already taken. A large calendar that includes all pertinent information could be placed on the church's website.

Planning can also help the church communicate. Many church members often complain that they do not know when a group will meet or what the church is presently undertaking. Sometimes this is the fault of the church because leaders have not planned far enough in advance to inform the congregation in time or have simply been derelict in making the congregation aware. Communication is a vital factor in a church's life, and the pastor and others who do the planning should strive to communicate effectively what the church is doing and how its people can be engaged. A failure in this area is inexcusable. Good planning is essential.

Pastoral Supervision

Pastors with staff members such as a secretary, janitor, or other staff ministers are charged with offering guidance and supervision. The pastor is
expected to offer supervision to committees as well.[10] The pastor is responsible for seeing that these people do their jobs effectively and honoring the
time they serve. Each position needs a job description that clearly spells
out responsibilities, hours of service, time off, sick leave, benefits, etc. The
pastor needs to affirm these workers, praise them when they do a good
job, and privately offer direction in areas where they may fall short. The
pastor must communicate often and clearly with his staff. "The relationship between a senior pastor and associate pastors is often the key to the
health and ministry of a church," Jason Byassee observes, "yet it receives
next to no attention in seminaries or in literature on ministry."[11] His article
presents ministry service from the perspective of associates who work with
the senior pastor. I have found through the years that good office administrators were worth their weight in gold. They made my ministry more
effective, conserved my time, and kept me informed about pastoral needs
and other matters. Custodians can likewise be most helpful not only in
caring for the building but also in apprising the pastor of matters regarding
maintenance that require the attention of the proper committee.

Leading for a Variety of Ministries

The pastor should seek to challenge the congregation to engage in a wide
variety of ministries both within and outside the church building. In one of
the churches where I was pastor, the church provided a tutoring program
and meals for underprivileged children. The same church had an effective
ministry to the deaf for many years. When I was called to be pastor of St.
Matthews Baptist Church in Louisville, Kentucky, it was with the understanding that its new multi-million-dollar building would offer ministries
seven days a week at any time in the day or night. That church engaged in
many servant ministries.

Some of these ministries came about through the visions of our own
laypeople. While I was pastor, one of our members, Mr. Clyde Carroll, who
founded our church's nursing home ministry, received a special citation
for his work. The nursing home ministry in our church began with the
vision of one layperson under the guidance of our minister of pastoral care,
Malcolm Marler, and that service was later conducted in seventeen nursing
homes with a hundred people serving weekly. They got no compensation

from it other than the joy of helping others. Our church also had a HUGG Ministry in which we went into the homes of our people who were unable to come to church and ministered to their needs.

Additionally, we had a job club that offered help to people looking for employment. We established as well the Wayne Oates Counseling Center in our church where people could come and find help in times of need. The counseling center continues to this day under the name of the St. Matthews Counseling Center. Our minister of pastoral care was responsible for establishing widow and widower support groups, divorce support groups, and many of the other programs that were instituted. Income tax preparation for the elderly was also provided. We had a clothing closet and an AA support group. We had an Alzheimer's Day Care Center, at that time the only one in the state of Kentucky, which offered an adult respite program for people with Alzheimer's disease. We had a kindergarten, nursery school, and a mother's day out program. We began a Spanish ministry, holding a Hispanic service of worship with a Spanish pastor who was a seminary student at the time.

Programs of all kinds reached out to the aging and needy. The opportunities for service were endless. These ministries arose as the laity and ministers in the church saw needs and responded to the challenges. They did not arise from the pastor's vision alone but through an atmosphere created for dreaming and responding to such challenges. Every church should assess the needs in their own community and find a way to minister to those needs. In some of my other churches we had ministries for the deaf, tutoring classes, programs for the mentally handicapped, welfare assistance, repair and service ministries to assist families with special needs, craft projects, exercise classes, and others. No matter how big or small your church is, and regardless of the types of ministries the Lord places before you, you as the pastor are charged with the responsibility to offer leadership in those efforts.

The Money Challenge

No pastor can lead a congregation effectively and yet be unwilling to address or get involved in the financial matters of the church. I believe the pastor has to preach and teach about stewardship and be willing to encourage tithing in the congregation. My book *The Forgotten Beatitude: Worshiping through Stewardship* offers examples of sermons I have preached in this area.[12] Pastors must set an example by their own faithful stewardship if they expects the congregation to follow them in this matter. Too many pastors are afraid to speak about money in the church, and I believe that is a mistake. The members of the congregation rarely give effectively if the church leadership does not take a positive stand on stewardship. The pastor needs to challenge the deacons and committee members to be faithful givers. In churches I have served, we had a policy that a person who did not give faithfully to the church was not eligible to serve as a deacon or on a committee.

I have always met with the finance committees and the budget planning committees as they engaged in their responsibilities, no matter the size of the congregation where I was pastor. The pastor's input is critical to ensure that the congregation has a budget that not only deals with physical and financial business but also focuses on the Christ-like way of ministry. The pastor, in my opinion, is charged with the responsibility of keeping the budget "spiritual" and not merely overseeing a list of figures. Pastors can hold up the model of servant ministry for the congregation in the area of finances.

The Toll and Reward of Leadership

Any time pastors offer leadership to their congregations, there is always the possibility of receiving criticism, of someone misunderstanding what they say, or of someone disagreeing with them and voicing opposition. Pastors should not be surprised by this but instead respond in a positive way, seeking to clarify or offer corrections where possible. Sometimes the criticism may be so severe that a pastor may experience a sense of isolation when others do not rally to her support. She may become weary and fatigued with the heavy burden of criticism. I will deal with the issue of conflict in chapter 12, but let me say here that the pastor needs to find support from the appropriate committees or people who have helped her lead in a particular matter. She need not stand alone if other church groups have supported her endeavors.

On the other side of this issue, however, I have found that when the pastor is willing to offer genuine, informed leadership, he is usually met with a positive response from the congregation. I have found that the congregation shows appreciation for the pastor's willingness to take a stand on an issue and not remain aloof or unconcerned. Sometimes they see the pastor's stand on social issues like race relations, war and peace, the environment, or some other matter as one of courage, and they respect him for taking such a position that might open him to criticism. The pastor's willingness to be a voice for a worthy goal gives others engaged in the same task assurance and a model for leadership. I have found that I earned a lot more respect and support when I took a stand on an issue or new program than when I did not.

In one of my congregations, I was away at a conference when the deacons met and voted to defund a mission project that our youth choir planned to undertake. When I returned and learned of this, I called the deacons into another session. Although I had only served as pastor at this church for a short time, I felt it was important to address the matter. I reminded the deacons that, according to our constitution and bylaws, when an item was approved in the church budget in a regular business session, they did not have the authority to change a program without bringing it back before the church and calling for a vote on the amendment. They decided to drop the matter. Later, one of the older deacons who had been in the meeting told my wife, "Last night your husband told us how a church is supposed to be run. And it's about time somebody did!" I have found that leadership at times may result in some criticism and rejection, but more often it brings us respect and support. When our goal as pastor is to serve as our Lord did, I believe the church will always function better.

Notes

1. Cecil Sherman, *To Be a Good and Faithful Servant* (Macon GA: Smyth & Helwys, 2010) 69.

2. Gil W. Stafford, *When Leadership and Spiritual Direction Meet* (New York: Rowman & Littlefield, 2014).

3. Ibid., 179. See Richard Rohr, *The Naked Now: Learning to See as the Mystics See* (New York: Crossword Publishing, 2009) 158.

4. Israel Galindo, *Perspectives on Congregational Leadership* (Vienna VA: Educational Consultants, 2009).

5. Ronald Heifetz, *Leadership without Easy Answers* (Cambridge MA: Harvard University Press, 1998) 2.

6. William Willimon, "Why Leaders Are a Pain," *The Christian Century,* 17 February 2016, 20–23.

7. Galindo, *Perspectives on Congregational Leadership,* 86.

8. Robert D. Dale, *Leadership for a Changing Church* (Nashville: Abingdon Press, 1998) 14.

9. Heifetz, *Leadership without Easy Answers*, 22.

10. In my chapters on "Church Committees" and "Healthy Staff Relations" (chs. 9–10), I offer specific guidance in these areas.

11. Jason Byassee, "Team Players: What Do Associate Pastors Want?" *The Christian Century*, 24 January 2006, 18.

12. William Powell Tuck, *The Forgotten Beatitude: Worshiping through Stewardship* (Gonzalez FL: Energion Publications, 2016).

9

Church Committees

I recently received a letter from a minister friend who wrote, "I can't find a replacement for the committee system, but I would be open to a suggestion on those nights with no end to the process in sight!" What pastor has not felt the same way after a long night in church committee meetings? Other than sermon preparation and pastoral calling, nothing so dominates a minister's time as preparing for and attending committee meetings. A pastor friend has a small placard hanging in his office that reads, "When God became incarnate, He didn't send a committee!"

Ministers often grow weary of committee work, but to this day it still seems to be the most effective way to conduct church administrative affairs. I have met with committees at breakfast, lunch, and dinner; Sunday afternoons before and after church; and in the mornings, afternoons, and nights of almost every day in the week. Sometimes we think we are going to meet ourselves coming and going. Most churches have dozens of committees to carry out their functions. These may include the following: personnel, nominating, finance, trustee, baptismal, Communion, worship, ushering, audio services, youth, children, preschool, public relations, property and space, food services, constitution and bylaws, and education. Some of these are active and others are almost nonexistent in many churches, even if they are on the books and people are elected to the committee. The larger the church, often the more elaborate the committee structure seems to become. What is the purpose of church committees? What kind of guidance should pastors offer them?

The Purpose of Church Committees

Committees are helpful to churches in several ways. First, they help effectively maintain the organized structure of a church. Without good committees, a church might soon fall apart. Lay workers are essential to carrying out the ministries. Second, committees help meet any problems that may arise in the life of the church. Third, the personal involvement of church members who plan and carry out church activities gives them a strong sense of "ownership" in the church itself. They are vitally involved in the life and work of the church on a day-by-day basis. Fourth, committees are agents of church training, growth, and spiritual renewal. They help set the direction, guidance, and function of the local congregation.

As much as some ministers complain about committees, they know deep down that they are essential to the life of a church. No pastor or staff can or should run a church alone. The ministry of laypeople is essential. Paul's epistles are filled with his acknowledgment of the role of laypeople in the life of the early church. The last chapter of his epistle to the Romans lists the laity who assisted him in ministry. Few laypeople are willing to support a church financially when they do not feel like they are a significant part of its ongoing work. They want "ownership" in the church's life and do not want to stand on the edge and admire the minister's programs and ideas.

Committees provide laypeople with avenues of services within the local church. Here they can exercise their gifts and render their services, whether working in the kitchen, carrying out building maintenance, keeping financial records, or directing a play. Committees also draw a variety of people into the ministries of the church so each one can use his or her talents. In one church where I was pastor, I saw a retired executive drawn into the life of our church when he was asked to serve as chairperson of the constitution and bylaws committee. He had never served in our church but was noted in the business and civic community for his leadership skills. The committee gave him an excellent opportunity to use his gifts, and he later became involved in the total life of the church.

This involvement of laypeople in the church life through committees enables them to get to know personally the pastor and other staff members. This builds better relations within the whole church. The "power structure" of a church does not belong in the hands of a few; it needs to be shared throughout the church by a wide variety of participants.

Establishing Committees

Committees are established in a variety of ways in churches. Some are established by the constitution and bylaws, and a committee on committees or a nominating committee chooses the members. Others might be appointed by the pastor or by the deacon council. Some are standing committees that continue year after year. It is wise to have committee responsibilities spelled out and the size of each committee indicated in the church constitution. Most committee members are elected for three-year terms, rotating off at the end of the third year and remaining ineligible for reelection for a year. It is also helpful to have a good representation of age and sex on the committee rather than any one age or sex dominating. It is especially useful to place people on committees that use their gifts, abilities, and interests rather than assigning them based on the length of their church membership and frequency of their attendance. When the committee gathers to conduct its ministry, the chairperson should have access to the guidelines or a description of the committee's work. The purpose of the committee and its particular goals should be set forth clearly for all to hear and understand. Sometimes this is done by giving each member a copy of its committee descriptions in the constitution and bylaws.

The Committee Agenda

The agenda for each committee meeting needs to be laid out carefully so all can see what will be addressed in a particular session. If the agenda can be provided to each member ahead of time, that is even more helpful. The chairperson should establish by mutual consent the length of the meeting and the best time for the next meeting or meetings. A few minutes can be used early in the meeting to determine both. Be sure to allot enough time for the session. Early planning can help by giving committee members advanced notice of the meeting so they can get it on their calendars and prepare ahead of time.

The Importance of the Chairperson

One of the keys to effective committee work is the role of the chairperson. He or she can make or break a committee. A *laissez-faire* leader who is too passive will let the committee waste time on everything but the issues before them, accomplishing nothing. An authoritarian leader dominates and manipulates those on the committee to simply agree with the leader's ideas and wishes and seldom gives an opportunity for real discussion or dialogue. This kind of leadership style often provokes hostility and frustration on the part of other committee members, who feel that they are not allowed a part in the process or decision making.

A more democratic leader seeks to involve all committee members in the discussion and work of the committee. This person tries to draw the best insights from everyone on the committee, aware that the contributions of all will enable the committee to arrive at the best possible decision for the whole group. No single person has the only or the best insight. That is the reason several people are chosen to be on the committee. An effective chairperson leads the discussion but does not seek to dominate, manipulate, or control the rest of the committee. He or she is a resource but not the only resource. Each person is allowed to express his or her opinion, and each opinion is heard with respect, whether one agrees with it or not. The chairperson works to avoid letting someone's hidden agenda dominate a meeting. Someone may have an old quarrel to interject. The chairperson should attempt to get the committee on the issue at hand and avoid problems unrelated to the committee's business. The chairperson needs to keep the purpose of the committee before the group and set the limits.

Conflicts can be overcome or avoided when freedom of discussion is allowed. Members need to feel that they can express themselves without restrictions in the discussion of the committee's task. Everyone may not agree on the conclusion, but if each person has a say, then all are more likely at least to be satisfied with the decision. John D. Rockefeller was a member of the Riverside Church in New York City, to which he gave millions to build. Often he opposed issues in committee meetings, only to be elected chairman of carrying out the very thing he had originally opposed. And he did that work graciously.

Detailed meeting minutes provide a record of each meeting and the committee's work. This will keep the committee on track and save time. Committee members can receive the minutes by mail or email to avoid using meeting time to read them. They can be approved or amended at the regular meeting.

The Goals of Committees

Every committee should strive to do at least five things. First, they should clarify the reason for being. What is the committee supposed to do? Second, once the committee knows its purpose, the group should brainstorm for creative ways of doing the task more effectively. Third, the committee should formulate goals and assignments. Fourth, they should determine the means for implementing duties and responsibilities. Fifth, they should find ways to check and evaluate their work to see they are fulfilling their goals.

The Pastor's Role

The pastor or staff member has at least two functions within every committee. First, she should see that the committee carries out its purpose in the overall church plan. Second, she should provide the chairperson and entire committee with any resources or guidance that will enable them to function more effectively in fulfilling their duties.

As a pastor, I have attempted to work with committees both behind the scenes and at committee meetings. I have met privately with the chairperson to talk about the purpose and function of the committee, offering suggestion for the agenda or goals. I have tried to help define the task of certain committees. People cannot do a task that they do not understand. I have sometimes freely shared my dreams, goals, or hopes for a committee. I have encouraged the chairperson to share his dreams, problems, difficulties, or frustrations with the committee's purpose or with various members. Other times I have listened to members of committees complain about the way the chairperson led the group.

Sometimes my secretary has prepared the agenda or other materials the chairperson wanted to give the committee. On other occasions I have simply discussed the meeting over the telephone with the chairperson and made suggestions or quietly listened. I have also tried to provide resource materials that the chairperson could read or distribute to the rest of the committee. Many denominational headquarters have pamphlets available on the work of typical committees in the church. If available, these can be a good source for a committee and chairperson.

When attending a committee meeting, I have tried to be supportive of the chairperson and the committee in their task. I have helped clarify their assignment. I have served as a resource and tried not to dominate a meeting or keep others from expressing opinions. I have drawn into the discussion people whom I thought were staying in the background, so we could get their insights and participation. I have listened and challenged others to listen to their brother or sister who wanted to speak. I am convinced that discussion is a healthy activity for a church.

I have attempted at times to mediate conflict and calm troubled waters. I have quietly tried to keep a committee focused on the issue. I have cautioned that we need to be fair and kind with one another. I have sought to encourage committees and express my appreciation for their time and involvement in a worthy use of their gifts in ministry. I also have tried to remind committees that their work, reports, or nominations must be presented to the church before any action is taken. If a committee is tasked with doing work or making decisions for the church as a whole, then the church must make the final judgment on that committee's work. When an issue goes to the church, it may still be discussed, revised, rejected, or adopted. But when a committee has done the best job possible, its members can be confident of a task well done.

Committees can sometimes be time-consuming for a pastor or other staff workers. But I wonder how we could carry out the ministry of the church effectively today without the involvement of laypeople. I thank God daily for them. They do much of the church's real ministry.

10

Cultivating Spiritual Gifts for Ministry

One of the essential ministries of the church is to help its members discover or use their spiritual gifts. In his fine book on spiritual gifts, Robert Cornwall declares boldly, "The theology of giftedness begins with the promise that all the gifts necessary for the people of God to serve are present in the community."[1] How are we going to run the church? The church should function today the same way that our Lord intended it to be run when he founded it—through the gifts of those who are his disciples. As each Christian contributes his or her gifts in ministry to our Lord, the work of the church will be accomplished.

A Variety of Spiritual Gifts

In Ephesians 4:7, 11-12 and 1 Corinthians 12:1-13, Paul says that there is a great variety of spiritual gifts. This has been true from the beginning of the church. Look at the first disciples. Simon Peter was radically different from John. Peter had gifts of leadership and courage but at times displayed an impulsive spirit, a fiery temper, cowardice, and indecision. Thomas came to a deep faith only through his questions, doubts, and fears. John, the beloved disciple, was loving, gentle, and quiet. Andrew served behind the scenes. He was always friendly, not seeking recognition, and always introducing others to Jesus. Mary and Martha had very different personalities. One was concerned about the preparation of food, the other with learning at her Master's feet. Paul arose on the scene, nurtured by rabbinic scholarship. Without question, he was a leader and organizer, but sometimes he was arrogant and uncompromising, other times gentle and loving, coura-geous and bold. Mary Magdalene celebrated her gift of service even to the point of public embarrassment when she washed the feet of Jesus. The early church began by drawing on the diverse gifts of these first believers.

In the Ephesian and Corinthian Scriptures mentioned above and in several other passages of Scripture, the variety of spiritual gifts is clearly noted. In Romans 12:6-8, Paul mentions seven different gifts: prophecies, service, teaching, exhortation, giving or contributing, leadership, and mercy. In 1 Corinthians 12:8-10, 28, there is an additional listing of wisdom, knowl-edge, faith, healing, miracles, discerning of spirits, tongues, interpretation, apostle, helps, and administration. The fourth chapter of Ephesians adds two other gifts—evangelist and pastor. Prophecy is mentioned in all three references. Prophecy is not so much telling what will happen in the future as "forth telling" God's word of judgment today. Teacher is mentioned in Romans and again in Ephesians. Most of the twenty are only mentioned one time. First Peter 4:10-11 has additional words about gifts.

Are these all of the spiritual gifts? I do not think so. These are not exhaustive lists of all possible spiritual gifts. Instead, they note the partic-ular gifts that were necessary to meet the needs in the life of the young church at that time. Special gifts should not be narrowly confined to these. Paul often gave a different listing himself. The varying situations in Rome, Corinth, and Ephesus demanded different gifts. Even from the beginning, the church had a variety of gifts.

The Necessity of Diversity

Rather than these gifts being merely incidental, it is likely that our Lord intended for the church to be diverse by nature. All Christians are not supposed to be alike. We all bring differing gifts to God to perform different functions. As someone once observed, "There is no one best way to do everything." Throughout the twelfth chapter of Corinthians, Paul stresses the diversity and interdependence of these gifts. All gifts are important in God's sight, and God seeks to draw out believers' gifts.

The church recognizes that all Christians have gifts. Some may be more gifted than others, but every single Christian has a gift that he or she can use in ministry for Christ. Several years ago, my wife Emily and I were in a circle along with others at a church function. The leader said to me, "Bill, would you take Emily's place?" "No," I responded, "I can't do that. I will change seats with her, but I can't take her place." I can't take Emily's place. She has her gifts and I have mine. The church must acknowledge the gifts that others have. As Romans 12:6 states, "Having gifts that differ accordingly to the grace given us, let us use them."

Provoking the Use of Gifts

One of the ministries of the church is to help provoke the gifts within us so we can use them in service for Christ. How do we discover these gifts? The Church of the Saviour in Washington, DC, includes these words in its statement: our church is a ship where "there are no passengers—all are crew members." One of the basic purposes of the church, as they understand it, is to evoke the gifts people have so they will be used in service for Christ. No one can be a member of that church and not use his or her gift in some ministry. Each person must discover his or her gift and use it. Sadly, in too many churches, people do not even know what their gifts are, and if they do know what they are, many of them are unwilling to use them. In a true church, there can be no spectators—all are participants in ministry.

Gordon Cosby, pastor of the Church of the Saviour until his death, observed three ways people can learn to discover their spiritual gifts. The first way you discover your gifts is with a sense of *eureka*. Aha! A light goes on within, and you feel a strong sense of excitement and satisfaction about the discovery. Second, you begin to dream about what you can do with that gift in ministry. Third, you realize that you need to talk about your gift because it is so important to you. This doesn't mean that every time we do something in church, we will find it exciting. We may have to discover our particular gifts by trying various tasks. We can be taught to grow in an area so our gifts can be nurtured and improved. Sometimes our work may be a burden, feel like an obligation, or be difficult and at times even painful. God has not promised that our service will always be easy. We might fail at some of our tasks. But we can be sure that when we discover our gifts and are willing to use them, God will help us serve others and experience an inner sense of blessing.

Spiritual Gifts Today

Yes, there are a variety of gifts. There is not only one way to serve Christ. What spiritual gifts might we see in the church today? Those using their gifts might be biblical scholars, theologians, church musicians, administrators, missionaries, dramatists, artists, writers, journalists, counselors, social workers, or preachers. There simply is no end to the variety of gifts that can be used as they are called forth in service for Christ.

A congregation needs many gifts in order to carry out functions within the church building. More than five hundred people served in many different ways in my Louisville church when I was pastor there. However, all spiritual gifts do not have to be used within a church building. Many people will use their gifts in the world for God. For example, the gift of evangelism ought to be used in the world to bear witness to God's saving grace. This gift is best used not in the church but in the world, outside the doors of the church building. We are also challenged to minister to the poor, hungry, sick, and homeless; to help overcome racism, injustice, crime, disease, and other problems. Our Scripture texts tell us that there are a variety of spiritual gifts. We are not all alike or gifted alike. Let's recognize that fact and be grateful.

All Gifts Come from God

Paul reminds us that all gifts come from God. We receive these gifts by the grace of God. God created the world, and we receive this gift of creation. Salvation is God's gift: "For God so loved the world that he gave . . ." (John 3:16). Handel wrote, "Unto us a Son is given." God's gift of his Son is a wonderful gift that we have to receive. Much of life comes to us as a gift from God. The sunshine, rain, air, and our own lives are all gifts from God. We have to assimilate, discover, motivate, train, and guide ourselves in the use of these gifts. First, however, we must acknowledge that they are indeed gifts.

Not a Call for Pride

As we affirm our gifts from God, this should not cause a sense of pride. We should have a feeling of joy that we can use our gifts in ministry for God. Some people say they do not want to discover their gift because it may make them prideful. There is no question of the real difference between spiritual gifts and human talents. Flaunting one's talent for personal reasons can be an expression of pride. Using your spiritual gift for God, on the other hand, is recognizing that your gift is to be used not for self-glory but to glorify God. I seek not to call attention to myself with my gift but to recognize that God has converted me; therefore, I am directing my gift to use in ministry for God. I may know my talents instinctively, but I discover my spiritual gift after I have been converted, and I dedicate that gift to

God. If my desire is to use my gift for a selfish goal or in order to receive gratification and praise from others, then I miss the point. Spiritual gifts are misused if they are focused on oneself. We are to point others to God, not seek more recognition for ourselves.

The church seeks to affirm the spiritual gifts in its members. What gifts have others affirmed in your life? For example, what are some of the gifts the church I served in Louisville affirmed about our minister of music, Milburn Price? We could acknowledge his musical gifts, administration, teaching, writing, the warmth of his personality, and others. From time to time our church recognized the spiritual gifts of others and affirmed them. We made a long list of particular gifts that God affirmed within the life of that congregation. I have felt the affirmation within my own life of certain gifts that this church and other congregations affirmed. Each of us seeks to dedicate his or her gifts to God because we realize that all gifts come from God.

One year when I was pastor at St. Matthews Baptist Church in Louisville, Kentucky, we had a deacons' retreat at the Sisters of Charity Nazareth Retreat Center at Nazareth, Kentucky. A small chapel there has beautiful stained-glass windows. On one side of the chapel, the windows represent God's gifts to humanity. These gifts are depicted as creation, nativity, crucifixion, resurrection, and Pentecost. On the other side of the chapel are windows that depict what the nuns say are their gifts to God. These gifts are teaching, nursing, obedience, chastity, and poverty. A small group of women have served God since about 1850 as nurses, teachers, and spiritual guides. They have offered their gifts in service for God in that part of Kentucky. Like these dedicated women, each of us needs to acknowledge that our gifts come from God and are to be used for God's glory.

Gifted for the Unity of the Church

Paul was also bold to affirm that spiritual gifts are to be used for the unity of the church. Today, people often use their gifts to fragment the church instead of unifying it. Can you imagine accepting the call to a church with a four-way faction? Paul went to the Corinthian church to try to heal such a division. Within that church, some wanted to follow the leadership of Apollos, others rallied around Simon Peter, others chose Paul, and others said they just wanted to follow Christ. In writing to the Corinthian church, Paul was striving for unity. He wanted to end the four-way split and draw the people together. He saw disunity as one of the worst things that could happen in a church. Paul felt that those who tried to use their gifts to divide the fellowship and bring about fragmentation or cause problems were working against Christ, whose body they were supposed to be. "The purpose of any individual gift always goes beyond the individual persons," Gary Harbaugh reminds us, "since it is to be used for the community, for the upbuilding of the church, and for the work of ministry to all people."[2]

One in Service

The church is Christ's body. Just as the human body is diverse and inter-related, so is the church. Paul wrote in 1 Corinthians 12 that the human body cannot say, "Well, I am the hand, so I am more important than the foot" or "I am the ear, and I am more important than the eye." All parts are important to the work of the whole. The human body has many different parts—eyes, ears, feet, hands, etc.—and all are important to the functioning of the body. If the body parts were at war with one another, we would destroy our body. We need to be unified. The church is supposed to be one in serving Christ. Every Christian is to work for the unity of the body. If we are working against the unity of the body, we are not seeking to do the will of Christ. We are working against him. Jesus laid down his life for the church, and as the church represents the body of Christ, who was the incarnation of God, so we seek to carry on his ministry through his body, the church.

Every Christian has a position in God's creation. We all have a place in God's grand design. All of us have a part in God's great orchestra—the church. The pastor needs to cultivate and help grow the variety of spiritual gifts so they might be used in building up the unity of the church and its ministry in the world.

All Gifts Are Important

In working for the unity of the church, we recognize that no ministry in God's sight is higher or lower than another. Part of the struggle Paul saw in the Corinthian church concerned those who thought their gifts were better than others. Some thought that because they could speak in tongues, they were superior to others in their gifts. Some may have thought that a pastor, an apostle, or some other function was superior. Paul's analogy of the variety of the parts of the human body was meant to affirm the diversity and importance of every part. All spiritual gifts are important to God. None ranks higher than another. All are important. As Kenneth Hemphill reminds us, "Every believer has a unique function in the body, therefore all are necessary and all depend upon the ministry of others."[3]

Every single one of us is an important part of the body of Christ. Our goal is to work for unity. If we are doing anything to work against unity, then we don't understand what the church is. We should seek to unify the body while we use our gifts as part of the whole. Our goal is never to be divisive; it is to be a united part of the whole.

Our Gifts Are for Service

Paul reminds the Corinthians that our gifts are to be used (see also Rom 12:6; Eph 4:12). We are not to bury our gifts in the ground like the man who had only one talent (Matt 25). We are not to bury our gifts within ourselves. We are to use our gifts for "the building up of the body of Christ" (Eph 4:12). We labor in the church so we can serve Christ more effectively. In his letters to both the Ephesians and the Corinthians, Paul stressed the importance of edification. In Ephesians 4:14-16, Paul confronted the immaturity of those who cause disunity in the church.

Paul devoted much of his writing to the problem of divisiveness in the church. Many of his epistles focused on the immaturity of Christians who were so intent on getting their own way that they caused strife and division. He encouraged the church to work for unity by reaching toward the "full maturity of Christ." In the fourteenth verse of Ephesians 4, Paul drew upon the image of an immature child to warn his readers about their behavior. Then he changed his metaphor to a ship caught on waves without a rudder. He turned again to another metaphor of dice in a game used by one who misled and cheated his victims. The mature Christian is founded on Christ, the solid foundation. He or she will "reach toward maturity." The church built on the foundation of Christ can withstand all kinds of doctrinal differences because its central creed is "Christ is Lord." The church will continuously labor to be a united church within, and then it will seek to be more united without.

The Pastor as Enabler

In striving to identify the gifts of the believers, the pastor is to be the enabler in building up the body of Christ. The pastor is not to do all the work of the church but to help equip others to do this work. The dean of a medical school will not practice all the medicine done in all the states. He trains others to practice medicine. The dean of a law school does not do all of the legal work across our state. She helps prepare others in law so they might do the necessary legal work. The dean of the school of music at one our divinity schools cannot lead all the music in our churches across the country. Instead, she helps train others to be ministers of music in our churches. Part of the function of a pastor and other staff members is to help train and equip other people to work to do ministry. We make a mistake when we think all we do is hire other people to do ministry for us. The church calls all of us to engage in ministry.

Our Ministry in the World

What is the work of ministry? Micah reminds us that our ministry is to do justice, to love mercy, and to walk humbly with our God (6:8). Paul writes in 2 Corinthians 5:18 that we have "the ministry of reconciliation." In this ministry of reconciliation, we are charged to bring people into a vital relationship with God when they have been separated by sin. We are also charged to reach out and bring people together who have been alienated from each other. We are to seek to restore relationships between individuals when they are broken so we can all serve God more effectively.

Personal Ministry

In Romans 2:16 and 2 Timothy 2:8, Paul uses the phrase "according to my gospel." You might want to say, "Wait a minute, Paul. What is 'my' gospel? Isn't it *the* gospel?" Yes, it is *the* gospel, but the gospel becomes most effective when it becomes *my* gospel and *your* gospel. It becomes this when we share our experience with Christ. We have all heard someone ask, "What can help me get over this particular physical problem I have?" People may offer all kinds of suggestions. Then somebody says, "Let me tell you what cured me." That is a different insight entirely. This person doesn't merely philosophize or guess about a cure; he says what made a radical difference in his life. When you and I experience the power of Christ and discover our gifts, then we are to go into the world and give our lives in service for him.

Connecticut has a state law that says all church doors have to open outwardly. I think that is a good spiritual law as well. After we gather together for worship, the doors ought to open outwardly so that we can go into the world to minister for our Lord. We are not to spend all of our time inside the church building. We are to carry our gifts of ministry into the world to glorify God.

Read the words from 1 Peter 4:10-11: "As each has received a gift, employ it for one another, as good stewards of God's varied grace: whoever speaks, as one who utters oracles of God; whoever renders service, as one who renders it by the strength which God supplies; in order that in everything God may be glorified through Jesus Christ. To him belongs glory and dominion forever and ever."

As pastors, let us strive to challenge our people that everything they do should glorify God, build up the body of Christ, and help them become better equipped for ministry in the world. Let us help them discover their gifts and use them for God's glory.

Notes

1. Robert D. Cornwall, *Unfettered Spirit: Spiritual Gifts for the New Great Awakening* (Gonzales FL: Energion Publications, 2013) 55.

2. Gary L. Harbaugh, *God's Gifted People* (Minneapolis: Augsburg Publishing House, 1988) 16.

3. Kenneth S. Hemphill, *Spiritual Gifts: Empowering the New Testament Church* (Nashville: Broadman Press, 1988) 203.

11

Healthy Staff Relations in the Church

"Supervising the church staff took most of my time," complained a pastor. "I often longed for the time when I was the only minister on the staff. It was easier and more fun then. The ministers of music, education, and youth were always at each other's throats." A minister of education related that he left his position with a prominent church because the pastor led like a dictator and always expected his staff to glorify him. "He acted like none of the rest of us had any sense," he stated, "or even made any real contribution to the work of the church." Such laments are heard across the country in every denomination.

Many fine churches have been hurt, frustrated, often fragmented, and sometimes even destroyed by unhealthy staff relations. This problem is as complicated as individuals. A church staff should be formulated with careful planning, guidance, and an awareness of the dynamics and circumstances involved in staff associations. Attention has often been directed to practical employment matters such as the job description, education, experience, salary, vacation time, work schedules, and personality. These matters are important and should be approached with care.

There are times when it seems apparent that staff leadership will be effective only when there is an awareness of motivational theory, interpersonal relations, and leadership role models. Yet there have been ministers without such training who have functioned well in leadership responsibilities, and some with management training have been unable to show effectiveness. Churches, of course, are concerned with many business affairs, but their chief end is religion, not business. The root cause of staff conflicts may lie deeper. It may arise from unhealthy theological assumptions.

In the total organizational structure of a church, it is essential that the paid professional staff base their understanding of each other and their varied ministries on a strong theological and biblical foundation. An understanding of the theological foundation on which healthy leadership rests will hopefully enable ministers to labor more effectively and to respect and appreciate the services of their fellow workers. Attitude toward and treatment of one's fellow staff workers are indications of one's theology. Relationships, then, with fellow staff workers become a theological action. Staff relationships involve far more than merely an awareness of educational and administrative techniques. One's views of God, self, and others are determinative for any meaningful performance of ministry. An understanding of the cardinal doctrines of reconciliation and the church are the foundational stones on which vital staff relationships are built.

Reconciliation

The work of reconciliation lies at the center of the Christian faith. In Christ, God took the initiative in bridging the chasm that separated God's sinful children from God. The supreme act of reconciliation culminated in the cross of Christ. "Reconciliation is a peace with God," Vincent Taylor notes, "made possible by the sacrifice of Christ."[1] In the mystery of the death of Christ, the bridge between the holiness of God and the sinfulness of humanity was spanned. Through the redemptive work of Christ, people are ushered into the presence of God. The Apostle Paul wrote, "For there is one God, and one mediator between God and man, the man Christ Jesus" (1 Tim 2:5). Frank Stagg has observed that the title "mediator" as applied to Jesus Christ means more than someone who is between God and humanity: "Jesus Christ came *to overcome the betweenness between* God and man."[2] Christ has reconciled sinful people with the holy God. James Denney stated it clearly when he observed,

> When reconciliation is spoken of in St. Paul, the subject is always God, and the object is always man. The work of reconciling is one in which the initiative is taken by God, and the cost is borne by Him; men are reconciled in the passive, or allow themselves to be reconciled or receive

the reconciliation. We never read that God has been reconciled. God does the work of reconciliation in or through Christ, and especially through his death.[3]

In the New Testament, Paul alone used the word *katallassein* to depict the totally new relationship that people can have with God.[4] In 2 Corinthians 5:17-21, Paul speaks of the radical change one undergoes to become a new creation. God's act of reconciliation does not indicate a change within the nature of God. God's loving nature toward people is already seen in the Old Testament. God did not have to be placated in order to be loving. God, as Paul noted, was the reconciler, not the one being reconciled. From first to last, this has been the work of God: "God has reconciled men and women to God's self through Christ" (2 Cor 5:18a). In Romans 5:10, Paul speaks of reconciliation as the work of God that established a new era in the relationship between God and people. The one decisive act that brought about this reconciliation was the death and resurrection of Jesus Christ. God, of course, was not an angry deity who needed to be appeased; he was a caring God who sent his Son because he so loved the world.

Through the centuries, theologians have debated various theories of the atonement, seeking to state how this reconciliation was accomplished. No attempt will be made here to define the "how" of reconciliation. In a sense, all the theories of the atonement fail to define the reality that was accomplished by the death of Christ. The fact of reconciliation is of paramount significance—not the various attempts to probe behind the mystery of this event. The cross of Jesus Christ is, then, the pivotal place for understanding the magnitude of God's love and grace. In God's work of reconciliation, the estrangement that separated human beings from themselves, others, and God has been overcome. The possibility for redemption and wholeness has been accomplished in the death of Christ. "God was in Christ reconciling the world to himself" (2 Cor 6:19a).

Writing about the work of reconciliation in 2 Corinthians 5:14-21, Paul affirms several things: first, God's activity accomplished reconciliation in Christ (vv. 14-15, 18-19, 21); second, anyone who has been reconciled to God in Christ has become "a new creation" (v. 17); third, those who are now in Christ are charged with the responsibility of sharing the good news with others. "All this is from God, who through Christ reconciled us to himself and gave us the ministry of reconciliation" (v. 18). "God was in Christ reconciling the world to himself . . . and entrusting to us the message of reconciliation. So we are ambassadors for Christ" (vv. 19-20).

Here then is one of the basic foundational stones in a theology for ministry. People who have experienced the forgiving grace of God for their own sins have now become "new creations"—new people in Christ. Having experienced personal reconciliation, their ministry is to guide others to a similar experience of reconciliation. As agents of reconciliation, they seek now to see people, understand them, and respond to them not from their old natures, a pre-Christian perspective, but from the viewpoint of those who seek to see, hear, and respond with the spirit of Christ, "for the love of Christ controls us" (v. 14). The guide for relating to others is not simply one's personal feelings or desires; it's the presence of Christ. "And he died for all, that those who live might live no longer for themselves, but for him who for their sake died and was raised" (v. 15).

Reconciliation has given us a new perspective on understanding our own relationship to God and to fellow Christians. In Romans 5:10f., reconciliation is depicted by Paul as the work of God. Men and women have often tried to produce reconciliation through various rites, activities, good works, and noble behavior. These attempts are again the result of the false idea that one needs to try to appease God in order to be reconciled. Paul declared that reconciliation was God's act that he accomplished through the death of Christ. By his death, Christ has removed all barriers that separated individuals from God (Eph 2:18) and also those that separated Jew and Gentile (Eph 2:14). Christ has overcome the hostility that separated people from each other and brought them into one family in Christ (Eph 2:16). This concept, as Taylor suggests, leads into the very heart of the New Testament, the good news of God for every person of forgiveness and reconciliation.[5]

All ministers need to be reminded that their present relationship to God was accomplished by God's act of reconciliation, which overcame their state of separation from their own selfhood, others, and God. No minister can assume, then, a superior attitude over others. Ministers are also sinners saved by grace. Having been reconciled to God, we are charged with overcoming barriers that separate individuals from each other, not with erecting new hindrances. Those who have been reconciled are commissioned to the "ministry of reconciliation." A clear understanding of this theological truth should remind ministers that often they have irresponsibly gone their own ways and, like all of God's estranged children, had to be drawn back into God's loving presence.

Since ministers are aware of their own "Jekyll-Hyde" characters, they should understand better and be able to be more compassionate toward fellow staff workers when any of them do things with which they may not agree or approve. It is easy to judge another's actions and assume that one's own behavior is always superior. But the willingness to judge so quickly denotes our personal state of separation from our fellow human beings. How easily ministers can forget their own sinfulness and need of forgiveness. Like our coworkers, pastors too stand in need of forgiveness and should not overestimate our own goodness and minimize others' actions. We all stand on the common ground of God's grace as fellow strugglers in need of forgiveness. Standing beneath the cross, we are united by our common need for forgiveness and are sent into our church, office, home, and all the world as agents of reconciliation.

The Church

The work of ministry cannot be separated from an understanding of the church. In the New Testament, writers describe the church using various images. Some of these images are drawn from analogies made by Jesus, Paul, and others. A parade of figures is evident in the New Testament: the household of faith, the family of Jehovah, the temple of God, a royal priesthood, a holy nation, the bride of Christ, and many others. Although the word *ekklesia* appears in Matthew 16:18 and 18:17 only, there is no question that Jesus intended to create a fellowship to carry forth his ministry in the world.

One of the richest and most useful images is Paul's "the body of Christ" (1 Cor 12; Ephesians). Christ is the "head" of his body the church, but believers are organic members of it (Col 1:18; 2:16-19; 3:15; Eph 1:22-23). Images such as "the flock" (Luke 12:32; John 10:16; 21:15-17; Acts 20:28; 1 Peter 5:2) and the vine and the branches (John 15:1-8) convey a similar picture. Christ is the Shepherd, his church the sheep. Christ is the vine, his church the branches. These images depict the unity and solidarity of the church but also the diversity of its members (Rom 12:4-5). Here is the great paradox of "the people of God." In using the analogy of the church as the body of Christ, Paul appealed to the significance of unity within diversity.

To speak of the church as the body of Christ is to acknowledge that Christ is the founder and head of the church. Images like the church as "the bride of Christ" (Eph 5:22-24), Christ as the "chief cornerstone" (Eph 2:19-22), and Christ as the vine (John 15:4-5) indicate not only that Christ is the head of the church but also that the church is utterly dependent on him. Lesslie Newbigin has noted that the church "derives its character not from its membership but from its Head, not from those who join it, but from Him who calls it into being."[6] Since Christ is the head of the church, his body, all the other parts find life and meaning only as they are subservient to the Lord of the church. Christian ministers labor, then, with an awareness that their commitment is to Jesus Christ as Lord of all of life and especially of the church.

To characterize the church as the body of Christ is to speak of the organism through which Christ is continuing his work in the world today. Just as the incarnate Christ had a body with which to carry out his ministry, so the church serves as the structure through which he continues his ministry now. If the church is true to its founder, then it exists to continue the work of reconciliation. The organization and structure of a church exist only for the purpose of enabling the church to fulfill its reason for existence. As a body, the church is a living organism through which Christ is the ever-present living Lord, speaking and working. No institutional shape or organizational form can completely contain the Christ who is always transforming and renewing the institutional church to perform his purpose more adequately. As Frank Stagg has noted, "The analogy may be taken too literally, but it cannot be taken too seriously."[7] My attempt is not to equate Jesus with the church but to affirm that the church is an extension of Jesus' ministry. Paul reminded us that Christ loved the church and gave himself for it (Eph 5:25).

Ministers need to be careful not to get so absorbed in the form or pattern of the institution that they forget the church's purpose: to serve and not to be served (Mark 10:44). No matter our position on a church staff, we must focus on the basic reason for the church's existence. To lose sight of the church's mission of continuing the work of reconciliation is to ignore its reason for existing.

At the beginning of his ministry in his first sermon at the Nazareth synagogue, Jesus announced that he had come to serve the poor, the imprisoned, the blind, and the oppressed (Luke 4:16-30). Throughout his ministry the servant image of the Messiah was dominant. "If any one would be first, he must be last of all and servant of all," Jesus said (Mark 9:35). In response to those who wanted to have the chief places in his kingdom, Jesus declared, "Whoever would be great among you must be your servant, and whoever would be first among you must be slave of all. For the Son of man also came not to be served but to serve, and to give his life as a ransom for many" (Mark 10:43-45).

Jesus has given to his church the ministry of joining him in service. As the body of Christ, the church loses sight of its mission when it exists to serve itself and forgets the commission to be Christ's instrument for service in the world. The credibility of the church and its ministers is diminished when its purpose for existence becomes self-serving. Too often, ministers become more concerned with what the church can do for them than with what they can do in service to the church. The church and its ministers, lay and ordained, are true to their purpose as they follow the example of Jesus. Paul wrote, "Have this mind among yourselves, which you have in Christ Jesus, who, though he was in the form of God, did not count equality with God a thing to be grasped, but emptied himself, taking the form of a servant" (Phil 2:5-7).

A Model for Church Staff Relationships

The ministers on a church staff can provide the congregation with a model of servant ministry through their relationships with each other and through the performances of their responsibilities. This may appear to be a heavy load for the staff to bear. But is it really? If church members see staff workers who are constantly putting each other down, circumventing each other for a place of greater recognition in the church, and unable to relate well with their fellow ministers, they will have great difficulty in understanding what it means to be servants in Christ's name. If staff workers are to function effectively in today's world, the model for ministry cannot be taken solely from business and economics but must also be drawn from the one who came to serve and who is still Lord of his church.

In the disputes among the disciples about who was to be the greatest, Jesus must have felt some sadness as he instructed them yet again in his way. For months he had taught them and modeled his ministry among them, but still they had not grasped his message. In contrast to the monarchs who ruled by "exercising lordship" over others, Jesus declared that his followers would rule, paradoxically, only by serving (Luke 22:24-27). The servant image provides a model patterned after our Lord's ministry. When the church staff is committed to this kind of ministry, they can serve as the catalyst for the whole congregation.

Probably no area in church staff relationships has caused more problems than the question of authority and power. Some pastors have led their church staffs in such a manner that the other members felt they had no opportunity to share insights or ministries except as they were directed to do so by the pastor. The pastor, they said, "ruled" with an iron hand. Others have longed for the pastor's guidance in the decision-making process of the church. Leaders are normally classified into three categories: (1) authoritarian leaders who alone plan, control, and execute the administration and ministries of the church; (2) democratic or cooperative leaders who involve others in the process with them; and (3) *laissez-faire* leaders who refuse to perform their leadership function.[8] All three types of leaders can be found in various churches today.

In most churches that have a staff, the chief leadership authority resides with the pastor or the one designated as the senior minister. Some have suggested the term "executive minister" for this person, but it has not won high favor. Richard Niebuhr offered the title "pastoral director" for this position, but it has not been well received either. Regardless of the title, if no one is in this role, the staff either soon disintegrates or some other leader arises from within the staff. To function effectively, every congregation must have someone designated as the individual with the final authority. Every staff has to have someone who is the leader. Someone must oversee the functions of the entire staff.

This does not mean the leader should be autocratic. The pastor or senior minister is part of a team ministry where each minister contributes his or her gifts. The leader needs to remember that he or she is *primus inter pares*, first among equals. One of the basic beliefs within Protestantism is the priesthood of all believers. The intensely personal relationship that each individual has with God removes any notion of an elite priestly class with special authority. This doctrine affirms that both the "professional minister" and the laity have ministries and that the distinction between them is only one of gifts and functions. Karl Barth brought this into clear focus when he observed,

> There can be no talk of higher and lower orders of specific services. There is differentiation of functions, but the preacher cannot really stand any higher than the other elders, nor the bell-ringer any lower than the professor of theology. There can be no "clergy" and no "laity," no merely "teaching" and no merely "listening" Church, because there is no member of the Church who is not the whole thing in his own place.[9]

Ministry is not a function of staff members alone but of the whole church membership. In the New Testament, the various ministerial functions in the church are seen as gifts (see chapter 10 above). Within the body of Christ, there is a variety of gifts that show diversity within unity. Paul wrote, "And his gifts were that some should be apostles, some prophets, some evangelists, some pastors and teachers for the equipment of the saints for the work of ministry, for building up the body of Christ" (Eph 4:11-12; cf. 1 Cor 12:27-31; Rom 12:4-8; and the longer passage in Eph 4:11-16). These passages speak not so much to the rise of any organized ministry within the church as they do to the variety of functions, gifts, and ministries within the corporate life of the church. The ordination of individuals is not to confer on them greater authority but is the church's way of acknowledging people's gifts and their callings to particular ministries for fulfilling those gifts.

Professional ministers do not do away with the ministry of the laity but afford the church an opportunity to draw from a variety of resources, experiences, education, training, and skills. There is no hierarchy within these ministries. In a multiple staff church, there is the recognition that all people are equal in their ministries. Each minister needs to have not only the responsibility to exercise his or her ministry but also the authority to fulfill that work. The pastor or senior minister labors as an equal among fellow ministers and serves only as the "executive" by selection, usually of the congregation in recognition of his or her pastoral, administrative, and/ or preaching gifts. Some congregations have gone so far as not to have any associate positions on the staff. Every staff person is recognized as a gifted minister in a particular church function such as music, education, administration, evangelism, counseling, outreach, youth, or some other area. In this way, the worth of every ministry is recognized. "Mature and self-assured leaders understand that they cannot provide leadership in isolation," Israel Galindo reminds us. "The most effective leaders solicit leadership from those around them."[10]

Each member of the team staff works as an equal among equals while recognizing that the church congregation has "called" one of their equals to serve as the "pastoral director," to use Niebuhr's image. This person, of course, is free to ask others to share in his or her responsibility, but responsibility must ultimately stop with someone. Each minister understands that his or her ministry is significant as part of the team, but, due to the variety in talents, experience, and training, responsibility may not always be totally equal. Sharing in this kind of team ministry will not happen when any staff member is easily threatened by the gifts of others or jealous because someone else receives recognition for differing gifts. The senior minister is key to creating a climate of cooperation, trust, support, communication,

mutual love, and understanding. "Early in my service of the church," Cecil
Sherman observed, "I did not praise staff enough. Later I recognized my
error and made a point of calling the work of the staff members to the
attention of the church."[11] This way, the senior pastor affirms his fellow
ministers, and the church sees their ministries more clearly along with the
senior pastor's support.

Taking their example from Christ, pastors lead their staffs and churches
with the awareness that the basic meaning of ministry is *diakonia*, "service,"
in strong contrast to the pompous priesthood often witnessed in Old Testament models. Any minister who follows Christ is his *diakonos*, his servant,
his minister (John 12:26; Matthew 20:26). Any conspicuous position in
the work of Christ is essentially a ministry or service to God and others
that might lead us to the supreme sacrifice of our very lives, just as Christ
did for us in his ministry.

Niebuhr, in his book *The Purpose of the Church and Its Ministry*,
discusses the question of ministerial authority. He traces the authority of
ministers to six possible sources. As official representatives of the church as
an institution, ministers have institutional authority. Command authority
arises more from ministers' relationship to the church as spokespersons
for the church's mind and spirit. Teaching authority is based on ability
to understand and interpret the Bible and theology for the congregation.
Judicatory authority arises from the ability to use the Scripture as a standard to guide and measure meaning and behavior. Spiritual authority is
drawn from ministers' experiences with God. Moral authority is derived
from ministers' personal character and behavior.[12]

Niebuhr has observed that the church has exercised authority in
different ways throughout its history. Outside the Roman Catholic Church,
the concept of institutional authority is usually weak. Within the Baptist
tradition, the final authority lies in the hands of the congregation. The
administrative authority ministers exercise within congregations arises from
the fellowships that give it to them and that can remove it at their discretion. Ministerial authority is derived from the congregations that have set
them apart in recognition of their gifts, training, and experience for the
task. The force of their personality, enthusiasm, and ability to function
effectively within their areas of responsibility often determines the kind
of support they receive from a congregation and other members of a staff.

Take, for example, the minister of music's authority within that sphere
of church life. Usually this individual is given "complete authority" to carry
out the music ministry of the church as he or she desires. But if, by lack

of gifts, ineffective planning, or moral misconduct, this person abuses his or her ministry, the church will not likely continue to award the authority necessary for the person to function effectively within that area. This can be true for any staff position, including that of pastor or senior minister. The congregation bestows limited "power" to its professional ministers and can recall this power at will.

Conclusion

Paul's concept of the body of Christ continues to be a helpful analogy for understanding the nature of the church and ministry. As head of the body, Christ is Lord of the church and its ultimate authority. Whatever authority church members have, they draw it from Christ's presence. Although the body is one, there is great diversity within this oneness. "For as in one body we have many members, and all the members do not have the same function, so we, though many, are one body in Christ, and individually members one of another. Having gifts that differ according to the grace given to us, let us use them" (Rom 12:4-6; cf. 1 Cor 12:4-6).

In Paul's analogy, he emphasizes everyone's importance within the church. Every Christian, lay or clergy, has spiritual gifts. Just as the human body would be overwhelmed if one part of its assemblage was dominant, the church would not function properly if one or a few members of its body totally controlled it. The same principle applies to church staff, which is a microcosm of the church. As leaders within the ministry of Christ, each staff worker shares his or her gifts as part of the body of Christ. Each is important to the functioning of the body. Diligently working together as a team of servants, the professional staff can help the church of Christ realize its mission of reconciliation.

Notes

1. Vincent Taylor, *Forgiveness and Reconciliation* (London: Macmillan and Co., 1948) 89.

2. Frank Stagg, *New Testament Theology* (Nashville: Broadman Press, 1962) 73.

3. James Denney, *The Death of Christ* (New York: A. C. Armstrong and Son, 1903) 143-44.

4. Cf. the discussion by Friedrich Buchsel on *katallasso* in *Theological Dictionary of the New Testament*, vol. 1, ed. Gerhard Kittel (Grand Rapids MI: Wm. B. Eerdmans Co., 1965) 254ff. See also "Reconcile and Reconciliation," in

A Theological Word Book of the Bible, ed. Alan Richardson (New York: The Macmillan Co., 1962) 185; Karl Barth, *Church Dogmatics, The Doctrine of Reconciliation,* vol. 4, pt. 1 (Edinburgh: T. &T. Clark, 1961) especially pp. 128ff.

5. Taylor, *Forgiveness and Reconciliation,* 223.

6. Lesslie Newbigin, *The Household of God* (New York: Friendship Press, 1954) 21.

7. Stagg, *New Testament Theology,* 196.

8. Cf. Kenneth R. Mitchell, *Psychological and Theological Relationships in the Multiple Staff Ministry* (Philadelphia: Westminster Press, 1966) 73–82.

9. Karl Barth, Files of Commission I, World Council of Churches, Geneva, first draft of Barth's article for *The Universal Church in God's Design,* quoted in J. Robert Nelson, *The Realm of Redemption* (Greenwich: Seabury Press, 1951) 145.

10. Israel Galindo, *Perspectives on Congregational Leadership* (Vienna VA: Educational Consultants, 2009) 101.

11. Cecil Sherman, *To Be a Good and Faithful Servant* (Macon GA: Smyth & Helwys, 2010) 90.

12. H. Richard Niebuhr, Daniel Day Williams, and James M. Gustafson, *The Purpose of the Church and Its Ministry: Reflections on the Aims of Theological Education* (New York: Harper & Brothers, 1956), 68–70.

12

Dealing with Conflict

Conflict is as inevitable as the sun coming up each day. There will always be differences of opinions on various subjects, because we all see and interpret things differently. The church community is not immune to conflict, either. Even the disciples of Jesus were often at odds on interpreting his message and even on who he was. Since the church is composed of human beings, we will see and respond differently to what happens or is said in our church. In the first place, we should not be surprised at this fact. And second, we should try to prepare our congregation to learn how to differ with one another and still love one another and worship and serve together. That is our goal, isn't it? As the pastor, we need to learn how to deal with stress and conflicts for our personal inner security. We need to teach our people to deal with it creatively and also, if possible, to avoid harmful interactions that fracture or divide the church. Dean Hoge and Jacqueline Wenger remind us that conflict in a church is a strong indicator that people are invested in their church: "Where conflict is present, apathy is not a problem," they assert.[1]

Types of Church Conflicts

Unfortunately, the subjects of church conflicts are almost endless. Conflict can arise over mission causes, budget items, worship or music style, something the pastor said or did not say in a sermon, the style of the pastor's sermon delivery, whether or not to be more evangelistic, the pastor's leadership style or lack thereof, a missed pastoral call, lack of supervision of a staff member, problems between the pastor and other staff members, deacons differing with a pastor's decision on some matter, different interpretations of a staff member's job description, who should chair a certain committee, where the piano should go, and on and on. I heard about a minister who came to a prominent church in Washington, DC, and was told by a fellow minister that he could preach heresy there, and even might be immoral, but for heaven's sake, he had better not move the candles on the altar! Sometimes the matter might seem that trivial; nevertheless, it is of importance to someone who may create an issue over it. Robert Dale believes that there are basically two types of church conflicts—conflicts over facts and conflicts involving feelings. He offers a discussion that can help pastors and their congregations find guidance in matters of conflict.[2]

Daniel Bagby, Theodore F. Adams Professor of Pastoral Care Emeritus at the Baptist Theological Seminary at Richmond, spoke at a ministers' conference I attended and suggested four great challenges that pastors had shared with him regarding conflict in their congregations. One focused on unrealistic expectations of the pastor or the congregation and on the congregation dealing with its past. Another was the toxic baggage that the congregation carried in unacknowledged and unresolved issues. A congregation, Bagby noted, is often in such a hurry to move to the next chapter in the church's history, such as calling a new pastor, that they cling to unprocessed grief and other layers beneath the surface that stymie their progress, like idealizing the past. Churches also struggle with unprocessed conflict through avoidance and denial or through destructive expressions of differences in dealing with conflict. Most churches, he believes, have poor resolution models and do not know how to deal with anger or to recognize the pain and concern behind it. Bagby encourages pastors not to be defensive in the face of church members' anger but to strive to get behind their anger and deal with the issue causing their concern, hurt, and fear.[3]

Often parishioners have an ideal or unrealistic image of their pastor or of the church itself. When the person or the institution is not able to live up to this ideal, then misinterpretations and differences quickly emerge. No minister is Superman or Superwoman, able to walk on water or leap tall buildings. The pastor is a human being with the frailties that all human beings possess. The congregation has to acknowledge this and not hold to unrealistic expectations. This is not an excuse for a pastor's lack of high moral and ethical standards. But all church members should adhere to a high moral standard as well.

Resolving Conflict

One does not have to be a pastor long before he realizes that the saints in the household of faith have not reached perfection but are still on the way to being saved completely. As the pastor and leader of the congregation, the minister has to be careful not to abuse his position and respond in a dictatorial or threatening way. She should not use the sermon or prayer as a means of chastising those who have raised a flag of concern about some matter. When the pastor tries to squelch or overrule another perspective from the pulpit, he usually fosters division and animosity, often driving the conflict underground and onto the parking lot or into church members' homes. Those who feel they are being attacked from the pulpit without an opportunity for rebuttal will likely organize their own power group. If the issue is a power struggle for leadership, then it may be confronted through the deacons, the personnel committee, or one-on-one contact.

On the other hand, if parishioners see the pastor as one who will entertain differences and dialogue about issues with the people who raise them, then the response will not cause alarm or cause anyone to feel threatened. "I understand church to be a place where we learn how to bring the depths of our convictions to the table; to agree sometimes and at other times learn how to disagree well together," Patricia Farris, a Methodist minister, declares. "Church is not about groupthink on matters temporal and political."[4]

Allan Rohlfs, in an article written in *The Christian Century*, suggests using an approach called "nonviolent communication" (NVC) to resolve conflicts. Marshall Rosenberg, who developed this approach, offers four steps: (1) Name the behavior that is a problem. (2) Name the emotions you feel when the behavior happens. (3) Name the need that is not being met because of the other person's behavior. (4) State clearly what you would like the other person to do.[5]

In one of the churches I served, I was asked to teach a course on preaching in a local college for one semester. In two previous churches, my congregations had welcomed this opportunity for their pastor and felt that the church benefited from it as well. This time, when I detected criticism from some about doing this, I asked the deacons to look at the issue and let me know whether they thought I should teach the course. I indicated that it would be taught on my day off and would not detract from my ministry time with the church. After a brief discussion, the deacons overwhelmingly approved my teaching the course and affirmed its benefit for the church.

By allowing freedom of discussion and dialogue with the deacons about the course, I avoided having a few negative voices talking about this matter behind my back. Some who had been against my teaching the course took a different attitude after the discussion and vote by the deacons.

Responding to Conflicts

Not all differences in churches lead to major conflicts. Some are misunderstandings, the result of a lack of information, or simply a mishearing of something. These instances can usually be resolved with open conversation or the correct information. But when more intervention is needed, I have found the following suggestions helpful in seeking to resolve various types of conflicts in the church. This list is certainly not complete; they are merely ideas for moving toward a solution that I have learned along the way.

Listen

Willingness to hear someone who differs from you can open doors. One of the worst things a pastor can do is refuse to listen to another perspective. Sometimes the mere willingness of the pastor to hear another perspective will disarm the other person. Even if you do not agree with the person's viewpoint, you are willing to hear it, and sometimes that is sufficient. On the other hand, I sometimes discovered that the person I took time to listen to had a perspective that I had not even considered, and I realized that it was indeed a better viewpoint than mine. Then I graciously thanked the person for the insight and acknowledged my indebtedness. The willingness simply to listen can solve many conflicts but of course not all of them. "Leadership," Jeffery Jones reminds us, "is always about relationships."[6] The more we seek to build healthy relationships with others, the more likely they will be willing to talk with us and listen to us—and we will do the same for them.

Control Your Anger

If you as the pastor are the focus of the conflict and the accusers have said unpleasant, untrue, or derogatory things about you, your anger is understandable. No matter how hard it is, pastors must control their anger and not slip into traps set by those who seek to show the ministers' lack of control. Unfortunately, many pastors carry old baggage from other church conflicts that feed present-day emotions. If someone causes you to lose your temper, then that person has exercised control over you. Don't give them that power.

In one of the churches where I was pastor, we had to remove a staff member for legitimate reasons. But no matter how incompetent or immoral people might be, they still have supporters in the congregation. Following this staff member's dismissal, a church member lashed out at me with vivacious and profane words. I held my peace and listened, giving little or no response, which only seemed to make him angrier. Nevertheless, I held my tongue and did not lash back. We cannot control the actions of others, but we should not let them control our responses. As much as we are able, pastors should strive to be peacemakers.

Share the Facts

When people inquire about a certain decision, respond with the real facts about the situation. They may not know the truth, and if they do, they may want to see if your interpretation is valid. Distorting or misrepresenting a situation will only harm you. Honesty is always the best policy. Your integrity may be at stake. Hold to the truth. If confidentiality is needed, then be honest and say so. At times you may not be free to disclose the necessary information without exposing some truth that you are not suppose to relate. In that case, simply state that fact.

Don't Attack Those Who Differ with You

As I said above, the pastor must restrain from attacking those who differ with her from the pulpit, in the church newsletter, in personal letters, or on Facebook or any other social media. This type of behavior is beneath a pastor. Ill-spoken or angry words in print can haunt a pastor and will not build good will even with supporters. Continue preaching in the appropriate way for your church and strive to be seen as a peacemaker rather than a warmonger. Attacks, sarcastic comments, and ridicule will harm rather than help your cause. You of all people need to exhibit a Christ-like spirit in the midst of conflict. You may be the victim of such attacks, but turn the other cheek and pray for those who demean you. Follow our servant Lord's model.

Compromise without Sacrificing Your Integrity

Sometimes the issue, struggle, or conflict allows the possibility for both sides to compromise without either side losing its integrity. The pastor or another appropriate leader who is open and willing to listen to both sides may chair the discussion. It does not always have to be a "win-win" or "lose-lose" situation. If each side is willing to give a little, then both sides still win because they have avoided a more severe conflict. Reasonable discussions and openness to each other can make this solution possible. The goal in this process is for adequate communication to take place so both parties can arrive at a consensus. If both parties come away with a sense of "victory," then the whole situation is a win-win for all. I have seen this happen on a number of occasions when the conflict was over church space, meeting times, or transportation matters. If the parties simply sit down and talk instead of arguing, the issue is often resolved.

Don't Turn Skirmishes into Major Battles

Be careful that you don't allow a small skirmish to be depicted as a major battle. Every disagreement pastors have with others should not be seen as an oversized problem. Quiet discussions on a face-to-face basis can resolve many misunderstandings or differences. Showing willingness for others to have an opinion that differs from yours and displaying the desire to converse about that difference can build bridges in communication and inspire intellectual and spiritual growth. Don't make a mountain out of a molehill when it comes to church conflicts. Choose your battles carefully, and don't engage in an argument or create an issue to quarrel about when there is none. Pleasant conversation about different interpretations can be an enriching experience and lead to strong bonds of friendships with other believers. Remain open and inquisitive. That's how real spiritual growth takes place.

Remain Positive amid Negativity

There is nothing harder than trying to remain positive when others around you are stressing the negative mood. But this is the pastor's challenge when the church wants to quarrel. The pastor has to be the voice reminding the church that we follow the one who brought good news, and we cannot let a negative perspective cause Christ's radiance to grow cold. We cannot allow the noise of bad news to drown out the beautiful melody of the redeeming good news. When it is appropriate, sometimes humor may help relieve tension.

Pray

Through the thick and thin of disagreements and conflicts, as pastor you need to pray for God's direction and presence in each struggle. Pray that you can maintain a Christ-like spirit amid the exchanges of opinions. Pray that everyone involved in the struggle may seek the truth that is the best solution for their church and will dialogue in a Christian spirit of good will and love. "When our faith gets out of focus, we tend to focus instead on ourselves," David Moffett-Moore reminds us. "This will always lead to conflict, as we each have counter-balancing egos. The corrective is to keep a steady focus on Christ as our head, on 'outdoing one another in affection,' 'counting others greater than yourself,' and remembering to love our neighbor as ourselves—'equal to' our love for ourselves."[7] Praying for one another can help us keep this focus. Do not, however, use prayer as a means of trying to manipulate others to your perspective, or allow others to abuse prayer in a similar distorted way. As the spiritual leader, you need to guide the church in its proper use of prayer in this critical time.

Refer to the Appropriate Group

On occasion, the differences or conflicts can be referred to a board or committee in the church that can help resolve the problem. The personnel committee, finance committee, church council, board of deacons, board of administration, board of Christian education, etc. may be the proper group to help reach a satisfactory solution for all. If the church has a large staff, one of the ministers can be asked to work with the various parties to seek a solution. An examination of the church's policy regarding the matters under dispute can be examined to see if it throws any light on the problem. Again, the goal may be to reach an understanding of the church policies or to reach a consensus. "Healthy leadership processes," Robert Dale reminds us, "have at least two qualities: credibility and openness."[8] Encourage all your group leaders to hold to those principles, and hold them as pastor too.

Hold Group Sessions

Sometimes a Sunday night or Wednesday night can be used for a listening and dialogue session. It is usually more effective if this discussion takes place around tables rather in a spectator setting. On a few occasions, I have conducted such sessions right after Sunday morning worship with a limit of an hour for discussion. Another approach might be to form a selected small group of about seven to eight people gathered around tables, with a trained leader, to explore the conflict and see if they can bring back assistance to the larger body of the church. The trained leader might ask the group to consider questions: "Where does our church seem to stand on the matter before us?" "What is the issue that is causing conflict?" "What do you hope for our church to do because of this issue?" "What difference does it make if we have different opinions on this?" "Is there a possible resolution to this problem?" Lay ground rules ahead of time, such as each person will have a limited time to speak; no one can judge or attack another; everyone must listen to another person's perspective, respect another viewpoint, control their tempers, and try to keep confidentialities. A selected person from the group can be designated to bring its suggestions or directions to the larger body, if appropriate.

Refer to a Called Meeting of the Congregation

The church may be called into a listening session to hear the report from the small group assigned to discuss the problem. Or it may be necessary to have a called meeting to hear the grievances from both sides and see if an open hearing would help resolve the conflict. The issue may have reached a stage beyond a committee or small group's ability to resolve it. It may now demand a wider hearing. Try to lay some ground rules for this open discussion similar to the ones mentioned above for the small group.

Recently I was asked to come into a church that was divided over an issue with its pastor, who was on a leave of absence, to see if I could help them come to a satisfactory solution to the problem. I led the church in two listening sessions on two different Sundays in which I gave them freedom to state the issue as they saw it. The tension on the first Sunday was evident, and several people spoke with a great deal of anger and were accusatory in their manner toward others in the congregation. The next week, we attempted to see if we could arrive at any areas of consensus that might enable them to communicate better. We made a list of several such areas, and I knew it was a small step in the right direction. Because I was an outside party, they knew I did not "have a dog in the fight" and wanted only what was best for the church.

Sometimes a church may need to ask a resource person from the church's denominational headquarters or seminary who has training in conflict management to lead the church's sessions. This is likely to involve the church in an extended period of seeking a resolution. If the church is willing to take the necessary time needed for such a process and will compensate the leader for this time, hopefully they can reach a harmonious solution and find healing. Here again, there will likely be some compromises if the group is to reach a satisfying solution.

Failure to Resolve Conflict

As a pastor, you may have to face the reality that all disagreements or conflicts may not come to a satisfactory resolution. No matter the format one uses, sometimes the conflict will continue until many members leave or the church splits. Some church members do not "play fair" and do not want to want to feel defeated, so they continue to carry on their complaints and gripes. Some of the members are like a man in one of my churches. He would introduce himself to visitors with these words: "I am the one in this church who keeps things from being unanimous." And he was indeed. He was a pain during my many years of ministry in that church. We learned that the congregation had to work around him to get things done.

Again, some people will continue in their negativity, and you will have to determine if there is any possible solution, whether you are the problem, or whether you are simply unable to achieve a satisfactory solution at the present time. There were times when someone came to me and said that the whole church was upset about me or some other matter. I learned to ask, "You and who else?" I quickly learned that this person was usually the only complainer and did not have an army behind her.

Richard Rohr reminds us that there are those who think that their evil ways are righteously justified. He summons us to remember that the very word *satan* means "the accuser." These accusing people, who are often overtly religious, "suffer no self-doubt or self-criticism, smirking at people who would dare to question them."[9] "Human nature always wants either to play the victim or to create victims—and both for the purpose of control," Rohr continues. "In fact, the second follows from the first. Once you start feeling sorry for yourself, you will soon find someone else to blame, accuse or attack—and that with impunity."[10] Unfortunately, there are those who will strike out and seek to diminish you and hurt you emotionally or professionally without real feelings of remorse. These people are often clothed in pious dress and language, assuming to be holier than you. This disguised self-righteousness is evil, nevertheless, and has to be exposed, or it will indeed cause precarious circumstances. Such people want to exercise control one way or another. Sometimes churches are willing to confront these people, but more often they continue in their devious roles unabated. And the church continues in one crisis after another.

As ministers, we are called to love the church as Jesus loved the church and gave his life for it. "This love doesn't mean agreeing with or approving of everyone's ideas or behavior," Henri Nouwen cautions. "On the contrary, it can call us to confront those who hide Christ from us. But whether we confront or affirm, criticize or praise, we can only become fruitful when our words and actions come from hearts that love the church."[11] If we truly love Christ's church, then we will seek to love those with whom we disagree or who mistreat or hurt us with their words and actions. This is never easy, but it is the Christ-like way. Of course, loving people does not mean we have to like or endorse them or their behavior. Jesus challenged us to love even our enemies, but surely that does not mean liking their attitudes or actions in hurting, harming, or even killing others.

Having to live with ongoing conflict can cause a devastating effect on your ministry. It leads to anger, depression, fatigue, and the inability to carry on effective ministry. It makes you question every decision and spend time looking over your shoulder to see if your detractors are coming again. It destroys your desire to lead the church into new possibilities because now you question if that is even possible. This negativity affects your preaching and sermon preparation and may cause you to question your calling into the ministry. Many pastors grow tired of the unending quarrels and conflict and finally look for another church to serve or leave the ministry altogether.

The Results of Church Conflict

Even pastors who have labored patiently to help a church resolve its conflicts may realize that they cannot succeed and have to leave, divide the congregation, or cause a split. If a pastor comes to this conclusion, I hope he or she has consulted with another minister, a pastoral counselor, or a denominational person who might also appraise the situation. I would discourage a pastor from resigning abruptly without any place to go or without any income. If the church is trying to force you to leave, indicate that you will leave if they provide salary and benefits for a year or at least six months. There are special support groups for ministers who have been terminated or forced to leave a church. I would encourage you to seek counseling from one of them and accept the special support they can give you. Remember that all churches are not continuously negative. Don't let one bad church experience cause you to abandon your sense of call to the ministry. Some churches, though, continue this pattern through every pastor without any correction or resolution because the same people are still there who champion the problems. Encourage the church you are leaving to get an intentional interim who will strive to bring healing to the congregation. Seek support from the Ministering to Ministers Foundation that I referred to in chapter 1.

Sometimes conflict leads a church to discover new ways of ministry and new lay ministers. Sometimes a spark is kindled that ignites the church into greater ministry. On other occasions, conflict kills the church, destroys its motive for service, splinters the membership into other nearby churches, causes the pastor to pack her bags and move on, and leaves an albatross of a building for a small handful of members to oversee. Jesus loves his church and gave his life for it. Why can't those of us who claim his name love one another as he commanded and then get on with the ministry he has called us to do? Remember that we are called to the ministry of reconciliation. This ministry will require patience, love, understanding, and faithfulness as we follow the Christ who declared that the "peacemakers are blessed." We have to begin with that message inside the church before we can carry it into the world.

Notes

1. Dean R. Hoge and Jacqueline E. Wenger, *Pastors in Transition: Why Clergy Leave Local Church Ministry* (Grand Rapids MI: William B. Eerdmans, 2005) 77.

2. Robert D. Dale, *Pastoral Leadership* (Nashville: Abingdon Press, 1986) 159–65.

3. Daniel G. Bagby, Virginia Network of Interim Ministers' Conference, Richmond VA, 10 October 2014.

4. Patricia Farris, *Five Faces of Ministry: Pastor, Parson, Healer, Prophet, Pilgrim* (Nashville: Abingdon Press, 2015) 74.

5. For the particulars of this approach, see Allan Rohlfs, "Beyond Anger and Blame," *The Christian Century*, 14 November 2012, 22–25.

6. Jeffrey D. Jones, *Heart, Mind and Strength: Theory and Practice for Congregational Leadership* (Herndon VA: The Alban Institute, 2008) 33.

7. David Moffett-Moore, *Wind and Whirlwind: Being a Pastor in a Storm of Change* (Gonzalez FL: Energion Publications, 2013) 46.

8. Robert D. Dale, *Seeds for the Future: Growing Organic Leaders for Living Churches* (St. Louis MO: Lake Hickory Resources, 2005) 152.

9. Richard Rohr, *Things Hidden: Scriptures as Spirituality* (Cincinnati OH: St. Anthony Messenger Press, 2008) 136.

10. Ibid., 134.

11. Henri L. M. Nouwen, *Bread for the Journey: A Daybook of Wisdom and Faith* (San Francisco: HarperSanFrancisco, 1997).

13

Officiating at Weddings

As a pastor, you will often be asked to officiate at wedding ceremonies. You may know the couple well as members of your congregation, or they may be strangers who want you to perform the ceremony. Most churches have a printed list of procedures for the couple to follow during a wedding ceremony. This includes requirements for the photographer, use of candles and flowers, moving of furniture, time of rehearsal, music that is acceptable, fees, etc. Most churches do not charge their members, but sometimes a fee for the janitor's service is required. I usually do not charge church members for my services, but if they want to give me an honorarium, I accept it graciously and give it later to my wife for her discretionary use.

Before I married a couple, I usually asked for at least three counseling sessions with them. In these meetings I discussed how they met and how long they had known each other. I asked about family backgrounds, plans for children, goals in marriage and life, medical history, their dreams and hopes for the future, career plans, and conflicts or disputes. I confirmed the date and time of the wedding, time of the rehearsal, details of the wedding service, clarification of the worship nature of the wedding, proper use of photographers, and any other issues.

I also required that the marriage license be brought on the night of the rehearsal or before. I learned to request this the hard way. When I was pastor in Louisiana, a young man who was in the military and his fiancée came by my office and asked if I would marry them. This was before I required several sessions of counseling. The next night when they came to the church for the wedding service, they brought a Mississippi marriage license. I told them that I could not marry them in Louisiana with that license. They had to drive over the state line into Mississippi and get another minister to marry them. I never forgot that lesson! Here are some other thoughts from my experiences in church weddings.

The Wedding Rehearsal

The wedding rehearsal is usually held on the night before the wedding. When the wedding participants were present, I asked that they sit in the front pews of the church. I spoke briefly about the happiness of the occasion and offered a brief prayer thanking God for the couple's love, for God's blessing on their marriage, and for the families that guided them to this special moment. Some churches have designated wedding directors, or couples may use their own. If there was no director, I provided the directions for the service, reminding the couple that it was a service of worship, and all activities should reflect that fact.

Seating arrangements and specific ceremony details may vary, but this is the plan I followed: I asked the mother of the bride to be seated on the aisle side of the second pew to my right in churches with a center aisle, or on the end of the pew to my far right in churches with two aisles. The groom's mother was seated on the end of the second aisle pew on the left. Then I asked the bride and groom to stand facing me in front of the church sanctuary, the bride on my right and the groom on my left as I faced the congregation. Next the maid of honor stood to the right of the bride and the best man stood on the groom's left. The various bridesmaids stood to the right of the maid of honor and the ushers or groomsmen to the left of the best man, usually beginning with the tallest and descending to the shortest on each side.

During rehearsal, I walked the wedding party through the ceremony, indicating what I would say at first, asking for the exchange of vows and then the exchange of the rings, with the best man placing the bride's ring in my hand, and asking the groom to place it on the bride's finger. After pronouncing the couple husband and wife, saying the benediction, and inviting them to kiss, I showed them how to recess from the front of the church.

The organist played the recessional, and the groom extended his right arm to the bride. They would move slowly down the aisle. If there were ring bearers or flower girls, they exited next, following the bride and groom. When they were about halfway down the aisle, the best man extended his arm to the maid of honor, and they proceeded down the aisle. One by one with a reasonable amount of space between each couple, the ushers extended their right arms to the bridesmaids and then proceeded down the aisle until the entire party was out. Then a designated usher came forward, extended his right arm, and escorted the bride's mother out with her husband following behind. Next an usher came forward for the groom's mother and escorted her down the aisle with her husband behind them. If there were grandmothers seated behind the mothers, the bride's grandmother was escorted next and then the groom's grandmother.

After this run-through, I asked them to practice the procedure in reverse. The ushers always extended their right arms to the ladies they escorted. The usher brought in the bride's mother first, then the groom's mother, next the bride's grandmother, and finally the groom's grandmother. When the wedding ceremony began, the minister came out of a door up front on the left facing the congregation and moved to the front of the church, standing before the center aisle or in the center of the front. Next the groom and best man came and stood by the minister facing down the aisle. During the organ processional, the bridesmaids came down the aisle one by one with a distance of about half the aisle length between them. The maid of honor followed next, and they stood to the right of the bride's place. The ushers usually came in two by two and took their place to the left of the groom. The ring bearer came next, followed by the flower girls who tossed their flower petals in the aisle. Having arrived at their proper places, the entire party was now facing down the aisle for the sound of the organ that announced the coming of the bride, who was usually escorted on the right arm of her father. With everyone in place, I went through the service briefly again and had them practice leaving once more. We rehearsed until everyone felt comfortable with the procedures.

I normally attended the rehearsal dinner, which always started late since some of the wedding party arrived late for the rehearsal no matter how much I stressed the importance of being on time.

Plan for the Unexpected

No matter how thorough a wedding rehearsal might be, the service seldom goes without some hitches. Don't be surprised by them, and learn to be flexible. One of the worst stories I have heard was about the time a bride and groom were kneeling for the prayer at the end of the service and the groom started to faint. The minister reached down to assist the groom, and the mother of the groom rushed up from her seat and yelled, "I'll take care of him," as she pushed the minister back. As the groom seemed to be recovering, the minister was ready to pronounce the couple husband and wife when the organist gestured to the minister and said softly, "Your robe is on fire!" The groom's mother had pushed the minister back into the candles, and they set his robe ablaze. After the minister put out the flames on his robe and pronounced them as husband and wife, the couple then proceeded down the aisle. As the bride reached the pew where the groom's mother was seated, instead of giving the special rose to her gently as she was supposed to, she threw it at her as hard as she could with a glowering look. I have often wondered how long that marriage survived.

Normally planning can help make this sacred moment in the life of a couple something to be cherished forever. I always found the occasion a happy and rewarding time with the couple getting married and with their families.

Same-sex Marriages

With the 2016 changing of the law by the Supreme Court in the United States that legalizes same-sex marriage, pastors will now have to choose whether they will perform these unions. This continues to be one of the most divisive issues confronting denominations and churches today. In an article in *The Christian Century*, theologian Gerald Schlabach wrote what he called "a Pauline case for same-sex marriage" in his article, "What Is Marriage Now?" Regarding people who struggle with whether or not to get married, he quotes Paul's line in 1 Corinthians 7:9—"it is better to marry than to be aflame with passion." He argues that this Pauline quote may offer a rare place for the church to meet for fresh discernment on this issue. He believes that conservatives will have to rethink and revise their concept of marriage to include same-sex marriages because he argues that "extending the blessings of marriage to same-sex couples will in fact counter the culture of contingency and promiscuity among heterosexuals as well as gays and lesbians. The blessings to all may encourage marriages among heterosexuals." He further asserts, "If Christians are going to continue to insist that public accountability within communal systems is an essential condition for greater and more permanent faithfulness, then weddings should be open to all."[1] This article by Schlabach can be a good place for pastors to begin reflecting on this challenging issue today.

Wedding Resources

There are, of course, various types of wedding services the minister can follow. Many standard ministers' manuals offer a variety of ceremonies, such as *Minister's Service Manual* by Samuel Ward Hutton, *Christian Minister's Manual* by Guthrie Veech, *Abingdon Marriage Manual* by Perry H. Biddle Jr., *Service Book for Ministers* by Joseph E. McCabe, and many others. A PDF file titled *A McAfee Marriage Manual for Ministers*, compiled by J. Truett Gannon, can be located on the Internet under *A Marriage Manual for Ministers—Mercer University*.[2] It is one of the most complete sources a minister might need.[3] The wedding service I used throughout most of my ministry in my latter years is given below as a sample. You, of course, can design your own as well.

The Wedding Ceremony

The following is the type of wedding ceremony I often followed. Many wedding resource books offer various services that one can follow. I liked to develop my own and make it personal for the couple being married.

Welcome

On behalf of the families of Mary and John, I welcome you to this wedding service. This is a time of special joy and celebration. We are glad that you can be a part of it.

Prayer of Blessing

Eternal God, who, out of boundless love, gave us the gift of life, bless Mary and John, who this day pledge their love to each other. May the excitement and joy of this moment remind them of the great adventure of love which lies before them. May the love which they have received from their families assure them of the wonder of the family they begin this day. In humility, we bow before the mystery of your presence in this glad hour. Amen.

Who represents the family in the blessing of this marriage? [The father or another designated person responds, "I do."]

Scripture Reading: 1 Corinthians 13

A Homily:
The Acknowledgment of the Sacredness of Marriage

We are gathered together this afternoon in the presence of God and in the fellowship of family and friends to join Mary Smith and John Jones in Christian marriage. Different paths have led you to this place of marriage today. You each have been loved and guided by your families. You have chosen this moment to consecrate your love for each other and establish your own family. As parents they acknowledge that this is a time of letting go and new beginnings—a time of joy and a time of different relationships. For you, it is a time of remembering strong family bonds, parents, brothers, and sisters who love you. It is a time of acknowledging friends who have supported you through the years. This sacred moment is a time of new devotions, consecrated promises, and enduring vows.

You come now before the altar of God to establish a Christian home.

Christian marriage is a Covenant of Faith and Trust between each of you. It begins in an acknowledgment by both of you of your covenant of faith in Jesus Christ. In a moment you will pledge to each other your faithfulness and affection. A covenant of trust will enjoin you to openness of thought, freedom from suspicion, mutual confidence in each other's devotion, and the willingness to speak your feelings kindly to each other.

Today you take solemn vows of loyalty to each other. As you trust each other in the little things of life, you will soon discover that the big issues will take care of themselves. This standard of fidelity begins in the simplest matters and extends to your most intimate relationship of love. Seek to be honest with yourself and each other and learn to trust each other implicitly; as the Epistle of John says, "perfect love casts out fear"—and suspicion.

Christian marriage is also a Covenant of Hope. You join hands today and pledge your love to each other with wonderful dreams and visions of what your marriage will be. Today you are no longer two but one. Of course, you will still have your distinct personalities but you now have each other. You are not alone. Your dreams, hopes, and thoughts can be shared with each other. Your family and friends gather today to affirm your happiness. Fill your life and home with the attitudes you want to have as a permanent part of your lives. As your lives are filled with love, trust, understanding, gratitude, and appreciation, you will not have room for the undesirable or negative. Let hope expand into reality as your devotion grows for each other.

Christian marriage, furthermore, is a Covenant of Love. You first experienced love from your parents. Out of this love for each other and you, you came into existence. Behind all human love is the love of God. The Epistle of John reminds us that "God is love," and "we love because he first loved us." You were drawn to each other out of love. Your love is deep and real, as it should be. In this moment you may feel that you love each other now as much as you possibly could. But remember, as the days lengthen into years, hopefully you will find that your love will grow and deepen. Cultivate your love for each other; do not take the other for granted. Always try to interpret each other's behavior with understanding and tenderness. To love is to understand and to understand is to love. Strive as husband and wife to empty yourself as much as humanly possible of your own concerns and take upon yourselves the concerns of each other. Let love reign and not selfishness. Pray, as Francis of Assisi voiced, "Lord! Grant that I may seek more to understand than to be understood . . . ." May your vows this day lead you into a great adventure where there is a continuous discovery of your love for each other and the profound love of the God who created and redeemed us. "Now abides faith, hope, and love, but the greatest of these is love."

The Promises

John, will you have Mary to be your wedded wife, to live together in the covenant of faith, hope, and love? Will you listen to her inmost thoughts, be considerate and tender in your care of her, and will you stand by her faithfully in sickness and in health, and accept full responsibility for her every necessity as long as you both shall live? Do you so promise?

John: "I do."

Mary, will you have John to be your wedded husband, to live together in the covenant of faith, hope, and love? Will you listen to his inmost thoughts, be considerate and tender in your care of him, and stand by him faithfully in sickness and in health, and accept full responsibility for his every necessity as long as you both shall live? Do you so promise?

Mary: "I do."

The Vows

You will now repeat your vows to each other. First you express your vows, John. Repeat the phrases after me.

"I, John, take you, Mary, to be my wedded wife, to have and to hold from this day forward, for better or for worse, for richer or for poorer, in sickness and in health, to love and to understand, till death shall part us, according to the design of God."

Now Mary, you express your vows.

"I, Mary, take you, John, to be my wedded husband, to have and to hold from this day forward, for better or for worse, for richer or for poorer, in sickness and in health, to love and to understand, till death shall part us, according to the design of God."

The Exchange of the Rings

Repeat after me:

John: "This ring I give, as a sign and pledge, of my constant faith and abiding love."

Mary: "This ring I give, as a sign and pledge, of my constant faith and abiding love."

The Pronouncement

Mary and John, you have now pledged to belong to each other in holy marriage before your families, friends, and in the company of this community. As a sign of your complete commitment to each other you have exchanged promises of faithfulness and have given and received rings from each other. I am happy to pronounce that you are husband and wife, in the name of the Father, Son, and Holy Spirit. May the unity which God has blessed this day remain forever.

Let us pray.

The Solo

"The Lord's Prayer" (Mallotte)

The Benediction and Blessing

May the God who has created life, bless you with long life.

May the God who taught us how to love, inspire your love for each other.

May the God who guides the stars in their orbits, direct your path.

May the God who is the author of joy, enrich you with much happiness.

May God be in your coming in and in your going out, both now and forevermore.

Amen.

Let me be the first to present to you Mr. and Mrs. John Jones.

(I attended the reception following the wedding to greet and chat with the parents and others I knew or had met for the rehearsal. I did not always stay until the reception was over, but left to attend to my other ministerial functions.)

Notes

1. Gerald W. Schlabach, "What Is Marriage Now? A Pauline Case for Same-Sex Marriage," *The Christian Century*, 20 October 2014, www.christiancentury.org/article/2014-10/what-marriage-now.

2. "A McAfee Marriage Manual for Ministers," ctc.mercer.edu/www/mu-ctc/ministry-manuals/upload/mariage-manual-2.pdf.

3. Also see these two articles: B. J. Hutto, "Why a Church Wedding?" and Steve Thorngate, "Church(y) Weddings: When Worship Is the Main Event," *The Christian Century*, 28 May 2014, 22–26.

14

Conducting Funerals

On a Friday night I received word that someone at the church I was leading had died. I was only a junior in college at the time, and was away with a youth revival team at another church. My grandmother's funeral was the only funeral I had ever attended, and I had no idea what I was supposed to do. None of my friends were able to help. As I drove toward the church, I tried to think about which Scripture passages I might use and what else I needed to do. I nervously completed a service that I am sure was like no other my church members had ever attended. Back at college on Monday, I sought out one of my professors and asked him how a funeral service was supposed to be conducted.

Since that first funeral service, I have conducted many funerals and have grown in my awareness of how important it is to the family of the deceased. I have also noticed, during these years, that many ministers have not given funeral services the time and attention they deserve. Many, like I was at my first funeral, seem poorly prepared, ill informed about the purpose of a funeral, and unconcerned about the family for whom the service is held. Death and grief are the greatest crises in a person's or family's life, and the pastor has an opportunity to minister to those going through such times. I have included a list of resources for grief and funerals in the Appendix.

The Purpose of the Funeral Service

Before a minister conducts a funeral service, he should ask himself the purpose of such a service. A Christian funeral should afford the bereaved a means of separating from the loved one who is dead. It enables them to face the reality of death and go on living with hope and confidence. A funeral service affords them an occasion to express their grief openly and experience the support of the Christian community. In a special service of worship, the bereaved family and Christian friends gather to affirm their faith in the love and presence of God in their time of need, to attest to the resurrection of Christ and the Christian assurance of life everlasting, and to draw on the comfort and support of God in the face of fears related to death.

Personal Visit

Before a minister can conduct an effective funeral service, it is important to visit the home of the grieving family as soon as possible after receiving word of the death. During this visit, I found it important to express my sorrow at the family's loss and assure them of the presence of God. I shook hands or embraced them to show my love and identify with them in their hurt. I listened, prayed with them, stayed with them, and did not try to offer easy answers to hard questions about the whys of suffering, tragic accidents, or the death of the young. I tried to share my love and concern for them. I believe that the minister's presence is often far more important than the minister's particular words. By being there, a minister shares the family's load of grief, hurts with them, and cries with them.

On this first visit, I usually did not work out the details of the service unless the family initiated it or it was the only possible time I would have with them before the service. Most often, I preferred to come back later that day or the next day and discuss the details of the service. I tried to guide them in deciding whether they wanted the service at the church, the funeral home, or the graveside; a possible day and hour for the service; what hymns, if any, they wanted in the service; whether they preferred only organ music or none; and what Scripture passages they wanted read. I also tried to get personal information about the deceased that I could use in the service. Sometimes I knew the person well enough to have most of this information, but other times I didn't. Regardless, I believe it is healthy for the family to think and talk about their loved one in this way. I have found that sharing stories, pictures, descriptive words, and ways they remember a loved one is therapeutic and beneficial to the healing process. I always pray with the family again before I leave and assure them of my love and support.

The Funeral Director

When I began as pastor at a new church, I found it helpful to meet with local funeral directors. At these meetings, I encouraged each director to contact me before he set the time for funeral services of any of my church members. This eliminated time conflicts. I also inquired about local funeral traditions and customs. I visited the chapel in the funeral home and asked where I would sit, whether they had a public address system, whether the casket would remain open during the service, where the family would sit, how the minister and pallbearers would leave at the end of the service, and any other matters I thought would be helpful in conducting a meaningful service. This visit also gave me an opportunity to meet and talk with the funeral director and the staff.[1]

The Funeral Service

The funeral service can be of great help to a grieving family, or it can be a heavy burden for them to bear. The minister should consider the family's needs in planning the service. In a large church, funeral services are often conducted in the chapel rather than the large auditorium. Few funerals attract enough people to fill up an auditorium that seats a thousand or more.

Sometimes the family desires only a graveside service. In this case, the service should be kept to an even shorter time than a service in a church or funeral home. I usually read a few passages of Scripture, deliver about a five-minute meditation, and say a prayer. I then greet the family members personally and step to the side so the funeral director can lead the family back to the waiting cars or give them time to speak with friends or relatives who have come for the funeral.

A funeral service in a church or funeral home is a service of worship and deserves careful planning and thought. As a general rule, I believe that the service should be relatively short, probably not more than thirty minutes at most. The service is primarily for the living and should affirm in a positive way the resurrection of Christ and the Christian assurance of life after death. Rather than allowing the gospel message to be absorbed into "a black hole of private grief," Thomas Long believes that "a good funeral works the other way, drawing private grief and personal loss so fully into the gospel that mourning becomes not only consoled but transformed."[2] That certainly should be our goal as pastors.

If the service is held in a church, the following order of service may work well: organ music; a spoken call to worship and an invocation; and a congregational hymn such as "Holy, Holy, Holy," "O God, Our Help in Ages Past," "Savior, Like a Shepherd Lead Us," or "Abide with Me"; Old Testament reading; anthem by the choir, a solo, or organ music; New Testament reading; some type of music; a brief meditation; a final congregational hymn; and then the benediction. When the service is in a funeral home or the funeral crowd will be small, this order may work better: organ music, an invocation, Scripture lessons, an organ hymn selection, a brief meditation, and the benediction.

The Purpose of the Service

I am convinced that one of the worst mistakes many ministers make at funerals is to let the service go on too long. The grieving family is already drained emotionally, and they do not need a long service. Much meaning comes from a few well-prepared moments. Do not attempt to play on the emotions of the family. Assure them that it is okay to cry and express their feelings, but do not try to make them feel guilty or sinful. I do not believe that funerals should be used as an occasion to try to evangelize the family. Any service in which a minister speaks about the love of God and the assurance of life everlasting for the Christian will share the good news of the gospel. But a funeral is not a revival meeting and should not be used as that kind of platform. Don't focus on the sins or faults of the deceased. Some family members may even be driven away from the church and feel hostile toward the minister because the service of their loved one was misused. Later, in the quietness of the home, the minister can talk privately with the family about their relationship with God.

The Importance of Scripture

Scripture should be a significant part of a funeral service. I read passages from both the Old and New Testaments, particularly Psalm 90:1-12; 130:1-6; 46:1-3; 121; 23; 1 Corinthians 15:42-57; Romans 3:35-39; 1 Thessalonians 4:15-18; Revelation 21:1-4; 22:1-5; John 14:1-6, 27. I have assisted in funeral services where the minister read only one verse of Scripture, but I advise letting God's word assure grieving families of

God's comfort and life everlasting. Our words are hollow compared to the comfort Christians have received for centuries from the Bible.

A Closed Casket

I discourage families from leaving the casket open during the service. This is too much emphasis on the body. Our attention should be directed not to the body but to life after death—the spiritual body that the Christian now has. I also believe we need to discourage families from coming by to look at the body after the service. That often emotionally undoes the focus of the service. The true person is no longer confined to that body; let the Christian affirmation of life everlasting have the dominant focus in the service and not the body of the deceased.

The Meditation

In the meditation itself, I always tried to limit my remarks to five to ten minutes or no more than fifteen at most. I spoke loudly enough to be heard in a conversational tone but did not yell. Yelling is out of place at a funeral. I drew a brief outline from a biblical passage and emphasized God's comfort, support, love, grace, concern, and presence in the time of grief. I affirmed the biblical view of the resurrection and life eternal in Christ. When appropriate, I tried to be personal by making references to the person and his or her faith and involvement in the church or community. When applicable, I referred to the concern and care of family and friends. I encouraged them to let this be the parting time when they could separate themselves from the deceased and slowly begin to rebuild their lives. I tried to speak to those who were living in order to bring healing, hope, comfort, and assurance. I always tried to address my message to the family, but I prepared it so that others who were part of the congregation would hear the Christian affirmations about God's grace, love, and everlasting life.[3]

At the graveside service, I read a few verses of Scripture, then spoke a brief word about committing the body to the earth and the spiritual person into the hands of God. I concluded with a prayer and asked the family and friends to join me in praying the Lord's Prayer. Following this, I spoke personally to each member.

Every funeral service should be treated individually. The deaths of a young child, a teenager, a suicide victim, an accident victim, a young mother, a soldier, and an aged person all require special emphasis. Care needs to be taken in the selection of Scripture, hymns, and the meditation one delivers.

The Follow-up Visit

One of the most important things a minister does in the time of grief for a family is make a follow-up visit. A few weeks after the service, visit the wife or husband, parent or child, and give the person an opportunity to talk and express feelings. You may discover they need more help or counseling. Our church had a widow support group and other groups to help people through their grief. You may want to give the person or family a copy of the service you conducted and your meditation (this was normally my practice) or a copy of a book like Edgar N. Jackson's *You and Your Grief* or Granger Westberg's *Good Grief.*[4] This gives the family a practical way to reflect on their grief. Assure them through your presence of your support and concern. It is also helpful to drop them a note a year later on the anniversary of their loved one's death.

Notes

1. See "A Funeral Director Looks at Death" in my book, *Facing Grief and Death: Living with Dying* (Cleveland TN: Parson's Porch Books, 2013) 129–43.

2. Thomas G. Long, *Accompany Them with Singing: The Christian Funeral* (Louisville: Westminster John Knox Press, 2009) 123.

3. My small book, *A Positive Word for Christian Lamenting: Funeral Homilies,* offers a number of examples of funeral meditations (Gonzalez FL: Energion Publications, 2016).

4. Edgar N. Jackson, *You and Your Grief* (New York: E. P. Dutton, 1961) and Granger E. Westberg, *Good Grief* (Philadelphia: Fortress Press, 1962).

15

Observing Communion

Depending on one's denominational identification, Communion or the Lord's Supper is considered a church ordinance or a church sacrament. The earliest record of the Lord's Supper appears in Paul's letter to the Corinthians (1 Cor 11:23-26). In the Synoptic Gospels, the event happens as Jesus observes the Passover Feast with his disciples in the upper room. (See Matt 26:17-30; Mark 14:12-26; and Luke 22:7-22.) The Lord's Supper is observed in various Christian traditions. Some, like Catholics, observe it daily as well as on Sundays. Most Disciples of Christ churches observe Communion every Sunday, while others, like Baptists, may observe it monthly or quarterly. Most denominations have special services of Communion during Lent, in particular on Maundy Thursday, on Christmas Eve, and some on Christmas day and other special liturgical days. The pastor or priest usually officiates, often with the assistance of deacons or other ministers or priests. In some traditions, the congregation comes forward and is served the cup and bread; in others, the Communion trays are passed down the aisles by deacons for the congregation to serve themselves. Much is involved in our observance of Communion. "The centre of Christianity is what Jesus did," William Barclay writes. "The Lord's Supper in its dramatic picture states that just as it is. Preaching talks about it; theology interprets it and conceptualizes it. The sacrament announces it."[1]

Our Attitude at the Lord's Table

As pastors we are charged to help prepare our people to commune at the Lord's Table. If we believe eating at everyday tables deserves manners, then think how significant our attitude should be when we come to the Lord's Table. We should strive to remind our people that the way we approach the Lord's Table reveals something about our religious development. Many approach in haste, without any thought or preparation. They sometimes remain detached during the service and simply go through the motions. It has become routine for them, without much meaning.

In Milan, Italy, there is a house where a group of priests lived years ago. On the wall of what was once a dining room is a painting by Leonardo da Vinci, one of the most famous artists of all time. When you examine the painting on the wall, you can see a place in the lower middle section where someone cut a doorway. Why? The priests were unaware of the significance of da Vinci's painting and thought it was much more important to be able to go directly into the kitchen from the dining room than to preserve the artwork.

Many of us come to the Lord's Table the same way: oblivious to the presence of the One with whom we are coming to commune. Some are simply not aware of the sacredness of the occasion, so they may sit through it and miss the beauty, mystery, and wonder of the event. The pastor needs to encourage a congregation to think about the way they are approaching the Lord's Table so they may commune with the Lord more effectively.

Penetrating Words

After Jesus feeds the five thousand in John 6:41-60, he tells the crowd that he is the "bread of life." Raymond Brown says that these words probably originate in the primitive preaching tradition and that John brings them forward here to tell us some truth about the Lord's Supper.[2] When we gather at the Communion table, what we do has a deeper significance than we can ever acknowledge about the presence of Christ in our lives. I have many books on my shelves. One of them is written by Jürgen Moltmann and titled *The Crucified God*. In this book, the German theologian describes what he believes the sacrifice of Christ means. But I can never learn anything from that theologian about the death of Christ if I never read his book. To learn from it, I must take it from the shelf, read it, and let it penetrate my mind and thoughts and become a part of me. I also have a recording of Handel's *Messiah*. As long as it stays on the shelf, I cannot enjoy the music. But when I play it, it can come into my life and become a part of me. It penetrates me and uplifts me with its power. Likewise, one can ever learn from the Gospel of John if he or she never reads it or never hears anybody discuss it. We must pick it up and read it and let it penetrate our minds and hearts. So Jesus is telling us, "Unless I come into your life and penetrate it, unless you take me into your life and I become a part of you (like the bread you eat), then I am really not yours and I do not influence you." As we lead a congregation through the Lord's Supper, we strive to remind people of the importance of opening their spirits to receive the presence of the abiding Christ.

Christ Is the Host

As pastor, I tried to remind my people that Jesus Christ himself is the host of the Lord's Table. The Lord's Table is not an individual's table or my table. It is not just a local church's table. It is the Lord's Table. Jesus Christ is the host. He is the one who took bread and broke it. He is the one who took the cup and shared it with his disciples. It was he who blessed the bread and the cup. It is he who is host at the table every time we gather together. Jesus Christ is not simply *on* the table. He is *at* the table. He is *presence*, and he is *present* with us. We celebrate the one who is host because he was victor over sin and death. We come to this table at his invitation. He extends his hands to all Christians, all sinners who will trust him, to come and commune with him. "Come unto me all ye who are weak and are heavy laden," he said (Matt 11:28). "Wherever two or three are gathered together in my name, there I am in the midst of them" (Matt 18:20). Remember that Jesus Christ is the host at the Lord's Table.

We Come to Receive

Remind the congregation that we come to this table to receive. It was Jesus himself who took bread and broke it and said that it represented his body. He took the cup and declared that it represented his blood. We are receivers of what he has given for us. As we come to this table, we acknowledge that we are sinners saved by grace. We are recipients of God's love, grace, and forgiveness. "For by grace are you saved through faith" (Eph 2:8)—not by anything you do. Grace is God's gift. We receive it. "For God so loved the world that he *gave* his only begotten son" (John 3:16). Grace is not something we earn but something we receive. We come to the Lord's Table today to be receivers—to receive his love, forgiveness, and redemption.

"This is my body," Jesus said (Matt 26:26). In Aramaic there is no verb for "is." Literally it reads, "This–body." "This–body" is not concerned with past or present but with identification. The bread and cup are representatives of Jesus' sacrifice. It is almost humorous how some theologians have wrestled for ages over the verb "is" and its meaning in this particular phrase. Jesus probably never even used it. He was declaring that he is present with us as we receive him.

"This [is] my body for you," Jesus said. "For you, Peter. For you, James and Andrew. For all you twelve who are gathered in this room. It is for you that I lay down my life." But it is also for you and for me. Martin Luther said that authentic religion is always best expressed in personal pronouns. God didn't love us abstractly. In Jesus Christ we have seen God's love for us, and each of us is able to receive it now.

In the Old Testament story found in Exodus 16:13-21, we read about the manna that was given to the children of Israel in the wilderness. The Israelites were told that they could not hoard the manna. They had to gather it fresh each day. What a powerful lesson for us about our relationship to God. Many people live with the notion that they can drop in on God anytime they want to. They think they can "feed" on God and then "store up" that experience without seeking a fresh encounter. They worship God occasionally and then wonder why their lives go stale and flat. They do not understand why their religion seems worthless and doesn't sustain them during difficult times. Our experience with God must always be fresh. We have to come again and again to the Lord's Table to be fed. We come again and again to worship, to confess our sins, renew our spirits, and go forth to serve. When we receive Christ's forgiveness, love, and grace, his presence is made real in our lives, and then we can live more effectively for him.

We Gather to Express Thanksgiving

Let us also remind our people that we gather at the Lord's Table to express thanksgiving. Jesus took the bread and the cup. He took; he broke; he blessed; he gave; he said; and he blessed. He blessed and so must we. We bless God this day for what God has done for us through Jesus Christ. We gather at this table as a sign of our thanksgiving to God, who cared enough for each of us that his son laid down his life that we might have life. One of the biblical words for the Lord's Supper is *Eucharist*. Eucharist means thanksgiving. We come to the table in thanksgiving for what God has done for us through divine love. As we take the bread and cup, it is a sign of our gratitude to God. "In the Lord's Supper," Markus Barth declares, "Christ and his death are remembered as the one good cause for joy, hope, and gratitude."[3]

The New Covenant

We also come to this table as a sign of a new covenant. Jesus said that the cup is the new covenant. That night in the upper room marked the end of the old covenant and the beginning of the new. The word "covenant" appears in the Scriptures from Genesis through Revelation. It is found 286 times in the Old Testament alone. God made a covenant with Abraham, with Moses at Mt. Sinai, and with other prophets. God established a covenant relationship with his people. But Israel broke the covenant again and again. They assumed that they had special consideration in God's eyes.

Jeremiah prophesied that the day would come when the covenant that was written in stone would be written on the human heart. In that upper room where Jesus took bread and broke it and took a cup and shared it, the New Covenant began. At that moment, the covenant was written on the human heart as a new community emerged. You and I are part of that covenant community when we commit our lives to Christ and pledge our loyalty to him.

As the new community, we covenant with one another to bear each other's burdens and support each other in times of need. We draw strength from each other and from the Lord of the new covenant. Each time we eat at the Lord's Table is a sign of the covenant. It is a sign of our covenant with Christ and his covenant with us, and of our covenant with one another as his people.

The Larger Christian Fellowship

Paul alludes to a common problem in 1 Corinthians 11:26-34. We often do not discern the importance of the unity when you and I come together at the Lord's Table. Communion should not be seen as a private affair. We come to commune with fellow Christians and affirm that we are part of the larger body of Christ—his united church. Paul writes in 1 Corinthians 11 that the Corinthian church showed careless disregard for others. Those who arrived early were only concerned with gratifying their appetites and had no care for their brothers and sisters who arrived later. Before you and I dismiss this as a problem from the past, let us be honest and admit that too often when we come to the Lord's Table, we are not really concerned about our brothers and sisters either. We seldom experience a sense of solidarity and bond with other church members or with the wider Christian church.

I am convinced that divisions in the body of Christ—the church—are a form of heresy. It is nonsense to say that the church is strengthened by divisiveness. It always destroys the fellowship and hurts the church. Walter Rauschenbusch reminds us that "humanity always crowds the audience-room when God holds court."[4] Our redemption is always personal, but it is never private. As Christians, we should also be concerned about where our brothers and sisters are in their pilgrimage of faith. If we have a quarrel with another Christian and are upset with them, it causes division in the body of Christ and hurts the cause of Christ.

The *Didache*, an ancient Christian writing, enjoined the Christians, "let none who has a quarrel with his fellow join in your meeting until they have reconciled, lest your sacrifice be defiled" (XIV: 2). Before you come to the Lord's Table, reconcile yourself with the person with whom you have a quarrel. Isn't that similar to what Jesus said? "If you are offering your gift at the altar, and there remember that your brother has something against you, leave your gift there before the altar and go; first be reconciled to your brother, and then come offer your gift" (Matt 5:23-24).

This effort to be reconciled with others might be accomplished by having a litany or Prayer of Confession in the worship service before the observance of Communion. A brief sample might be the following:

Minister: Before we gather at the Lord's Table, let us confess our sins.
People: *We acknowledge that we have sinned against others, our self and especially God.*
Minister: We come to the Lord's Table grateful that God forgives our sins.
Unison: *We lift our hearts in gratitude for God's mercy and love.*

The Table Sometimes Divides Us

One of the tragedies and heresies of the church is that the Lord's Table, which should depict our unity, is often the example of our worst dividedness. When I was a pastor in Kentucky, I served as the chairman of the Commission on Christian Unity for the Kentucky Council of Churches. One fall, our commission sponsored a conference where we had a service of worship and Communion. One of the most satisfying features of this worship service was to see people from all denominations—Catholics,

Lutherans, Episcopalians, Presbyterians, Methodists, and others—gathered together to take Communion at the Lord's table. But a sad fact was that some were present who would not—could not—partake of Communion. The Roman Catholic priests and nuns were forbidden by their church theology from sharing in the sacraments with anyone who was not Catholic. In the place where we should be the most united, often we are the most divided. It is sad, but I also believe it is heresy. The Lord's Table that should unite us has too often divided us.

In the small group discussions at this ecumenical conference, most participants expressed pain about those who did not share in the Eucharist at the service of worship. Some suggested that allowing Communion at inter-denominational weddings would help build bridges between traditions. It was also suggested that more frequent ecumenical sharing of the Eucharist would affect the wider activity of service and ministry.[5] In his discussion of the disputes and divisions over the Lord's Supper, Geoffrey Wainwright observes, "In connection with the Lord's Supper itself, the doctrinal matters have mainly touched on the nature and mode of Christ's presence at the Supper, and on the relation between the eucharistic action and the unique sacrifice of Christ." He continues, "The disciplinary matters have had to do with authority to preside at the Lord's Table and with competence to receive the sacramental bread and wine in communion."[6]

Forgiveness and Unity through Christ

Paul instructed the Corinthians, "Let me tell you what you need to remember about this meal. I am passing on to you a tradition, not merely my words, but a tradition which goes back to our Lord himself. He took one loaf and one cup which symbolized the unity of his Church—the togetherness of his people. He broke the bread and shared it with his disciples. And then the cup" (cf. 1 Cor 11:23-26). Remember the unity of the church that the bread and cup represent. Remember Christ, who laid down his life so that all people might experience redemption. Remember that we are all brothers and sisters in Christ as we gather at his table. Remember that he has commanded us to love one another. As pastors, we need to work for unity of the church and seek to overcome our differences and quarrels with one another. Let us learn to love each other, even as Christ loved the church and gave himself for it.

In a New Year's Eve worship service, the pastor of a church in Atlanta invited members of his congregation to come to the altar that night and confess silently any sins that related to a fellow church member. Two men who had quarreled with each other for years met at the altar rail that night. They stood before the altar looking at each other. They hesitated for a moment, and then they embraced and began to weep. Each asked the other to forgive him. They forgave past sins and began their lives as different men. The Communion table should be the place for us to forgive others as we have been forgiven.

Several years ago, Andrew Wolfe visited West Berlin. One night, as he was walking from his hotel, he passed a bombed-out cathedral. Nothing but the shell of the cathedral was left. As he approached, he noticed a statue standing in front of the church. He could see that the figure was chipped and battered in many places, and one hand was missing. On drawing closer to the figure, he realized that it was a statue of Christ. The statue stood with his hands outstretched. At first, he thought it was sacrilege and wondered why they didn't replace it with a new statue. But as he got closer to the statue, however, the eyes of the Christ figure seemed to telegraph a message. "It was for this, exactly this, that I had to come; to bear in my own body the signs of a broken world and a broken humanity." At that moment the words of Jesus at the institution of the Lord's Supper came to Wolfe: "This is my body, which is broken for you." The words took on new meaning for him. "Before they had been simply words out of a ritual, but there in the bombed-out shell of a church in a city divided by hostility, I understood their real meaning. A broken body for a broken world; that's what they mean."[7]

Don Harbuck, a minister friend of mine who died too young, penned the following lines about the Lord's Supper before his death:

The Table

Two worlds—
One to believe in
One to live in
And between
No bridge but a dream
Root out of dry ground
Heat-choked at midday
Impatient, parched
In the long afternoon just begun.
Memory-haunted
By bread and wine around the table of togetherness

Where presence is real
Body and blood and word
Felt and touched and tasted.
Yet always
At the end
A parting into night
With frail souls
Clutching crust and cup
In fingers of hope.
Stumblers in the dark
Spoiled by light
Condemned to search
Endlessly
For love's table
Where belief and life
Embrace.

Christ was broken for the brokenness of humanity so that we might be drawn back to God. Let us invite our people to come to the Lord's Table, aware that we are all, in so many ways, broken—sinners, all of us— but through Christ's broken body we find wholeness and redemption. Encourage them to come to the Lord's Table with faith and expectation.

A Service of the Lord's Supper

The Lord's Supper is administered in different ways in the many Christian traditions. In some churches communicants come forward to the front of the church and kneel or stand to receive Communion. Sometimes when they are down front, they are offered the bread and cup separately or asked to dip the bread in the cup. In some traditions, they receive the bread from a common loaf by tearing off a small portion and also drink from a common cup. There are other variations of these practices. In most traditions, only an ordained minister or priest is allowed to serve Communion. In a wide number of traditions, like Baptists and Disciples of Christ, Communion is normally received in the pews where the church members are seated. These churches, of course, at various times may engage in other forms of Communion as well, especially on Maundy Thursday, Christmas Eve, and other special occasions. The following is a typical observance of the Lord's Supper that I often practiced in churches where I served as pastor.

A Typical Service

The trays of the bread and wine are prepared ahead of time, usually by laypeople who serve on the Lord's Supper or Worship committee. They arrange the trays in stacks that have lids with some of the bread and cups on both ends of the Communion table. I normally have a small loaf of bread and a chalice or cup in the center of the table that I use symbolically in the service. The deacons are usually seated on the first pews of the church during the worship service and will come forward later when the Communion service begins.

The Invitation to Commune

To begin the Communion service, the chair of deacons and I move from our seats to stand behind the table and face the congregation, with the deacon chair on my left. I then invite the congregation to share in the service of the Lord's Supper: "This is the Lord's Table. We come at his invitation. It is not my Table or yours but the Lord's Table. He invites all Christians to commune with him at this Table. So let us come now to celebrate Christ's presence with us." I then pick up the loaf of bread and begin to tear it in half, and as I do, I say, "On the night when Jesus gathered with his disciples in an upper room to observe the Passover, he instituted what we call the Lord's Supper. The apostle Paul gives us the earliest account of the Lord's Supper in 1 Corinthians 11. He tells us, 'For I received from the Lord what I also handed on to you; that on the night when he was betrayed he took a loaf of bread, and when he had given thanks, he broke it and said, This is my body that is broken for you. Do this in remembrance of me.'" (I give the Scripture from memory in all the places in the service.) Then I offer a brief prayer: "Loving God, we thank you for the sacrificial love Christ had for us which is represented in this bread broken for us. As we eat this bread, may it remind us of the depth of his suffering and love for us. Amen."

The Passing of the Bread

The deacons come forward, half on my side and the other half on the chair of deacon's side. We remove the lids and pass the bread trays to the deacons one by one, and they go down the aisles by twos, passing the bread trays to the congregation in the pews by extending them to the people on the ends. The trays are then handed down the pews, and the deacons collect the trays and continue until they gather at the back of the church. Then they move forward to the front by twos. The deacon chair and I have been seated next to the Communion table, he on the left and I on the right. We rise when the deacons start back down the aisles. Again they divide as they did before, half coming on my side and the other half on the chair of deacon's side, and hand us their plates. The deacons go back and sit on the front pews, and the chair of deacons and I each take a bread tray, and he serves the deacons on his left and I serve the deacons on my right. Coming back behind the Communion table after serving the deacons, I extend my tray to the chair of deacons and he takes his bread, and then he extends his tray to me and I take my bread.

I then face the congregation again and say something like this as I lift up my piece of bread: "This bread represents the One who is the Bread of Life. As we eat this bread, we acknowledge our desire to be nourished and fed by Christ. May his abiding presence strengthen us to serve him faithfully." Next I remind them that Jesus said, "Take, and eat; this is my body." We all then eat our bread together.

The Passing of the Cup

After pausing for a moment, I move to the center of the table and lift the chalice while I say, "In the same way, Jesus took the cup also, after the supper, saying, 'This cup is the new covenant in my blood. Do this, as often as you drink it, in remembrance of me.' For as often as you eat this bread and drink the cup, you proclaim the Lord's death until he comes." I then offer a short prayer like the following: "God of grace and love, we pause to acknowledge the wonder and mystery of your great love. May this cup remind us of the blood Jesus Christ shed for us and the costly nature of our redemption. Such love is beyond our understanding, but we express our gratitude and devotion. Amen."

The deacons come forward again, half on my side and the other half on the deacon chair's side. Removing the top lids, we pass the wine trays to them and they in turn serve the congregation pew by pew. Again the deacon chair and I take our seats until the deacons start back. The deacons return again to the front by twos, and the deacon chair and I gather the trays once more. After the deacons are seated again on the front pew, the deacon chair and I serve them as before, he those on his left and I those on my right. After we finish serving them, I extend my wine tray to the deacon chair, and after he takes his cup, he extends his wine tray to me. I take my cup and move to the middle of the table, where I lift my cup and say, "This cup represents the blood Jesus shed for us. We drink it acknowledging our indebtedness to him for such sacrificial love. We drink it as a sign of our continued commitment to follow his redeeming way. Jesus said, "Take and drink all of it."

Concluding the Service

After the service is concluded, many congregations sing a hymn, such as "Bless Be the Tie that Binds Our Hearts in Christian Love." In some congregations, they hold hands with fellow Christians as they sing. Following the singing of the hymn, they greet one another and share in fellowship for a while. Other congregations conclude with a benediction instead of a hymn.

All denominational service books offer some guidance in observing the Lord's Supper. I would suggest that a pastor purchase several different kinds from various denominational perspectives. There are many ways the Communion service can be observed, and the pastor needs to determine what approach works well for her and her congregation. Most congregations have a tradition they have normally followed, and it would be wise for the pastor to learn what that is and follow it for a while before suggesting changes.

Notes

1. William Barclay, *The Lord's Supper* (Nashville: Abingdon Press, 1967) 113.

2. Raymond E. Brown, *The Gospel According to John* (Garden City NY: Doubleday & Co., 1966) 287.

3. Markus Barth, *Rediscovering the Lord's Supper* (Atlanta: John Knox Press, 1988) 22.

4. Walter Rauschenbusch, *A Theology for the Social Gospel* (New York: The Macmillan Company, 1917) 48.

5. William Powell Tuck, ed., *Ministry: An Ecumenical Challenge* (Lexington KY: Kentucky Council of Churches, 1988) 59.

6. Geoffrey Wainwright, *Faith, Hope & Love: The Ecumenical Trio of Virtues* (Waco TX: Baylor University Press, 2014) 47.

7. Andrew R. Wolfe, "Broken Bread for a Broken World," *Pulpit Digest* (September-October 1984): 3–4.

16

Administering Baptism

Think about baptismal services you have observed or in which you have participated. I remember vividly my own baptism. I was fifteen years old and had made a clear and conscious commitment to Jesus Christ. I remember that our pastor, Dr. P. T. Harman, was elderly at that time and could not administer the baptism, so another Baptist pastor, Dr. Warner Fusselle, performed the service. It was a meaningful moment to me, and I have never forgotten it.

Years later when I was a junior in college and pastor of the Good Hope Baptist Church in northern Virginia, I led my first baptismal service in a pond on Joe Good's farm. I baptized thirty people that warm Sunday afternoon in August. The young men were dressed in white shirts and jeans, and the young ladies wore white dresses. We stood around the pond and sang, "Shall We Gather at the River." I have never forgotten that baptismal service. Nor have I forgotten the occasion when I baptized my two children, Catherine and Bill, and later my grandchildren, J. T., Michael, and Emily. Through the years I have shared in literally dozens of baptismal services, and they have all been meaningful to me.

Defining Baptism

Baptism is one of the church's richest traditions and practices. The word "baptize" comes from the Greek word that means to dip or immerse. No scholar of any denomination debates that baptism was originally by immersion. It is unlikely, according to many scholars, that baptism other than immersion took place until the fifth century, though some believe that infant baptism may have begun as early as the middle of the second century. But generally, all scholars consider immersion to be the standard way the church baptized believers for centuries. Renowned theologian Jürgen Moltmann calls the church to a "more authentic baptismal practice" by moving from infant baptism to adult baptism of those who believe and confess their faith.[1]

Baptism as an Acted Parable

Baptism provided the early church with a powerful picture of the radical nature of the change in one's life. When believers were to be baptized, the catechumens, as they were called at that time, would walk into the baptismal pool, strip off the old clothes, and enter the waters naked. They would be lowered under the water as though losing their lives by drowning, and then they would be raised up from the baptismal waters washed clean. They would then put on a white garment, indicating that the old man or woman had been taken off and they had now put on the new. This was indeed a radical picture to describe what happens within a person who becomes a believer.

H. Wheeler Robinson, the noted Baptist historian, and Karl Barth, considered by many the foremost theologian of the twentieth century, have both called baptism "an acted parable."[2] Let's explore this helpful image.

The "acted parable" of baptism focuses on the past, the present, and the future.

The Past

Baptism is an acted parable about the past. When a believer is lowered under the baptismal waters, this act presents a parabolic image of Jesus being nailed to the cross and giving up his life for us. It pictures Jesus' sacrificial death and then his being buried in the tomb. Further, baptism depicts the believer as being raised from the baptismal waters as Jesus Christ was raised from the grave. Rising out of the waters—the resurrection—affirms that the grave was not victorious. Jesus was triumphant over death, not defeated by it. Baptism points to the past, reminding us of the church's great message that Christ died for our sins. He was buried. The grave was not victorious; Christ was triumphant over it. And he continues to live today.

The Present

Baptism is also an acted parable about the present. It is an image of what is happening within a believer's heart. It is a description of the transformation that takes place in the life of one who commits his or her life to Jesus Christ. This is the reason that Baptist churches require a conscious commitment on the part of the person being baptized. It is the believer's response of faith to the grace of God. Baptists do not believe that someone else can be baptized for a believer or that someone else can make that decision for a person. Our experience with God is never secondhand or passive. It has to be a conscious decision that each of us makes as we give our lives to Jesus Christ as Lord. The candidate for baptism, as Karl Barth notes, is "freely confessing, declaring on his part his willingness and readiness."[3] As an acted parable for the present, baptism also represents other aspects of our conversion to faith.

A Picture of Confessing Sin. Baptism is a picture of making a confession of sin. Paul declared, "If you confess with your mouth that Jesus is Lord and believe in your heart that God has raised him from the dead, then you will be saved" (Rom 10:9). A believer is one who acknowledges her sins, confesses them, receives God's forgiveness, and turns to walk in a new way of life, following Christ as Lord. Baptism is a parable whose image affirms that one has made a confession of sin and a declaration of faith. Being lowered under the water is a picture of dying to the old way of sin and being raised up as a forgiven sinner, saved by God's grace as revealed in Jesus Christ. The church boldly proclaims to one who is aware of his sins, "Repent, and be baptized in the name of Jesus Christ" (Acts 2:36). Baptism is the dramatic picture of a changed life.

A Picture of the Conversion Experience. Baptists believe that immersion is the most beautiful image of the conversion experience. Karl Barth, not a Baptist but a Lutheran, threw down a theological gauntlet before the whole church when he affirmed that the Baptist practice of baptism by immersion rather than infant baptism was the correct biblical teaching. He called for the church to acknowledge its error and repent.[4] Infant baptism, he stated, was based on a "very slim thread."[5] Baptism by immersion is a vivid picture of a person turning away from his or her sins to receive God's redeeming grace, and it should be done by someone with the maturity to understand the decision.

A Picture of Cleansing. Baptism is a picture of cleansing. It is an image of being washed clean of our sins. As we are lowered under the baptismal waters, the image is that of being washed in the blood of Christ, who cleanses us of our sins. The act of cleansing is not our doing. It is something that God does for us and in us. It is not the water that removes our sins but God, the Father of Jesus Christ (1 Pet 1:3-5; Acts 22:16).

A Picture of Our Identification with Christ. Baptism is a picture of our identification with Christ. When we trust Jesus as our Savior, we are united with him. Baptism is an acted parable to express this union. We join Christ in his dying, in his burial, and in his rising. As we are lowered under the baptismal waters, we die to the old way of life. We die as Christ did. We die to the way of sin, and then we are raised up from the baptismal waters as Christ was raised from the grave. We are raised up to live a new life. The symbolism of this union is clear in immersion. Believers identify themselves with Christ who died for them, and as they rise up out of the water, they identify with the risen Christ. The Christ-like life is a call to follow him as Lord and Master. The Scripture text, Colossians 2:12, affirms this identity. Baptism is a sign of total surrender in turning from sin to committing oneself in union with Christ.

Paul wrote about this in the sixth chapter of Romans:

> Have you forgotten that when we were baptized into union with Jesus Christ, we were baptized into his death? By baptism we were buried with him, and lay dead, in order that, as Christ was raised from the dead in the splendor of the Father, so also we might set our feet upon the new path of life. For if we have become incorporate with him in a death like his, we shall also be one with him in a resurrection like his. (Rom 6:3-5, NEB)

Here is the vivid symbolism of identification. Here is the pictorial parable. As we are lowered under the baptismal waters, it depicts the way our Lord died and that we identify with him and his way. Again Paul states, "If we died with Christ, we believe that also we shall live together with him" (Rom 6:8). Baptism pictures both death and life like that of Jesus. Paul writes, "I am crucified with Christ, nevertheless, I live yet not I but Christ lives in me" (Gal 2:20). Here is the rich symbolism of our union with Christ in the watery grave. Jesus asked his disciples, "Are you able to partake of the baptism that I am?" (Mark 10:38) He declared that his baptism would be one of suffering and death. Our baptism is our union and our identification with Christ in his sacrificial death and glorified resurrection. It is a radical picture to declare a costly commitment on the part of the believer who follows a crucified Lord.

In the ancient ruins of the city of Leptis Magna in North Africa, the remains of a cathedral and a church dating from the early centuries of the Christian movement were discovered. Inside the cathedral and outside the church are well-preserved baptisteries shaped like crosses with steps going down into the crosses from all four sides. There is a pool in the center of each cross for baptism. The picture of these cross-shaped baptisteries is clear. It looks like a person is walking down into an open grave. Here believers clearly depicted their identity with Christ in his death and their rising from the watery grave to walk with the Risen Savior. This is the symbolism of the mystery and wonder of baptism.

A Picture of the Sign of God's Spirit. Baptism is also declared in the Scriptures to be a sign of the Spirit of God. In almost all instances, except a few, water baptism is the occasion where the Spirit of God comes upon those who are baptized. The Spirit is linked with baptism. Baptism and the coming of God's Spirit were not two events but were almost always seen as one event. When a believer is immersed, God's spirit comes into that person's life. Peter made this association in his Pentecost sermon: "Repent and be baptized, every one of you, in the name of Jesus Christ, so that your sins may be forgiven. And you will receive the gift of the Holy Spirit" (Acts 2:38).

A Picture of Obedience. We are baptized also out of obedience. Jesus has commanded his disciples to go and baptize in his name (Matt 28:12-20). We have received a commission from our Lord to go into all the world and tell people the good news about Jesus Christ, and then to baptize converts in the name of the Father, Son, and Holy Spirit. Baptism is no optional matter for the church; it is a direct response to our Lord's command. It is part of the "great commission." I like the story about the frontier preacher who went out West. The people in the community noticed that the preacher was busy digging a hole for a baptistery. "What is that for?" someone asked him. "To baptize people," the preacher responded. The reply was, "But there are no Baptists here!" "No," said the preacher, "but I'm digging this hole for the Baptists who will be here."

Jesus has commissioned us to go into the world and bring others into his kingdom. We are not to linger long near the baptismal pool. We are challenged to move into the world to bring others to Jesus Christ. We cannot do that if we hang back near the place where we begin our walk with our Lord. We have to strike out across the world to share what we have experienced.

The Future

Go another step with me and note that baptism is also an acted parable about the future. Baptism declares that a new age has begun in Jesus Christ. When Jesus was raised from the dead, something radical and transforming happened in the practice of the first believers. They changed their time of celebrating worship from the Sabbath day to the first day of the week, Sunday. This was a most dramatic change. The early Christians taught that a new age had begun: "Therefore, if any persons are in Christ, they are new creations: old things have passed away; behold all things are new" (2 Cor 5:17). The early church also thought of worship and work in seven-day units, so the new era was called the "Eighth Day." This was one day past the seventh-day Sabbath. In the Eighth Day, the past, present, and future are caught up into one. Sunday is a day of remembering the death, burial, and resurrection of Christ and of looking ahead and celebrating the reign of God in the world today. The Lord's Day on the Eighth Day united the past, present, and the future.

A Call to Respond. As a parable about the future, baptism calls us to respond. Every time there is a baptismal service, those of us who have been baptized should see it as a call to personal reflection and a time of recommitment. Every baptism is a summons to remember your own baptism, to remember the commitment you made to Christ on that day. Every baptism is my baptism and your baptism in its call to remember that we are identified with the believers who are lowered under the water by faith. Every baptism reminds us that we are one body and that we are renewed by every observance of this act. In remembering our own baptism, we recommit ourselves to serving Christ as Lord. We also link our lives with those being baptized as part of the body of Christ—the church. And in supporting, loving, and ministering to them, we strengthen not only them but also ourselves and the whole body of Christ.

A Picture of Hope. Baptism is a picture of hope for the future. There is more to life than we have here in this world. For Christians, death is not the end but a doorway that opens into new life. Just as baptism is the doorway into church, so baptism by death is the doorway into eternal life with God. Christians live with an eschatological hope. "But if we have died with Christ, we believe that we shall also live with him" (Rom 6:8). We believe that God is moving toward bringing history to completion. And we have a confident hope that life will go on after death in another dimension.

But this belief is more than hope. For Christians, there is an assurance. Jesus declared, "Because I live you will live also" (John 14:19). He said, "I go to prepare a place for you" (John 14:2). You and I, as Christians, have the assurance from our Lord that death is not the end. Our "baptism" by death will raise us up to the new life that God has prepared for us. We die as we have lived, with complete confidence in Christ.

More than a Symbol

Some people say that certain Christian groups make too much of baptism and the Lord's Supper. But I am convinced that most Baptists make too little of baptism and the Lord's Supper. Baptism is not a "mere sign" or a "mere symbol." To say that baptism is only a symbol is not to understand its rich meaning. Baptism cannot be fully defined as a symbol. Baptism is, to use Paul Tillich's term, a "dynamic symbol."[6] The believer is participating in something that is happening in the baptismal service. Our faith brings us to an event in which God is present. The water is not magical; nevertheless, the action of God is working within the soul of the person being baptized as that individual makes his or her response to God's grace. From the believer's perspective, one enters the baptismal waters out of a faith commitment. God accepts this commitment at the moment of baptism and fills the believer with the divine Spirit.

As Baptists, we are often frightened of the word "sacrament." But it originally comes from a Latin word that referred to an oath a Roman soldier made to the emperor as he enlisted in the army. Simply put, a soldier was often asked annually to reaffirm his allegiance to the emperor. Christians saw this parallel and adapted the word "sacrament" to describe the pledge, oath, or commitment to God the believer made at baptism. Nothing magical is done at baptism. But surely God is actively present in what is happening.

As much as I believe in "believers' baptism," I think we have to be careful that we do not turn it into a modern-day version of the battle the Apostle Paul had over circumcision. The church continues to be divided over infant baptism and believers' baptism. Many Baptist churches continue to insist that people of non-Baptist churches who practice infant baptism must be baptized again by immersion. I believe the real question should be about whether the person seeking membership in the church has made a commitment of faith in Jesus Christ as Lord. Some Baptist churches recognize infant baptism as the rite of affirming the family's support of a child who will later confirm that faith in some way through a program or study that leads to personal commitment. Today, some Baptist churches recognize this kind of spiritual journey and do not require baptism by immersion if a person has already made a commitment to follow Christ as Lord in another Christian fellowship.[7]

The Presence of God

Since it is an acted parable of the remission of sins, reception of God's grace, and incorporation into the death and resurrection of Christ, surely we want to confirm God's dealing with the human heart in the profound moment of baptism. Surely God is in the event. Let's not make too little of baptism. Let's not exclude the power and presence of God. Mere symbol is not enough to contain all that is transpiring.[8] God is present in a mighty way. Paul's reminder of the importance of baptism underscores this: "As many of you as were baptized into Christ have put on Christ" (Gal 3:27). There is human participation, but let's not forget divine participation. Our words to describe this significant event are inadequate. It is filled with mystery. Baptism is a sign of God's redeeming action and presence and of the cataclysmic change in the life of the one baptized into Christ.

Recently I stood at the altar of our church with a couple who were getting married. They came to the altar having already pledged a commitment to each other. At the altar, they said vows and exchanged rings. A wedding ceremony does not make a marriage. But I don't believe that you have a real initiation into marriage without some symbolic or acted parable to note its beginning. Commitments need to be made. A real marriage will take a lifetime of living together and living out the vows made at the wedding. The initial wedding vows mark the point of beginning.

What happens in the baptismal pool is likewise a picture of the allegiance we make to God and our desire to follow God. It takes a lifetime of faithful discipleship to show others how deep that commitment was and is. Baptism is our initiation into the church and our desire to grow in the community of faith in the likeness of Christ. Baptism is an acted parable about the beginning of the Christian life.

A Baptist Baptismal Service

In the Baptist tradition, Christian baptism involves immersion of a person under water after he or she makes a confession of faith in Jesus Christ as Lord. The word "baptism" comes from the Greek *baptizo*, which literally means to dip or immerse. John baptized Jesus, and Scripture indicates that it was by immersion. Matthew 3:16 reads, "And when Jesus had been baptized, just as he came up from the water, suddenly the heavens were opened to him" (see also Mark 1:9-10). Paul's reference to baptism in Romans 6:4 indicates baptism by immersion when he writes, "Therefore we have been buried with him by baptism into death" (note also Col 2:12).

It is essential to meet with the person being baptized before the service and explain the process, such as how to bend his knees when it's time to go under the water. This way, people know what to expect and will be less anxious. Churches may order baptismal services differently. The following is how I usually conducted them when I served as pastor.

The Introduction to the Service

In most churches, the baptismal service is usually a part of a regular worship service, often held at the beginning of the service after the call to worship. Sometimes, however, it is observed as a separate service in the afternoon or in the evening. In these cases, there are usually several people to be baptized, Communion may be observed, and often a reception follows the service to honor those who were baptized. When the service was part of a regular service of worship, I put on my baptismal robe and waders ahead of time. I wore my shirt and tie under the robe and entered the baptismal pool, which was filled with warm water in advance.

In some churches, a curtain separates the minister from the view of the congregation until it is pulled back when the baptismal service begins. I entered the water before the curtain was pulled back and carried my Bible with me. After the curtain was drawn back, I read or quoted two passages of Scripture to begin the service. The first was from Matthew 26:18-20 and the second from Romans 6:3-5. Both Scriptures address the importance of baptism in the life of the new Christian. Jesus has commissioned us to disciple others and to lower them under the baptismal waters to symbolize the new Christian's identity with Christ and the way he or she will follow after Christ.

After reading the Scriptures, I related three meanings that baptism conveys to us. First, it shows that the person being baptized is "dying" to her way of sin as she is lowered under the water. Then she is raised to symbolize that she is forgiven by the grace of God to follow Christ as Lord. Next, baptism reminds us of the death and burial of Jesus and his resurrection from the grave. The lowering under the water represents Jesus being lowered into the grave, and being raised from the water depicts Jesus being raised from the grave by God the Father. Finally, baptism symbolizes the human death of a Christian as one is lowered under the baptismal water, and then one is raised out of the water to represent the assurance of life after death.

The Baptism

Following this brief explanation of the meaning of baptism, I handed my Bible to an assistant who was hidden from the congregation's view, and then I invited the first person to come down the steps and enter the water. I usually extended my hand and assisted them as they walked in front of me, and then I had them stand in front of me facing to my right. They usually wore a white baptismal robe and no shoes.

After they were in place, I quoted a verse of Scripture from memory, a different verse for each candidate, and then asked a question: "Do you profess Jesus Christ as Lord?" The candidate replied, "I do." At this point I raised my right hand and said, "On the profession of your saving faith in Jesus Christ as Lord, and in obedience to our Savior's command, I baptize you, [the name of the person], in the name of the Father, the Son, and the Holy Spirit." I then assisted them in putting their hands around my right wrist, freeing my hand so I could gently cover their nose and mouth. Next I placed my left hand around the back of the shoulder area and lowered them under the water, then quickly raised them out of the water. I assisted them to the steps and then welcomed the next candidate, if there was one, and continued in the same manner with each until all were baptized.

The Invitation to Others

After all were baptized, I addressed the congregation: "The baptismal waters await anyone who wants to walk with Jesus Christ as Lord. He gladly welcomes all those who come by faith." I closed the service with a prayer: "Loving God, bless those who have been baptized this day. Strengthen them as they begin their walk with you. May they be drawn to your presence in times of temptation and stress so that they feel the sustaining power of your presence. Guide us as a congregation to help nurture them in their faith along with their families. May the beauty of this service remind us of our call to witness and serve you faithfully. This we pray in the name of our risen Lord. Amen."

After I dressed, I returned for the rest of the worship service. We often had a service of Communion later in the service on baptismal Sundays.

When the Communion elements were given to the congregation, I would serve the bread and cup to the people who were baptized and encourage them to take the Communion cup with them as a reminder of the service. Following the worship service, those who were baptized received a baptismal certificate to commemorate the occasion.

As pastor, you may lead your congregation to devise other ways to celebrate such a beautiful and memorable occasion.

Other Traditions

In other Christian traditions, the practice of baptism has developed a variety of forms. Some denominations baptize infants who may be the children of parents affiliated with the local church. The children are blessed in a service of worship that expresses thanksgiving for the gift of the child and the willingness of the parents or guardians to commit to guiding the child to make a personal faith response at a later age following catechetical instructions. This service of infant baptism also assures the family that their child is now a part of the Christian community. The personal confession of faith is expected to come at a stage in the child's life when she has been guided in knowledge of the Christian faith by the corporate Christian community and has grown in her own awareness of what it means to be a Christian.

The policy, practice, and procedure of baptism in other traditions can be found in denominational service books like *The United Methodist Book of Worship, Book of Worship: The United Church of Christ, The Book of Common Worship, Lutheran Book of Worship, The Book of Common Prayer, The Revised Common Lectionary,* and resources like *Holy Baptism and Services for the Renewal of Baptism: The Worship of God* (Philadelphia: The Westminster Press, 1985), and *Baptism, Eucharist and Ministry* (Faith and Order Paper no. 111; Geneva: World Council of Churches, 1983).

Notes

1. Jürgen Moltmann, *The Church in the Power of the Spirit* (New York: Harper & Row Publishers, 1977) 240.

2. H. Wheeler Robinson, *The Life and Faith of the Baptists* (London: The Kingsgate Press, 1946) 77; Karl Barth, *The Teaching of the Church Regarding Baptism* (London: SCM Press, 1963) 18.

3. Barth, *The Teaching of the Church Regarding Baptism,* 54.

4. Ibid, 40f., 49.

5. Ibid., 44ff.

6. Paul Tillich, *Dynamics of Faith* (New York: Harper and Brothers, 1958) 41ff.

7. See the discussion by Fisher Humphreys in *Baptists Today*, September 2014, p. 39 where he encourages Baptists to finds ways to mend the division that has come about by insisting on believers' baptism for those who practiced infant baptism. See also E. Glenn Hinson, "Baptism and Christian Unity: A Baptist Perspective," *Baptism: An Ecumenical Starting Point*, ed. George A. Kilcourse (Lexington KY: Kentucky Council of Churches, 1986) 20–31.

8. Several Baptist New Testament scholars speak of the importance of using the word "sacrament." See George R. Beasley-Murray, *Baptism in the New Testament* (Grand Rapids MI: Wm. B. Eerdmans, 1988); R. E. O. White, *The Biblical Doctrine of Initiation* (Grand Rapids MI: Eerdmans, 1960); Warren Carr, *Baptism, Conscience and Clue for the Church* (New York: Holt, Rinehart and Winston, 1964).

17

Overseeing the Deacon Ministry

When we turn to the Scriptures for the origin of deacons or for the source of early church leaders, we do not find a set pattern. There is no simple approach. The New Testament shows that the early Christians had various ways of worshiping and of organizing themselves. There was one method in the Jerusalem church, another in the Corinthian church, and even other ways in Paul's Pastoral Epistles.

In his commission, Jesus challenged his disciples to go into the world and share the gospel with all people (Matt 28:19-20). But he did not tell them exactly how to do that or how to organize themselves as a church. He chose twelve disciples, and then later the disciples and other apostles appointed a group called elders (Acts 14:23; Titus 1:5). In the book of Acts, we discover that seven were set aside to serve the early church in a particular way (Acts 6:1-6).

The Beginning of Deacon Ministry

No clear picture is given in the New Testament of how deacons came into existence. In fact, the New Testament contains only four references to deacons: Philippians 1:1; 1 Timothy 3:8-10, 12-13; Titus 1:5, 7; and Romans 16:1.[1]

Acts 6 is probably not, according to most scholars, the origin of deacons. The seven are not called deacons anywhere in this passage. Although these seven are not called deacons, it is interesting that the early church soon limited the number of deacons to seven. One of the early church fathers,

Irenaeus, wrote that the deacons in churches should be seven in number. Later the Council of Neo-Caesarea, which met in AD 315, set seven as the official number of deacons in the church. In Jewish thought, seven was a perfect number. But the church down through the ages has had a varied number of deacons and has not been so limited.

In Greek, the root word for deacon means servant or minister. In none of the references are deacons are described in terms of power or prestige. They are spoken of as servants. Jesus said, "Whoever would be great among you would be *diakonos*," the Greek word for servant (Mark 10:43). Jesus used the same word that we have for deacon to describe his ministry. "Deacons derive their name from the idea of the servant," Dale Moody writes, "a term most closely related to the Messianic ministry of our Lord."[2] The word used for servant and deacon is the same in the New Testament.

Even if Acts 6 is not the origin or source of the deacon ministry, it can still serve as a model for what deacons should be like in the church. Most early Christians were Jews. The Jerusalem church was composed mostly of Jewish and Palestinian Christians. These people spoke Aramaic, which was a derivation of Hebrew. But there was also a group called Hellenists. These were Jewish people who had moved away from Jerusalem or Palestine to foreign countries, and they no longer spoke Hebrew but Greek. So in the early church, some of the Christians spoke Aramaic and others spoke Greek. The latter group stayed in Jerusalem usually temporarily. But all of these people were still Jews.

A common practice among the Jews of this time was that on the Friday before the Sabbath, a group of two from the synagogue would go around to the various members of the synagogue and ask for food or money. They would carry a basket, called *Kuppah* in Hebrew, to hold the food or money. Then they used the gifts to take care of the poor people in their congregation. They wanted these poor people to have food for the Sabbath and into the week beyond.

It may be possible that the appointment of the seven, in some ways, bears similarity to what the Jewish synagogue had done for many years. The early church may have modeled their practice after this one. Thus, the passage in Acts 6 it is at least a model of what deacons should be like. Below, I offer some lessons that I see clearly in this passage. You may see others as well.

A Practical Need for Leadership

First, if we look closely at Acts 6, we find that the leadership within the early church began in order to fulfill a practical need. There was no theological discussion about which "holy" people should serve. The church members simply recognized a need in the congregation: the widows of the Hellenists, the Greek-speaking Jews, needed support and care. People were chosen to distribute food to those who were needy in the church. These people were selected primarily to put their Christian faith into practical action. This is still a basic function of Christian leaders, especially those who serve as deacons. Deacons need to engage in the practical service of visiting the sick, the homebound, and the grieving. For this reason, ministry to the congregation is the paramount work of deacons. This kind of servant leadership is based on the biblical model. From the beginning, deacons have been servants.

Laity Called to Serve

Second, notice that the leadership in Acts 6 was not chosen from those in high, holy positions like bishop, priest, or pastor. The people chose servant leaders from among themselves—from the laypeople of the church. Those chosen were leaders who arose to fulfill practical needs. One of the problems in churches is the idea that authority has to come from the top down. In Acts 6, we see leadership arising from the laypeople in the church.

George W. Truett was one of the great preachers of an earlier generation. When he was a schoolteacher in North Carolina, the congregation where he was a member literally said to him, "We believe that God has called you into ministry. We are setting you apart as a minister." At that time, Truett hadn't felt a call, but the congregation felt that God was calling him. They anointed him to go and serve. This model may be the best way for leadership to arise in the church—from the everyday, ordinary laity in the congregation.

Vote of the Congregation

Third, note that the seven men in Acts 6 were selected by a vote of the congregation. When the apostles had to choose a disciple to take the place of Judas, who had hanged himself, they cast lots. Based on the lots, they selected a person named Matthias (Acts 1:23-26), who never appears again in the New Testament. But in Acts 6, leaders were not selected by the casting of lots. They were chosen by a vote of the congregation. The question was, "Who is it you want?" The congregation then chose people as they let God's Spirit guide them. The local people in that church made the decision.

Authority of the Congregation

Fourth, Frank Stagg observed that the election of the seven by the congregation "is the first clear evidence that the authority was in the church as a whole and not in individuals."[3] The authority in the local church is not in the hands of one individual, whether he is the pastor, bishop, pope, associational director, or convention president. In the Bible, the election of servant leaders takes place within the congregation. The local congregation chooses these leaders. This is an early reference to the autonomy of the local church that continues to be the practice in our Baptist churches today.

Involvement in the Church

Fifth, Acts 6:3 says that the early church chose individuals who were very involved in the local church. They were "from among you" (6:3). These people didn't come from someplace outside the local church; they were individuals who were involved in the church they were chosen to serve. They had been converted, their lives had changed, and they were active in that local church. We want such people ministering in our churches.

People of Good Reputation

Sixth, the seven were people of "good reputation." The King James Version says that they were persons of "good report." What does that mean? It means that they had Christian character. We don't want characters, but you want people *with* Christian character. We want individuals who are not apologetic about saying, "I am Christian and my faith permeates my life." The Christian character of servant leaders should be beyond reproach.

One deacon at a church I led was an auto mechanic, a simple man named Lewis. He was a loving and caring person who repaired many of the seminary students' cars for free when they could not pay. His son, Bob, went into the ministry, came back to Virginia, and served for many years there until he retired. Bob said that he never saw any conflicts in the Christian lifestyle of his father, either in his business as a mechanic or in what he said and did as a deacon. What a marvelous testimony for every Christian. What you do in your business shows also in what you do as a deacon. And what you do as a deacon is reflected in what you do in your business. The

Greek word for witness can mean "one who shares the faith well," but it can also mean "a person of whom a good witness is given." A Christian deacon not only bears witness to the faith but also bears witness by the way he or she lives.

Sharing Faith

Seventh, notice that the seven were people who shared their faith with others. They were not apologetic or embarrassed about witnessing to someone else about Christ. They wanted to share the good news of what God had done. Two of the seven, Stephen and Philip, are prime examples. Stephen and Philip shared their faith freely with other people. They were both witnesses. Stephen spoke before the Sanhedrin and the Jewish people in the synagogue. The Jewish leaders eventually put him to death. Scripture records that he was "full of grace and power" (6:8), charm and charisma, but he also revealed the grace of God. The stoning and death of Stephen influenced Saul, who later became Paul. Even in his death, Stephen was able to bear witness.

Philip shared his faith with the Ethiopian eunuch (8:27-40). He was willing to cross racial and cultural barriers and travel a long distance to let God's spirit guide him. He witnessed from the Scriptures to the eunuch, and then he allowed the man to respond. Stephen even baptized the eunuch after he committed his life to Christ. Neither Stephen nor Philip was frightened and embarrassed to share their faith.

Full of the Holy Spirit

Eighth, note that the seven were "full of the Holy Spirit." The disciples knew that they could not do the work of Christ by their own strength. They opened their lives so that God's Spirit could fill them and guide them. They were not merely devout people; they were spiritual people in the sense that they had felt the power of God's Spirit—the zeal, the fire, the enthusiasm of being a Christian. They responded to the continued presence of Christ. Today, we need individual deacons who have this sense of enthusiasm. Enthusiasm literally means "God breathed." God has breathed into us the challenge and inspiration to do the work that God wants us to do.

Full of Wisdom

Ninth, the seven were "full of wisdom." I don't think this necessarily means that they were great scholars. I believe it is a reference to practical wisdom.

They had the wisdom mentioned in James 3:17: "The wisdom that is from above is first pure, then peaceable, gentle, and easy to be instructed, full of mercy and good fruits, without partiality, and without hypocrisy." They were filled with wisdom in knowing how to minister in Christ's name. I think they were also aware that they needed to keep learning. They knew they had not arrived spiritually. All of us—deacons, pastors, and other Christians—need to continue to grow in the faith and knowledge of Christ.

A former deacon in First Baptist Church in Bristol, Virginia, where I served as pastor, was a medical doctor who became so affected by arthritis that he had to quit his practice and finally became bedridden. When I went to visit him, he would tell me about his study of the Scriptures. This man had literally become an authority in the Scriptures. He could no longer do his medical work, but he continued to study the Bible, commentaries, and other books. I was astounded at the wisdom and continuous growth of this man who was confined to his bed. He became an example for those of us in good health of the need to find ways to continue learning more about God and how we can serve God better.

Full of Faith

Tenth, the seven were also "full of faith." Stephen was the first one named among the seven who was declared to be a man full of faith (6:5). Surely we don't want deacons who do not have their own sense of faith. We want deacons who have committed their lives to Jesus Christ, who have had a conversion experience, who acknowledge that Christ is Lord of their lives. I believe deacons should affirm that "Christ is the foundation, the cornerstone of my life and the one whom I want to be my guide and source." It is not enough to be a good person, a good businessperson, or a nice individual. "Confidence of faith was . . . established as a crucial characteristic from very early on," New Testament scholar James D. G. Dunn asserts.[4] Deacons are expected to be people who are "filled with faith."

Devoted to Prayer

Eleventh, notice that the seven devoted themselves to prayer. Prayer is one of the primary functions of deacons. We take prayer for granted and don't draw on its power enough. We need to spend more time learning how to pray. We need to spend more time praying. We need deacons and others who will devote themselves to upholding our church, our ministers, and those in need through prayer. Every deacon should be open to God, that they might know how to serve God more faithfully.

The Laying on of Hands

Twelfth and last, note that the seven were set apart by the laying on of hands. In the Old Testament, the laying on of hands was a sign of the blessing of another person. It was a sign of setting them apart for service. In their worship practice, the Jewish people often used a scapegoat on whom they would place their hands, confessing their sins, and then they would send it away to carry their sins. In ancient Judaism, the laying on of hands was a sign or a symbol of transferring something from one person to another. The Jewish Mishnah indicated that people were admitted to the Sanhedrin, the official Jewish body, by the laying on of hands.

In Christian circles, we are not absolutely certain what the laying on of hands meant. We know that the symbolism originates in the Jewish tradition. I am not convinced that it means the transmission of authority. More likely it is a sign of blessing or a sign of prayerful support. It is a symbol of setting a person apart for a particular service in a particular place. It is a sign that this person is called to a certain kind of leadership—a servant ministry. It is also not clear whether the laying on of hands was done by the apostles only or by the congregation as a whole. Either is possible. I do not believe it is helpful to be dogmatic.

It is recorded that the famous Russian novelist, Leo Tolstoy, used to go around and ask great thinkers and ordinary people this question: "What is the purpose of life?" He never seemed to find a satisfactory answer until a peasant man responded one day. "The purpose of life," the peasant said, "is to serve God." Tolstoy said this was the highest wisdom that he had ever heard. Above all else, deacons—and all who wish to live as Christ lived—should focus on serving God.

Deacon Responsibilities

I have found that deacons almost always need guidance in the particulars of their ministry. The best way for me to offer this guidance was at a deacon retreat, which I usually held on Friday night, Saturday morning, and Saturday afternoon at a retreat center away from the church. It might take place at a denominational location like Eagle Eyrie or at a secular retreat spot. During this time, I taught or had a seminary professor or another pastor offer sessions on the biblical view of deacons and their role in the church today with particular attention to our local church and the proper way to do "pastoral" calls. I would lead rehearsals for taking up the offering and administering Communion. A quiet time for meditation and prayer was built into the agenda. Special sessions for deacon spouses were also offered.

Listed below are deacon responsibilities from one of the churches I served as pastor. I offer these as a guideline for churches. Each church should develop guidelines that work well for them. It was my custom to give the deacons on the day of their ordination a small towel embroidered with the church's symbols. This was a tangible symbol for them to remember that, as Jesus washed his disciples' feet and dried them with a towel, they too are called to be servants and humble themselves on behalf of others. The list below contains suggestions for ways to carry out this servant leadership.

Deacon Organization and Administration

1. Chairperson
• provide spiritual leadership and direction for the deacon body
• facilitate monthly deacon meetings
• attend monthly church council meetings
• facilitate monthly (day and time to be determined) deacon meeting agenda with deacon officers

2. Vice Chairperson
• provide spiritual leadership and direction for the deacon body
• facilitate monthly deacon meetings in the chairperson's absence or co-facilitate monthly as required
• coordinate the updating of deacon family photos with new deacon class at the beginning of each year
• attend monthly church council meeting in chairperson's absence

3. Secretary
• provide spiritual leadership and direction for the deacon body
• read and ask for vote of approval of minutes from prior meeting
• record minutes of current meeting
• facilitate monthly deacon meetings in the co-chairperson's absence or co-facilitate monthly as required
• mail reminder notes to deacons who miss monthly meetings

- distribute minutes and all pertinent correspondence discussed at the deacons' meeting via e-mail or mail on or before Friday of the following week
- include all church staff and church moderator on distribution lists

4. Family Ministry Coordinator
- provide spiritual leadership and direction for the deacon body
- assign new families to deacons at each monthly meeting, determining number of families assigned to each deacon and level of individual knowledge and desire to work with a particular family
- update family lists monthly and distribute them to the appropriate deacons via e-mail, with copies sent to the church secretary and deacon officers
- call any deacon not present at a meeting with a family assignment during that first week

Deacon Body

1. Deacon Steering Committee
- consists of one deacon officer and up to four active deacons
- meets and makes recommendations to the deacon body regarding specific deacon business to be addressed at future deacons' meetings
- meet in January of each year and plan the annual deacons' retreat
- meet every August to lead in the nomination of deacon officers for the next year to be presented for election to the deacon body and to the church staff by September

2. Deacons of the Month
- chair the 8:30 a.m. and 11:00 a.m. Communion services
- assist the pastor in Wednesday evening services as requested
- present deacon family ministry prayer concerns to the pastor and give support during the prayer service as requested by the pastor
- take an active role in the service prayer time

3. Deacon Scripture Reading
- chairperson of the 11:00 a.m. worship service reads Scripture and says prayer each month

4. General Advice
- work together, at least in pairs, at deacons' meetings, devotionals, prayer times, and visitations
- seek to welcome visitors to church after service
- cultivate spiritual gifts among deacon body and church family
- strive for spiritual growth and leadership within the church
- provide additional pastor support
- have a Sunday morning prayer time with the pastor each week
- hold an "open dialogue" deacons' meeting once per quarter

Caring Contacts

Listed below are suggestions I gave deacons in one of my churches regarding visitations. Many are also appropriate for pastors during their visitations.

Types of Contacts and Their Purposes
1. Initial Visits

Make an initial visit. Build these visits around something other than inviting the person to Sunday school or church. Use the time to get acquainted, to find ways to pray for them, to follow up on earlier prayer requests, to honor special events (birthday, new job, promotion, Christmas, etc.), to share what you learned during Sunday school and church the past week, and/or to inform them of upcoming events.

2. Cards and Letters

Send personal cards to your families occasionally. Make the cards personal, and use them to relate that you're praying for specific situations, honor special occasions (birthdays, Christmas, etc.), or as invitations to class functions (cook-outs, fellowships, etc.) or Wednesday night supper.

3. Times for Intentional Contact
- Crisis
- Illness
- Death of family member
- Birth of child
- Retirement
- Graduation in family or other important event

4. Prayer

Pray, if appropriate. Use prayer as a means of communicating to our Lord. Prayer is the most vital part of outreach, and you should pray specifically for a person's needs.

5. Special Events or Needs
• Sit with the person or family in church.
• Have lunch together after Sunday service.
• Invite them to your home for a meal or dessert.
• Sit together at Wednesday night meal.
• Offer transportation when needed.
• Discover their special interests and talents.
• Invite them to your Sunday school, if not already attending.
• Make the family aware of various opportunities for each age.
• Report changes of address or new telephone number.

6. Dos and Don'ts of Contact
• Do contact a person in a spirit of interest and concern.
• Do mention that you would like for them to be part of Bible study and worship on Sunday morning.
• Do talk about the good things happening at church.
• Do listen with your ears rather than with your mouth.
• Do verbalize your concern and love for the person with a need.
• Do offer the ministry of your church, your Sunday school class, or yourself in a situation of need.
• Do pray for a member who is absent.
• Do share something special from the Sunday school lesson or pastor's sermon that meant something to you.
• Do share about upcoming events in the class, department, or church that the absent person might not have heard about.
• Do take church bulletins, Lenten or Advent materials, etc.
• Do be informed about the church's ministries and programs.
• Do remind them, if needed, that ministers and other church members are human.
• Do make a graceful exit.
• Do bring back information on the person or family if church staff or pastor needs it.
• Do give them a new member packet, if applicable.
• Do fill out and turn in your report.

- Don't contact people in an accusing attitude about their being out of Sunday school or church.
- Don't contact people for the sole purpose of telling them they missed Sunday school or church.
- Don't lecture.
- Don't pry into or discuss people's problems or business unless they offer to do so.
- Don't argue.
- Don't be defensive.
- Don't reassure someone that everything will be all right unless you can personally guarantee it.
- Don't visit an absent member when you are not feeling well.
- Don't stay too long.

Notes

1. The debate of whether or not women should serve as deacons was a big issue several years ago. Most churches have determined where they stand. My only comment will be to point to Romans 16:1, where Phoebe, a woman, is called a deacon or a minister in the church at Cenchreae. This designation, according to David Bartlett, indicates that she "has a role of some importance in the early community" (*Romans*, Louisville: Westminster John Knox Press, 1995, p. 140).

2. Dale Moody, *The Word of Truth: A Summary of Christian Doctrine Based on Biblical Revelation* (Grand Rapids MI: William B. Eerdmans Publishing Company, 1981) 455.

3. Frank Stagg, *The Book of Acts: The Early Struggle for an Unhindered Gospel* (Nashville: Broadman Press, 1955) 90.

4. James D. G. Dunn, "The First Letter to Timothy," *The New Interpreter's Bible*, vol. 11 (Nashville: Abingdon Press, 2000) 807.

18

Working for Christian Unity

Throughout my years in ministry, I have chosen to belong not only to my local and state or regional Baptist ministerial group but also to the local ecumenical ministers' organization and to a statewide organization like the Kentucky Council of Churches or the Virginia Council of Churches. I have chosen also to join an intra-faith group composed not only of various Christian denominations but also of other world religious groups. Additionally, I continued my membership in the Academy of Parish Clergy, which crosses ecumenical lines and has representatives from other world religions. I would encourage any minister to join in working for Christian unity of churches. Denominational divisions, I believe, are a fracture in the body of Christ, his church, and we should strive for unity. I am a Baptist but much more. I love the way Walter Rauschenbusch, one of our noted Baptist theologians, put it over a century ago:

> I should do harm if I gave Baptists the impression that "we are the people and that there are no others." We are not a perfect denomination. We are capable of being just as narrow and small as anybody. There are fine qualities in which other denominations surpass us. I do not want to foster Baptist self-conceit, because thereby I should grieve the Spirit of Christ. I do not want to make Baptists shut themselves up in their little clam shells and be indifferent to the ocean outside of them. I am a Baptist, but I am more than a Baptist. All things are mine; whether Francis of Assisi, or Luther, or Knox, or Wesley; all are mine because I am Christ's. The old Adam is a strict denominationalist; the new Adam is just a Christian.[1]

I have learned from many other Christian and religious thinkers. Religious bigotry and narrow-mindedness should not be a part of our proper perspective. One of the most powerful movements sweeping across the Christian world today is the quest for church unity. I want to encourage pastors to join in that important effort. Since the Second Vatican Council and the establishment of the World Council of Churches, many Christian bodies have labored diligently to see if the broken body of Christ, the church, could be united. Many Christians view the fragmentation of the church as a scandal and a factor that harms its witness to the world. Many believe that the wide variety of denominational expressions of the faith hurts the cause of Christ. The fighting between Christians about correct doctrines and church practices is an affront to our Lord.

Those of us in the Western world need to be aware of the increasing diversity in the church. Since the middle of the last century, the majority of Christians are now of ethnicities other than Caucasian. People of other races will likely continue to grow in number in the Christian community.

A High Priestly Prayer

I believe that our Lord's high priestly prayer for his disciples and the future church can guide us in our quest for unity (John 17:20-26). Jesus' prayer begins with a personal plea that he might glorify his Father in the ultimate sacrifice on the cross that lies before him (17:1-5). Next he prays for his disciples, that they might be consecrated to God's truth in order to serve Christ as he sends them into the world (17:9-19). Jesus then offers his prayer for all future believers, which includes you and me and other Christians around the world. All believers who read these verses (vv. 20-26) overhear the Lord's prayer for them. What does his prayer tell us?

A Quiet Trust

Even as Jesus faced the most difficult experience in his earthly life, his prayer revealed a quiet trust in his Father's presence and guidance. With the certainty of the cross before him, rejection by the crowds around him, and desertion by the disciples who were closest to him, Jesus maintained confidence in what God would do in the future.

Confidence in His Disciples

Jesus' prayer reflects not only certainty about his Father but also confidence in the disciples. Even knowing his disciples' fears, ambitions, struggles, and weaknesses, Jesus did not lose trust in them. He had chosen them after long hours of prayer, and he was convinced that God would use them as instruments to spread the good news throughout the world. And indeed later they did.

Jesus' Basic Desire

Jesus prayed for the unity of the future church. He prayed that the future growth of the church would not inhibit its unity. Why then do we debate about whether or not the church should be united? The last will and testament of our Lord was a prayer for unity. All the debate about whether or not the church should be united is superfluous, if we really want to follow the intention of our Lord. I believe it is clear that the unity of the church was our Lord's basic desire.

Efforts to bring about the reunion of the church have never been easy. Anyone who has labored within ecumenical circles knows the difficulties and obstacles to unity. But we have to start someplace to reunite separated Christian churches. Any small step is at least a step in the right direction.

In a CBS special several years ago, Bill Moyers told a story about a man in New York City who decided to do something to help the hungry. As he went to work each day in New York, he distributed one hundred sandwiches to the homeless. They soon learned about his kindness and began to line the sidewalks, waiting for him to hand them a sandwich. After a TV segment that showed the man handing out sandwiches to the people, Moyers observed, "New York City's population now runs in excess of eleven million people. A hundred sandwiches will hardly scratch the surface in the need. But while Sam may never move his world very far, at least the direction he is moving it is forward."

Every effort we make to move the church forward to be united is at least a step in the right direction. With every step we take to fragment the church, we move away from our Lord's intention. That's the reason I believe every minister needs to be a vital part of that effort toward unity.

A Unique Kind of Unity

Jesus also prayed for a unique kind of unity for his church. He prayed that the future disciples in the church would be united as he and the Father were united: "May they all be one, as you, Father, are in me and I in you" (v. 20). Jesus' unity with God was based on a unique personal communion of the Son with the Father. The Church's unity is a reflection of unity within the Triune God.

The unity Jesus prayed for extends beyond organizational or ecclesiastical uniformity. This unity is not simply organized under a giant administrative group that brings various factions together; instead, it rests on openness to the Spirit of God who works in our lives as God worked in the life of his Son, Jesus Christ our Lord.

The basis of the church's unity, as it is modeled after our Lord's unity with his Father, is rooted in the nature of God and in Jesus' obedient love. The Father was "in" Jesus, and Jesus was "in" the Father. As the Father has "sent" the Son, so Jesus "sends" his disciples into the world (John 17:18). Jesus mediated the presence of God through the temple of his body (John 17:6-19), and the flock was united under Jesus, the one "Shepherd" of his church (John 10:7ff). The unity of the church in today's ecumenical movement should not be void of all diversity of theology or administrative form. Instead, should be based on the Triune nature of God, characterized by the diverse unity of the Father, Son, and Holy Spirit.

It is sad to listen to various theological discussions about the reunion of the church and realize how inflexible many people are in their stance on various denominational traditions. Dick Sheppard, a leading Anglican churchman of several generations back, gathered a group of church leaders together to discuss the question of the reunion of the church. He thought the meeting was successful until he heard the two clergymen who were the speakers for the night make a comment to their own followers. One of them remarked to his minister friends, "I don't think I gave anything away, did I?" The other minister observed, "I rather fancy I held my place all right. Didn't I?"

How unlike our Lord, who laid down his life for the church, is that approach? Too often we are more concerned with "Can I get my way?" or "Is my position well-established?" If unity is to be achieved, each side must seek to see what the other gives and not what they can hold on to. To recover unity, sacrifice is necessary.

The Model of Divine Love

If Christians loved one another as Jesus loved his Father and the Father loved the Son, this same expression of love would be evident in the life and work of the church. The motivating power of God's love that guided Jesus' ministry would be the dominating expression of the church's mission. The way Jesus revealed the Father to his disciples convinced them of his Father's love. In a similar way, the unity of the church, which rests on the redemptive love of God manifested through the incarnate Christ, will convince the world that its mission is really from God (v. 21). The disunity of the church continues to be a compelling argument to the world that believers have lost sight of their redemptive mission to share God's love as they claim to have experienced it in Christ.

Our model for unity in the church comes from our Lord. Jesus Christ extends God's grace to all people. Jesus called all people to experience the Father's love. Instead of exhibiting Christ-like love, we often draw circles and exclude others from the church. We want to include only those who think like we do or act like we do, only those who fit in certain theological boxes or believe along our rigid patterns. Jesus encountered this attitude in the Pharisees, who built their religion on exclusiveness. Their religion erected walls and fences to keep people out. But this was not the kind of religion Jesus proclaimed. Rather than excluding people, Jesus reached out to include them. Rather than pushing people down, Jesus reached out to lift them up. Rather than crushing people with heavy burdens, Jesus sought to liberate them. Rather than hating people, Jesus sought to love them. Rather than trying to destroy people, Jesus wanted to redeem them. The Christ who reaches out to all of us with his love is the same one who instructs us to reach out to our brothers and sisters across all barriers. He does not want to build walls that separate but doors that open to include others.

Joseph Fort Newton once told a story about a deacon who was excommunicated by his church in New England. But the deacon refused to leave the church. For twenty-five years, this deacon came to every Communion service. He sat in the privacy of his own high pew with a piece of bread and a small sip of wine that he brought with him. He communed with the church when the church would not commune with him. The church might have excommunicated him, but he was still present in church, communing with the God who was open and responsive to him.

Men and women may exclude people from the church for reasons that are of major or minor importance. But God seeks to include. The uniqueness of the unity of the church is realized in our relationship to being in God as God was in Jesus and Jesus was in God. The oneness of the church rests on a theological base of the Triune nature of God. God's love and grace are open to all who will respond.

Discerning God's Glory

The reason Jesus prayed for the unity of the church is so the world might know the true nature of God as one. Note the three stages through which God manifests his glory. *First, Jesus received glory from his Father.* What was this glory? It was revealed through Jesus' incarnate life, words, and ministry. This glory may have been a reflection of Jesus' obedient love of his Father. Glory may have been a reference to Jesus' death on the cross. When Jesus spoke about his death, he usually spoke of being "glorified" (John 11:4; 12:23).

Second, Jesus transmits this glory to his disciples (John 17:22-23). As Jesus had reflected the light from his Father, the disciples were to be lights to show others the way to the Father. Sometimes the disciples would suffer as the Lord had suffered. The ministry of the church is not to call attention to itself but to lead people to God.

The church's task is not to erect fences so that we can keep out those who don't think like or act like us. Instead, our role is to glorify God and lead other people to find God. Isn't it sad when we think about what divides the church? Across all Christian theological lines, we worship one God, the Father Almighty; acknowledge Jesus Christ as Lord; and affirm the Holy Spirit as the One who inspires the church and works within our lives. We read the same Bible, which we all believe is inspired by God's Holy Spirit. We sing hymns from each other's traditions and read books, prayers, and devotional literature from various denominations. What divides us? It is primarily church order and polity. Each religious group declares that only their perspective is the correct one.

In my book, *Our Baptist Tradition,* I said that I was reluctant to write or preach about the Baptist denominational line because I did not want Baptists to push themselves further into a private corner and assume that we alone have all the truth about God. We do not. No group has all the insight![2] Let us labor as one alongside others within God's kingdom. We labor not as isolated Baptists with all the truth but as Christian ministers working with others for the unity of the body of Christ.

Third, ultimately Christ's glory will not be realized in this world but in the eternal glory that he has gone to prepare for his disciples. During times of tribulation, the disciples can find hope in the love and promise of God (see Rom 8:18-25; 2 Tim 2:11-12). God's glory will not be fully manifested in this world, but it will be known as we depart this life to dwell eternally with God.

I served for a number of years as chairman of the Commission for Christian Unity for the Kentucky Council of Churches. This was a fascinating but sometimes difficult experience. Our goal had been to explore ways Christians from across various denominational lines might work to restore unity in the church. One of the most moving experiences I had as a member of that commission came when we gathered together at Barren River Lake State Resort Park in Kentucky for a conference several years ago. At one of the night services in this conference, we observed Communion. It was ironic that at a place named Barren River, my life was enriched. Christians from all denominational lines—Catholics, Episcopalians, Disciples, Methodists, Presbyterians, Baptists, and others—communed together at the Lord's table. We put aside our denominational differences. Some shared in the service by using wine, while others used grape juice. But we all communed together at the Lord's Table. I was deeply moved by the service. Others were likewise moved emotionally as we gathered before the Table of our Lord. At that moment, as Christians, we affirmed the things on which we agreed and did not focus on how we differed.

The divisions in the church are a scandal in Christianity. Our disunity must break the heart of God, whose Son continues to pray for the unity of the church he founded. As a pastor, make your efforts a part of the force that works for this unity. A writer has expressed his longing for the church's unity in these lines:

What care I for caste or creed?
It is the deed, it is the deed.
What for class, or what for clan?
It is the man, it is the man!
It is of love and joy and woe,
For who is high and who is low,
Mountain, valley, sky, and sea
Are for all humanity.

What care I for robe or stole?
It is the soul, it is the soul.
What for the crown or what for chest?
It is the soul within the breast,
It is the faith, it is the hope,
It is the struggle up the slope.

It is the brain and the eye to see
One God and one humanity.[3]

May this be our goal as well.

Notes

1. Walter Rauschenbusch, "Why I Am a Baptist," *A Baptist Treasury*, compiled by Sydnor L. Stealey (New York: Thomas Y. Crowell Co., 1956) 183–84.

2. William Powell Tuck, *Our Baptist Tradition* (Macon GA: Smyth & Helwys, 2005) 2.

3. Robert Loveman, *The Builder Magazine* 12/3 (March 1926), http://www.phoenixmasonry.org/the_builder_1926_march.htm.

19

Looking Back
If I Could Do It All Again

I became pastor of my first church when I was twenty years old, a junior in college. I was young and couldn't begin to imagine what ministry and church life were all about. My first church in Northern Virginia and other churches through the years have helped me grow in my understanding of ministry. I have had the privilege of serving many different kinds of churches for more than sixty years—country churches, a fast-growing suburban church, a university church, a downtown college church, a semi-nary church, and a downtown church in a small Southern town. I have also had the privilege of teaching part-time at two colleges, full-time at the Southern Baptist Theological Seminary in Louisville, Kentucky, and as an adjunct professor at the Baptist Theological Seminary at Richmond.

As I reflect over the years, I feel a great sense of satisfaction, but to be honest, if I had to do ministry all over again today, I think I would do some things differently, maybe even radically so. Nevertheless, we each respond with the sense of calling and sight we have at the moment. One of the lessons I have learned through the years is that my labors in God's kingdom are only a small part in the continuing effort to advance God's work. I could not do everything I wanted, but I could do something, as small as it might be, and then leave the rest to others and especially to God. I know that looking back gives the benefit of hindsight. It is the clearest vision we have for most of our lives. I look back to look forward better. Here are some things I would do differently if I could do it all again.

Graduate School Education

First, I might pursue my education a bit differently. I worked my way through college and seminary and wanted to do graduate work abroad at Edinburgh University or at some place like Oxford. Frankly, I don't know if I could have gotten into those schools, but it was a dream that I always had. I did not get to study at these universities until I received a mini-sabbatical from St. Matthews Baptist Church in Louisville, Kentucky. For several months, I had the privilege of studying at Oxford University and St. Andrews University. I had written my doctoral dissertation on John Baillie, who had been the principal at New College, Edinburgh University. If I had studied there, I could have had many primary sources to draw upon. If I had my education to pursue again, I think I would find a way to borrow the money so that I could have studied abroad.

I was fortunate, however, that I was married during my graduate study, and Emily worked so that I could complete my graduate courses. I did some supply preaching, but most of our salary came from what she made during those years of graduate study. Even so, I think that if I had gone abroad, my perspective would have been broader, and I would have gained a different outlook on life and ministry altogether. I think every young minister should have the opportunity to study abroad and especially go to the Holy Land early in his or her ministry.

Personal Friendships

Second, if I had to do ministry over again, I believe that I would work harder at developing personal friendships in my church. Many church members are often reluctant to establish friendships with their pastor. I know there are many reasons for this, but what they don't know is that this attitude often creates a lonely life for the pastor and his family. I have been privileged to have some older members in various congregations who have taken the initiative to establish friendships. In some churches, people my own age have wanted to build those kinds of friendships with me. When we were in Louisville, Kentucky, I had many seminary friends in our church and in the community. As I look back over my ministry, though, the people who took the initiative to make friends with Emily and me have continued to be our friends through the years. Every pastor and his family need friends. They need a supportive group that cares for them as people and not just as their pastor and family. I think I would try to develop more personal friends without fear of what someone in the congregation might say. I would encourage people in the congregation to seek ways to reach out and show friendship to the pastor and his or her family.

Ministry Outside the Church Building

Third, if I had ministry to do over again, I would seek to help the church recognize that its reach extends beyond the walls. We often spend too much time on committee work and activities that confine us to a building. Much of that may have nothing to do with extending the kingdom of God. The Roman Catholic concept of the parish is probably a more authentic understanding of ministry. In the Catholic tradition, wherever a church is located, the priest (pastor) is responsible for the whole parish. The pastor ministers to the entire community where the church exists. A good pastor would be responsible for knowing that he or she has a role in the total community and is not confined merely inside the local church building. Too much of the work of church life is busy work, just keeping the machinery running. That work is important, but it is certainly not the main essence of ministry.

I believe that the important ministries of the church need to be done in the community where the congregation reaches beyond the boundaries of the church walls and seeks to make a difference in the city where it lives. That was the reason I became involved in establishing the Boys and Girls Club and the Pastoral Counseling Center in Lumberton, North Carolina. These were vital ministries our community needed, and they made an ongoing difference in people's lives. In other places I have seen Alzheimer's day care centers, grief support groups, divorce support groups, alcohol support groups, assistance to the elderly, tutoring programs, food pantries, HIV/AIDS support groups, and many other such groups make a radical difference in the church and community where I served. I believe that much of this type of ministry is done in the true spirit of Jesus.

I know that some people in the church will object to the minister being involved in such work. They do not believe that the pastor's responsibility should extend beyond the church's building or the church family. But I do not believe that the main reason I was called to ministry was to be confined within the church's walls or to serve only those on our rolls. I was called first as a minister and second as a pastor of a local church. I believe that if I had ministry to do over again, I would seek to help the churches where I served as pastor to see the importance of ministry in the community all around them.

Hands-on Missions

Fourth, if I had to do ministry over again today, I would try to get my church to be more involved in hands-on missions. I would not let them be content just to study or pray for missions, as important as both of these are. I would try to challenge my church to be involved in local, state, national, and worldwide missions. Too often church people are unwilling to do mission work in their own community. We think of missions as work to be done someplace else, somewhere far off. I think that is a shame. Jesus challenged us to begin our ministry in our own Jerusalem and then go into Galilee, Samaria, and the rest of the world. But first we begin at home to meet needs near us. One of the finest things one of my churches did was the "Inasmuch" ministry. This was a small way for our church to be involved in missions. Adults, youth, and children did local missions. This ministry focused on two weekends a year when our church got involved in dozens of hands-on ministries—repair work, roofing jobs, painting, yard work, nursing home care, food delivery, fire wood delivery, and many other projects. If I had to do ministry over again, I would be much more involved in this kind of hands-on ministry. Too often the church focuses on its chores, keeping the organization going. The real ministry begins in our community around us, extends to our state, and finally moves into the rest of the world. I think we need to open our eyes to see the real ministry to which Jesus has called us.

Disciple Church Members Better

Fifth, if I had to do ministry over again today, I would seek to disciple people more in my churches. In our churches today, we have too much emphasis on programs. There is seldom a call to real commitment. We put too much stress on getting people to join something, but we need to ask *What has really changed in a person's spiritual life?* The Church of the Saviour in Washington, DC, is a model for this type of discipleship. No person can join that church until he or she has been in attendance for a year of specialized study in which one seeks to understand what it means to follow Jesus Christ. After that year, if a person wants to be a part of that church, he or she has to make a commitment to Christ and a commitment of money, worship, time, and service for Christ. The final commitment indicates that a person is willing to do some kind of genuine ministry on an ongoing basis in his or her community.

I like that concept of church. I think Jesus is calling us not just to join something but to be his disciples. Our understanding of missions and evangelism should not be "come sit with us in church," but "come share with us in our mutual call to serve." I don't think we work very hard in our churches to disciple people. Starting fresh, I believe that I would have a requirement that a person had to reunite every year with the local church and make a renewed commitment to follow Jesus Christ. To commit one's life to Christ would not be something that was done just one time. At the end or beginning of a new year, I would invite those who really wanted to continue growing with Christ to reaffirm that commitment.

Develop Stronger Staff Relationships

Sixth, if I had to do ministry over again, I think I would work more closely with my fellow staff members. I have been fortunate through the years to have many wonderful staff people with whom to work. Some of these are still dear friends, and we have shared much of life and ministry together. I have often spent time with staff members over lunch and in private conversations, talking about the church, setting goals, and planning ministries together. Most of the time I have had cordial relationships with other staff members—but not always. Some staff caused conflicts and actually worked behind my back to create difficulties.

For difficult staff members, I believe I would exercise closer supervision. I would ask these people to come in and see me each Monday morning. We would sit down and go over their goals in ministry and how the goals work together with my goals and those of the other staff members. I would talk about areas where we need to improve, where there are conflicts or difficulties, and about our own relationship. I would address some of the problems created in the church by this particular staff member. Some difficult staff members are not truly team members, and I would encourage them to be a part of the ministry team. I believe that close supervision might have helped overcome some of the problems I had with staff members and possibly made them a stronger part of the team.

I know that no pastor can do his or her work without the full support of staff. I believe that every single minister should be free to exercise his or her own gifts, but there is no question that some staff members need closer supervision than others. If someone on the staff does not support the senior minister, obviously that individual needs close supervision. If I had ministry to do over again, I would exercise that supervision more rigidly for such staff members and seek to build a stronger team and create a greater sense of loyalty to each other and to our Lord.

Personal Spiritual Development

Seventh, if I had to do ministry over again, I think I would focus more on developing my own spiritual growth and inner life. I would work harder on my prayer life and spiritual growth. I think I have always worked at this, but never enough. I think too many ministers take our spiritual growth for granted and do not labor at it. I know that I have a long way to go in my spiritual development even now. I know I have not arrived.

I would also labor more intently to help develop the spiritual lives of people in congregations where I served. I do not believe any of us can really be genuine Christians without working harder at our personal spiritual lives.

When I was pastor in Louisville, Kentucky, I was a part of an ecumenical group. A young woman, who was an Episcopal priest, was also a part of this group. The leader of our ministerial organization indicated that he wanted all of us to come to a breakfast meeting at an early hour several weeks in the future. The Episcopal priest indicated that she could not come at that time. "That is my quiet time," she said, "and I never let anything interfere with that time." That's real commitment. She wouldn't let even a religious meeting get in the way of her devotional life and spiritual growth. She is the model that many of us should follow. I think that I would follow her example and try to teach people to honor more the time I set apart for my personal spiritual life. Too often, church people do not honor the quiet time of a pastor's devotional life, spiritual nourishment, Bible study, and prayer. Even ministers, maybe especially ministers, need to set aside the time in their lives to grow more deeply in the things of God.

More Time with My Family

Eighth, if I had to do ministry over again, I would make more time for my family. Too often in ministry I have worked seven days a week. This has meant that I did not often have enough time with my wife or with my children. Sometimes I took no time off at all. I think that too many ministers, me included, have suffered from what I would call a "God complex." The demands of ministry are always upon us, and if ministers are not careful, churches can take every bit of the time they have, and they may never have time for their own families.

I confess that in all my years of ministry, I have never had a church member tell me not to work so hard or advise me to take some time off. Pastors need to know that their congregations support the time they spend with their families. I believe this is one of the reasons that divorce affects more minister families today. Church work can be all consuming. Many ministers do not have a spouse who is as understanding as mine has been. Emily has been deeply devoted to ministry herself and understands that commitment.

As I look back on my life, I thank God for a strong sense of calling, for the opportunity to serve, for a loving wife and good children, for churches that have nurtured me and have been supportive of my leadership, and for opportunities to do ministry locally and in many other places. I have tried to make some small contribution as I committed my life in following the call of God that I received in Jesus Christ, my Lord.

20

The Minister as a Star Thrower

Several years ago a tramp comedian named Bilbo was a genius at panto-mime. His audiences loved him. He always finished his act with a pair of oversized yellow shoes with big toes sticking out under the stage curtain. All the audience could see from behind the closed curtain was Bilbo's big yellow shoes with a spotlight shining on them. As long as the spotlight was on the shoes, the audience continued to applaud.

When Bilbo thought the audience had applauded long enough, he would step on stage in his stocking feet and take a bow. The audience realized that they had been fooled by him, and they loved it. Unfortu-nately, Bilbo's life had a sad ending. He was booked into the Hammerstein's Victoria Theater on 42nd Street and Broadway, the palace theater of its time. He opened on Monday and was never better. He had a heart condi-tion but no one knew it. At the end of the performance, he stepped out of his shoes, as he had at every performance, but this time had a heart attack. The audience was wildly applauding his shoes, but Bilbo never came back for his last bow. The star performer was dead.

Acknowledging Our Humanity

Although most clergy would not like to admit it, there is a star factor in ministry. Like Bilbo, many ministers end up being performers in a spotlight before their congregations. Like the star comedian, some kill themselves by pushing too hard and seeking applause. Unfortunately, too many ministers seek to be a "star" instead of following the high calling that brought them into ministry in the first place.

Many ministers are unwilling to acknowledge their own humanity. They have fallen into this "star" trap by yielding to a "God complex." All of us suffer from the basic sin of pride that Reinhold Niebuhr calls our "God Almightiness," "the effort to usurp the place of God."[1] Some ministers seem to have taken second or third helpings of such a dish.

Congregations often put the minister on a pedestal and expect him or her to walk on water. Ministers themselves often assume that they are not supposed to be sick, express emotions, or have time for their families or themselves. This attitude often leads to burnout and to what I would call "ministerial shooting star" syndrome.

At the annual church night at Hampton Baptist Church in Hampton, Virginia, where I served as interim pastor, I was asked to put on a Superman shirt with a big S in the center under my dress shirt and coat and enter the congregation through a phone booth that was placed on the stage. At the moment when I was introduced as the interim pastor, I burst through the phone booth pulling my coat and shirt back to reveal the Superman S in the middle of my chest and yelled to the people, "I have come to save Hampton Baptist Church!" The congregation broke out both in laughter and applause. This, of course, was all done in good fun, but unfortunately many churches do expect their ministers to be a superhero and save them from their problems, struggles, and difficulties.

A Reality Check

But no minister can solve all the church's problems or challenges. No minister can be everywhere at once. Believe it or not, you cannot really walk on water. Every minister needs a reality check. We need to make the distinction between our role and reality. Our identity and our identification are not the same. We are ministers by calling and profession, but our identity is male or female, married or single, husband or wife, mother or father. We are not fully what others say we are or think we are. Our robes, stoles, and clerical garb do not fully define who we are internally. These trappings indicate who we are as ministers, but they do not remove from us our humanity, emotions, instincts, and drives. The question looms within us, "Who is this I/me/he/she/you/they?" We are pulled in many directions. We are more than we think we are and yet less than we think we are.

All Christians Are Called to Minister

Ministry is not for a selected few star performers; it is a community of faith serving the one who is the bright and morning star—Christ, the light of the world. You and I are called, Paul says, "to help equip others in ministry to build up the body of Christ." As we share our gifts, whatever they are, we seek to minister in the name of Christ. Every single Christian in a congregation is a priest. Each has a ministry. All have gifts, and there is a great diversity. No one expects the dean of a medical school or law school or seminary to do all the work. Each person uses his or her own gifts and helps train and equip others to minister effectively. That is one of our leading roles as well: to equip all people to serve Christ more effectively.

The Church of the Saviour in Washington, DC, affirms in their membership statement that the church of Christ is the ship on which "there are no passengers, all are crew members." Every Christian needs to be engaged in ministry. If we are members of the church of Christ, a member of any congregation, then we seek to find what our gift is and commit that gift in service for Christ. Karl Barth, the noted German theologian, wrote a number of years ago that within the church there are many different functions, but the preacher does not stand any higher than the elders, nor the bell ringers any lower than the professor of theology. There are differences of functions, but each offers his or her gifts to Christ.[2] As a minister, you too offer your gifts, and you seek to equip others to use theirs.

Ministering Outside the Church Walls

A church has many essential functions: worshiping, training, leading Bible study, equipping church members for ministry, comforting, celebrating, and others. But we need to be aware that we are called to minister outside the walls of the church as well.

Bill Jones, a noted New York preacher, told about a time when he was a small boy and visited his grandfather's farm. He had grown up in the city and was unaware of all that one needed to do on a farm. His grandfather got him up early and they spent a lengthy time feeding the chickens, milking the cows, and feeding the other animals, then finally they came back to a bountiful breakfast. As a small lad whose eyes were beaming with enthusiasm and excitement, Bill Jones said to his grandfather, "Granddaddy, we have really worked hard, haven't we?" His grandfather looked back at him and said, "Son, what we have been doing are just the chores; the real work is out in the fields. That begins now."

Do not forget that Christ has called all of us to authentic evangelism, to share the good news of Christ with others in the world and seek to minister to the hurting people in the world around us. Many are looking for meaning, purpose, and hope. We need to share our faith unashamedly through words and deeds. Let the banner of your faith proudly wave in the winds of change and struggle. Travel your journey of faith joyfully as you share your faith with Christ. Respect all religions and traditions. Acknowledge that every person has the right to have religious faith or to deny it, but do not be ashamed of the gospel that you proclaim. Proclaim it boldly with the assurance that the living Christ is with you.

We Are Called to Serve

We are called to serve and not to be served. We are not performers but servants. One of my favorite writers is Loren Eiseley, the anthropologist. I love one of his stories where he writes about walking along the beaches of Costabel. As he walked along the beach an hour before dawn, he could see flashlights gleaming off in the distance along the shore. Making his way around the altered edges of the cove, he saw a stooping figure moving along in the gloom. On the sand he saw long-limbed starfish strewn everywhere as though the night sky had showered down. He came closer to the figure of a man in front of him. He saw the man stoop down and fling an object beyond the breaking surf. Eiseley moved toward him to see what was happening.

In a pool of sand and silt he saw a starfish, its arms up stiffly. "It's still alive," Eiseley ventured. "Yes," the man said. With a gentle movement he picked up the star, spun it over his head, and flung it out into the sea. It sank into a burst of spume and the waters roared once more.

"It may live," the man said, "if the offshore pull is strong enough." "Do you collect?" Eiseley asked the man. "Only like this," the man said softly, gesturing, "and only for the living." He stooped again, oblivious of Eiseley's curiosity, and skipped another star neatly across the water. "The stars," he said, "throw well. One can help them." Eiseley wrote later,

> I turned and as I neared the bend in the coast and saw him toss another star, skimming its skillfully far out over the revening tumultuous water. For a moment, in the changing light, the sower appeared magnified, as though casting larger stars upon some greater sea. He had, at any rate, the posture of a god . . . . He is a man, I considered sharply, bringing my thought to rest. The star thrower is a man, and death is running more

fleet than he along every seabeach in the world. . . . On a point of land, as though projecting into the domain beyond us, I found the star thrower. In a sweet rain-swept morning, that great many-hued rainbow still lurked and waved tentatively beyond him. Solemnly I sought and picked up a still-living star, spinning it far out into the waves. I spoke once briefly. "I understand," I said. "Call me another thrower." Only then I allowed myself to think. He is not alone any longer. After us there will be others.[3]

Eiseley's account of the star thrower reminds me that every minister is called to be a star thrower. We are to reach out to help those who have been washed ashore in the currents of sin, depression, conflicts, hopelessness, and the endless other struggles of living. We reach out as a "wounded healer," as Henri Nouwen has reminded us. We are to assist, care, listen, support, love, give attention, give a shoulder on which a person can cry, give encouragement, offer tolerance, and render comfort, guidance, or whatever the need may call for.

As star throwers we seek to serve. At the banquet for graduating seniors at Baptist Theological Seminary at Richmond, each graduate was given a towel. This towel symbolizes that they were a servant. They were reminded that they are called to minister. When a minister puts a stole around his or her neck, that stole is a symbol of the towel. That was the original significance of the stole. It is the recognition that we are all servants. As Jesus said, "the greatest of all is the servant of all." He said he came to minister and not to be ministered to. And as ministers, you and I have come to model and serve the one who is the greatest servant of all.

Our Learning Is Never Complete

As a star thrower, you are still en route educationally. Your education was not completed when you got your seminary diploma! You have a lifelong journey before you. No one ever arrives educationally. In one of his comic strips, pop theologian Charles Schulz depicted Lucy and Charlie Brown engaged in conversation about school. Lucy asks Charlie Brown, "Are you smarter this afternoon than you were this morning?" "Yes, Yes," Charlie Brown replies. "I think I am a little smarter." "But are you a whole lot smarter?" she asks. "No," he responds, "just a little smarter." "See?" Lucy exclaims. "See what?" Charlie Brown asks. Lucy then asserts, "There are serious flaws in our educational system!"

There are indeed many flaws in any educational endeavor. The biggest flaw of all, however, is to think that one has arrived educationally. It is a lifetime process. Paul says we are always reaching toward the maturity of faith and for deeper knowledge of Christ. The psalmist reminded us that the fear of the Lord is the beginning of wisdom, but this awesome, mysterious encounter and relationship is a lifelong journey in which we are seeking to grow. "To think and to think hard," Hegel reminds us, "is a religious duty." William James asserts, "I like tender hearts but I also like tough minds." Down through history there have been great thinkers who have given their minds as well as their hearts in service to God and truth. Christians like Paul, Augustine, St. Teresa, Thomas Aquinas, Luther, Wesley, and thousands of others have believed that to love God with all of one's mind is not separate from what it means to be Christian. To be a believer is not divorced from being a "thinker." To love God with one's entire mind is indeed a sacred duty.

Our education is always in process. We are reaching toward "maturity" to measure ourselves by the stature of Jesus Christ, as Paul says in Ephesians 4:13. We need to continue to study, read, learn, and observe. Sit, stand, walk, and run by the doorways of the past and present and listen to the voices that are whispering to you their continuous wisdom. Our minds, spirits, and souls are dead when we cease to hunger for more knowledge and insight about life and its meaning.

Remember that we are on a quest; we are voyagers, adventurers, seekers, dreamers—like the Magi, seeking to follow the star wherever it may lead. Walk near the edge of heresy as you seek truth. Be open, flexible, and unafraid of truth wherever it leads. Creeds, affirmations of faith, or statements of belief are only individual or group renderings where people have attested to their faith in any given moment or age. Drink from their wells of inspiration, but do not see these statements as binding, final, or inerrant. We follow a living Lord who goes before us to open new pathways, new insight, new truths—the One who gives a new birth and a new heaven. He is the Lord of the living not the dead, the future not the past.

We are all in the process of becoming, being, and learning. True believers want to live with God at our elbows, directing us to the next step, phase, insight, and challenge so we realize that learning is ever before us and beyond us. When we reach toward Christian maturity, we sense that whether our study is religion, math, science, literature, medicine, psychology, physics, or any other endeavor, we have not arrived. Something or Someone is ever pulling us toward the not yet realized.

Nurture Your Own Spiritual Life

As a star thrower—a servant of the Bright and Morning Star—you will have to continue to nurture your spiritual life. Open yourself through personal meditation and prayer to the numinous Other, the mysterious presence of God. No one ever reaches spiritual maturity. We always need to be open and continuously growing. How can anyone dare say that he or she is able to measure up to Jesus Christ?

There is an old story about a woman who got religion at every revival meeting. She would be challenged to repent and exclaim, "Fill me, Lord, fill me!" But after hearing this for about twelve years, an older member of the congregation called out, "Don't do it, Lord, she leaks!"

But so do we all. No one is ever fully filled spiritually. Remember to set aside a quiet place for reflection, Bible reading, and prayer. Read and meditate on the Scriptures, the great devotional classics, and selected contemporary writings. People who have been meaningful to me have been Harry Emerson Fosdick, Leslie Weatherhead, C. S. Lewis, John Killinger, Elton Trueblood, Barbara Brown Taylor, and Joyce Rupp. Jot down the thoughts, prayers, ideas, questions, or longings that are stimulated by your reading. In your praying, focus on God's greatness, confess your sins, accept the forgiveness of God's grace, and spend time listening for God's voice. You may do this in a quiet place at home or during a walk in the park or the woods.

One of the people who modeled the quest for intellectual and spiritual growth for me was John Baillie, the Scottish theologian and principal of New College at the University of Edinburgh. In his study were three objects that symbolized his faith and ministry. One was the desk on which he did his theological writing, the second was a chair where he did his reading, and the third was a cushion near a window and bookcase where he would kneel, meditate, and pray. This great theologian knew the importance of developing the inner life and never assumed that he did not need to spend quiet time in worship before God. Each of us has that same challenge.

Continue to Respond to God's Call or Vision

Remember that, as a star thrower, you must follow the Bright and Morning Star wherever it leads. Do not be disobedient to your heavenly vision. You came into ministry out of a sense of call, a vision, a pull, an urge, and a drive that could not be satisfied without your making a commitment. You are here because of that vision. Down through the centuries, men and women have felt pulled toward God. They have climbed mountaintops, crossed deserts, sailed vast seas, marched down familiar avenues at home, taken strange routes in foreign lands, struggled inwardly, followed lighted paths, and agonized gropingly down dark paths to understand and know the love of God. Paul's vision gave him a faith that endured. Each of us needs to have a vision that will enable us to endure.

Have you ever thought about what the world would be like without vision? Everything that has come into existence has come because somebody had a dream or a vision. Columbus had a dream of a new world, and he set sail. Galileo had a vision of a new scientific approach. Edison had a dream that sound could be recorded and that electricity could produce light. Ford had a vision of a horseless carriage. The Wright brothers dreamed that men and women could fly. Von Braun believed and dreamed that men and women could go to the moon and beyond.

What would religion be without vision? Abraham followed his vision of God and went looking for a city without foundations. Moses saw God in a burning bush. Jacob wrestled with God at Peniel. Ezekiel had a vision of God at the river Chebar. Isaiah had a vision of God high and lifted up in the temple. Esther had a vision of how to save the nation of Israel. Ruth had a vision of how to save her family. Elijah experienced God in the sound of gentle stillness in a mountain cave. Paul had a life-changing vision on the Damascus Road. Augustine had a vision of "the city of God." Luther had a vision of a reformed church. Wesley had a vision of a church in revival. Albert Schweitzer had a vision of reverence for all of life. Martin Luther King Jr. had a dream that all men and women could be brothers and sisters together. Mother Teresa had a vision of the church's concern for the poor and outcast of society.

What would the church be without vision? Without vision, the church would cease to exist. It has been said, "Without vision, the people perish." Only when men and women dream dreams, see visions, formulate plans, follow stars, and prophesy do we see real living. Christ has summoned us out of complacency into adventure, from apathy to enthusiasm, from the settled to the pioneer, from safety to risk, from comfort to danger, from death to life. The singer in *The Man of La Mancha* declared that we are "to be willing to march into hell for a heavenly cause . . . to reach the unreachable star."[4] So live with expectancy, wonder, mystery, hope, faith, and love as you follow that vision and star. Continue to go back, at least in your mind, to the meeting place where you were first surprised by God's presence.

A number of years ago in England, a man stood reading a plaque on a church door. It read, "Here God laid his hands on William Booth." The man stood there a while, looking at the plaque. Finally the custodian came over and said, "I'm sorry, mister, but it is time to close the church. You need to move on." The man said, "Give me just another moment, please."

"Okay," the custodian said, "just another moment." The man read the plaque again: "Here God laid his hands on William Booth." The custodian suddenly realized that the man reading the plaque was William Booth himself, the founder of the Salvation Army. Then he heard Mr. Booth praying, "Oh God, do it again. Do it again!"

In some place, quiet or noisy, God laid the divine hand upon your life, and you committed your life to God. That is not the only time that God will touch your life. You need to pray, "Oh God, do it again and again."

Continue then on your journey of faith, but come back and warm yourself over and over in the light of the Bright Morning Star so that you will know how to be a star thrower.

Notes

1. Reinhold Niebuhr, *The Nature and Destiny of Man* (New York: Charles Scribner's Sons, 1949) 179.

2. Karl Barth, *The Universal Church in God's Design*, quoted in Robert Nelson, *The Realm of Redemption* (Greenwich: Seabury Press, 1951) 145.

3. Loren Eiseley, *The Unexpected Universe* (New York: Harcourt, Brace & World, Inc. 1969) 72, 89.

4. "The Quest," in *The Man of La Mancha*, lyrics by Joe Darion, Cherry Lane Music (Greenwich CT, 1965).

Appendix

1. A Wedding Homily

This wedding took place outside in North Carolina with a lake and Grand-father Mountain in the background.

A Psalm of Blessing—Psalm 121

Angela and Bill, you have chosen for your wedding canopy the majestic Blue Ridge Mountains. They rise tall above us and are reflected in the lake behind you. Having been born and raised in the mountains, you look to them, like others of us who love the mountains, for strength and inspiration. To those of us who love the mountains, there is nothing more sacred and secure than looking out from or up to the hills. The mountains anchor us and remind us who we are and to whom and where we belong. The mountains attest to God's majesty and the assurance of our Creator. We gather this afternoon in the shadow of this great mountain for you to begin your married journey together and to express your vows of commitment to each other. Let me encourage you to take Psalm 121 as a Psalm of Blessing for your marriage.

Psalm 121 is a dialogue between two persons, a pilgrim and a priest or a father and a son or a husband and a wife and the priest. The psalm was originally written as pilgrims traveled to the city of Jerusalem to worship in the temple. As they approached the city on a hill, they were asked to "lift up their eyes and look to the hills." They looked with expectancy as they asked where their help came from. An elder responded that their help came from the God who made the hills and who also took the time to watch over them as well.

Today you begin a journey of marriage. As you travel this road you may encounter trials and difficulties, but the psalmist assures you that you can look to the God who created the mountains for assurance and protection. Look upward, he assures you. *Sursum corda.* Look upward to God, who made heaven and earth, who never rests, who will not let you stumble who does not leave his post, who never goes to sleep, who is your shade in the heat of the sun, who is your guard in the dark, who will keep you from all evil forever and ever.

The psalmist reminds you as you travel your journey together that you are not alone, but God is constantly present to preserve and bless you along this pathway. The folk song assures us that God has the "whole world in his hands," and the writer also muses, "he's got you and me, brother and sister, in his hands." God is personally concerned about each of us. Look ahead then with confidence. The assurance of blessing does not remove all obstacles and problems; it gives you the reassurance that you never face any of these difficulties alone but with the power, providence, and preservation of God. So this day, lift up your eyes to the hills as a gesture of trust in the God who will be with you in your going out and in your coming in during all your life. To the ancient Hebrew people, this last phrase was a reference to the doorstep in their home that was stepped over and not on marking a division between the home and the rest of the world. The psalmist is reminding us that no matter where we are, God will ultimately preserve us.

This psalm in its metrical version is popular in Scotland and sung to a tune that links it to the Huguenots and the Continental Reformation. As the Scots sing it, they are reminded of their Scottish mountains, the hills of home, which assure them of the Lord from whom their help comes. As you remember your Scottish roots, may you be assured of that providence and support as you take steps on your journey of marriage today. God bless your marriage with the assurance of his providence and loving grace. Receive this blessing today with a trustful heart.

2. A Funeral Homily

A funeral service should be biblically based, reassuring and comforting for the family, and personal. The following homily was for a minister of music who had served for forty-five years in the same congregation.

Memorial Service for Joann Feazell
"The Music of Life"
Psalm 100; John 11:25-26

Unamuno, the Spanish Christian writer, once wrote, "The proper use of a temple is to provide a place to grieve together." We gather this afternoon to express our grief but, much more, to celebrate the notable life of Joann Feazell. Early in her life, she affirmed her gift of music and devoted that gift in the service of God. For forty-five years she used that gift to help adults, young people, and children come into God's presence with joyful hearts and with songs of praise and thanksgiving. Music was her medium to direct others to sense and love God.

The 100th Psalm offers us some guidelines for understanding the music of Joann's life. Reflect with me on its message for us in this time.

1. Make a joyful noise unto the Lord. The Scriptures, especially the Psalms, are filled with the ringing echo of praise and song, both with the voice and with instruments to God. Jesus hallowed music as he and his disciples sang a hymn together in the upper room before he left to go to the garden of Gethsemane.

Music is a part of nature itself. From the songs of birds and the chirping of insects to the rhythmic beat of ocean waves breaking on the sand and the streams flowing down the mountainside, nature seems to be filled with the continuous sound of music from its Creator.

Martin Luther wrote that besides theology, "music is the only art capable of affording peace and joy of the heart." Carlyle wrote, "Music is well said to be the speech of angels; in fact nothing among the utterances allowed to man is felt to be so divine."

When the writer of the book of Job sought to describe the beauty and harmony in God's universe, he declared that in creation's dome, "the morning stars sing together." On the night when God's son was born, the glorious prelude to the birth of Jesus came about as angels sang together on the plains of Bethlehem. Charles Kingsley has stated, "Music has been called the speech of angels; I will go further, and call it the speech of God himself."

Have you thought how bland our worship services would be without music? Imagine a worship service absent of hymns, organ, piano, or other instruments. I have discovered that most people can quote more hymns than they can Scripture. Why? I think the simple answer is because thy have sung hymns over and over again. As we sing together, our theology is communicated on the wings of a hymn. Through singing, our faith is nurtured and we grow spiritually. Joann dedicated her life to helping people worship through the medium of music. This way she was a teacher not only of music but also of theology and, by her lifestyle, a teacher about the mystery of life and how one can dedicate and use one's own gift in service for God.

2. Serve the Lord with gladness. We cannot have music without notes. Notes are a tone of a definite pitch that give meaning and direction to music. Joann found within music her sense of direction in life, using music to express one of her many gifts and to call out the gifts she saw in others— young and old. She was committed to excellence in her personal organ and piano playing, in choir directing, and in seeking the best from her choirs. Having studied under great organists and teachers like John Finley Williamson, Dr. C. C. Loomis, Dr. George Markey, Marcel Dupré, and Nadia Boulanger, she never took her gifts for granted but spent hours practicing the organ day after day and week after week and year after year.

Joann's use of her musical gifts was not to direct attention to herself but to point others to God and to offer praise to God. She used her gifts to touch the lives of others. At one time she had over eighteen different choirs—including three handbell choirs. These choirs ranged from small children to senior adults. At various times, these choirs averaged over 500 choir members, with several dozen choir assistants and a dozen or more accompanists. Every child, young person, and adult grew to love Joann as she affirmed them, challenged them, disciplined them, and called them to a higher commitment to Christ.

For forty of her forty-five years as minister of music, Joann took choir tours all over the country and abroad. During these choir tours, our young people grew in their faith and spiritual awareness.

Through a word, a smile, laughter, or a song, Joann lifted the spirits of others. She was one of the most enthusiastic people I have ever known. Her radiant smile would light up a room, her contagious laughter would invite others to join her, and her warm, friendly spirit always conveyed, "I've never met a stranger. Come be a friend of mine." I never knew her to be discouraged or downcast for very long. She was enthusiastic about working with children, young people, adults, the Boys' Club, The Civitan Club, or a stranger on the street. Enthusiasm comes from a Latin word that means "God breathed." God breathed into Joann a wonderful breath of enthusiasm, and it gladdened the hearts of others. These lines about music are often attributed to Thomas Gibbons:

> Our lives are songs;
> God writes the words;
> And we set them to music at leisure;
> And the song is sad or the song is glad.
> As we choose to fashion the measure.
> We must write a song,
> Whatever the words,
> Whatever the rhythm or meter;
> And if it is sad, we must make it glad,
> And if it is sweet, we must make it sweeter.

3. The Lord is God, and God made us, and she was God's. Joanne had a quiet personal faith that sustained her all her life—in good times and in times of personal struggle, and in the times of grief with the deaths of her parents, her brother Landrum, other family members, and Dr. Loomis.

She had her own quiet time each day with special devotional books that nurtured her. In addition to the Bible, she used the devotional writings of John Baillie, Harry Emerson Fosdick, John Killinger, Elton Trueblood, C. S. Lewis, and many others.

She sought to grow in her own faith and helped nurture the faith of others. Through her music, she attempted to deepen her faith and the faith of others, or to lead them to faith in Christ. She reached for excellence in her faith journey as well. She was never content to rest where she was but always reached higher in her spiritual growth.

4. Voice thanksgiving to God when you come into God's temple. Joann's organ music would often swell to a toccata as she expressed her sense of thanksgiving to God. We pause in this hour to acknowledge our thanksgiving for the life of Joann Feazell. We are thankful for her gift of forty-five years of music ministry and the thousands she touched. We are:

Thankful for the hope and encouragement she gave many,
Thankful for the joy she shared,
Thankful for the guidance given,
Thankful for the faith she quickened,
Thankful for the friendship she gave,

Thankful the for gifts she awakened in others—young and old,

Thankful for her willingness to listen to a child, young person, or an adult in need of an ear,

Thankful for free piano and organ lessons,

Thankful for her personal dedication,

Thankful for her loyalty to her family,

Thankful for words and notes of affirmation,

Thankful for small words of thanks and support,

Thankful for her disciplined, practiced organ music,

Thankful for the young people she inspired to find places of spiritual service,

Thankful for the rich example of a single woman who lived a full and productive life,

Thankful for her forty-five years of ministry in one place—Bristol, Virginia—and her impact on this church and city,

Thankful for her witness of what one person can do when she dedicates herself fully to God.

You know many other reasons we are thankful for Joann's life. I know you can express them yourself.

Thanks be to God for this good woman, who was a marvelous organist, a beautiful spirit, a dedicated Christian, and a good friend to many.

Fred Anderson, in his article about Joann in the July 14, 2004, edition of the *Religious Herald*, titled his piece, "A Scrapbook of Memories." Joann had told Fred that she never had time to keep a scrapbook, yet her scrapbook is all over this church, this city, this state, and in other states and countries. I am thankful today for that countless collection of people she touched through her ministry in this church and city. Her scrapbook is not pasted in a book but revealed in the lives of people she influenced through her forty-five years of ministry. Her legacy is a living one—many of you are here today.

I am thankful to God for that legacy. Joann has blessed God's name through every life she has touched, affirmed, nurtured, guided, and supported with prayers, encouragement, and good will.

5. *"For the Lord is good, his steadfast love endures forever, and his faith-fulness to all generations" (Ps 100:5)*. Joann has now passed from this earthly life to the eternal realm. We affirm today that "the Lord is good." Joann lived to be eighty-seven years old and served as a minister of music until nearly eighty. She was alert almost until the end. She is now free of her

suffering and has entered her spiritual rest. In music there is an important place for rest. In childlike trust, Joann has yielded her life into the arms of Christ.

In Mendelssohn's oratorio *Elijah*, there is a section titled "O Rest in the Lord." Here are the lines:

> O rest in the Lord,
> Wait patiently for Him,
> And He shall give thee thy heart's desire;
> O rest in the Lord.
> Commit thy way unto Him,
> And trust in Him,
> And fret not thyself because of evil doers,
> O rest in the Lord, wait patiently for Him.

Joann now rests in the Lord. We affirm "God's steadfast love and his faithfulness to all generations."

Joann lived by faith and died in faith. As she had put her hand in quiet trust in Christ's hand many years ago as a small child in the Christian church, so she placed her hand in the hand of Christ to bear her through "the valley of the shadow of death." She trusted the words of Christ who said, "I am the resurrection and the life." Death is a birthing from the material world to the spiritual realm. Death opens the door from the physical world into the eternal world. For the Christian, we affirm that death is not the end but the beginning of a new stage of existence.

The music she shared in this life will be played on in the lives of others today. As the sun sets tonight, it will leave an afterglow. The sun will pass out of sight, but its rays are seen for some time. The afterglow of Joann's life will vibrate in the lives of people like Steve, Sam, and Beth Boyd; Kay Dodson Congdan; Eric Barber; Susan Keith; Terri and Tracy Paris; Karen Sherfey; Kevin Flannagon; Beth, Jimmy and David Bell; Eric Hicks; David Hicks; Tom Makress; Vic Barrett; Dennis and David Cross; Sam Morlay; Karen Tate, and countless others.

The impact of her music, service, love, devotion, and smile will continue to be felt long after she is gone. Her influence will leave an afterglow that will continue to be felt through the lives of thousands of people.

The custom in our Baptist church, when one moves to a new community or a different city, is to grant them a letter of transfer to the new church. So today we grant to Joann Feazell a letter of transfer from the church mortal to the Church Immortal—from the physical church to the Church Eternal, from the earthly church to the Spiritual Church of God.

Enter into your rest and your new opportunity for service, Joann Feazell.

I don't know what picture you have of life after death, but I don't think of it as a picture of idleness. Joann, as much as she loved to be busy, would certainly not like to sit around and do nothing. I think the words of Rudyard Kipling describe something of what life might be beyond death for her.

> When Earth's last picture is painted and the tubes are twisted and dried,
> When the oldest colors have faded, and the youngest critic has died,
> We shall rest, and, faith, we shall need it—lie down for an aeon or two,
> Till the Master of All Good Workmen shall put us to work anew.
>
> And those that were good shall be happy; they shall sit in a golden chair;
> They shall splash at a ten-league canvas with brushes of comet's hair,
> They shall find real saints to draw from Magdalene, Peter, and Paul:
> They shall work for an age at a sitting and never be tired at all!
>
> And only the Master shall praise us, and only the Master shall blame;
> And no one shall work for money, and no one shall work for fame,
> But each for the joy of the working, and each, in her separate star,
> Shall draw the Thing as she sees It for the God of Things as They are![1]

And so, calmly and quietly today, we note the homegoing of this good, dedicated woman, Joann Feazell. May God give us strength and comfort to guide us as we face the future without her presence among us. As the cool breezes blow upon our faces, may we sense the quiet music of God's abiding presence. As we look upon the beauty of flowers, may we detect the whisper of God's love and grace. As we hear the songs of birds, may we hear the pulsating sound of God's melody of support. As we look at the stars in the dark sky, may we sense the constancy of God. As we listen to the bubbling brook or the waves breaking on the beach, may we be reminded of the ever-flowing grace of God. As we listen to the sound of an organ, piano, anthem, or solo, may it recall to our minds the dedication of Joann and our own call to faithfulness and service.

Grant, O Lord, that we may open the window of our soul and sense the music of your eternal peace and the assurance of life everlasting. Through Jesus Christ, our Lord, we pray. Amen.

3. Resources for Funerals and Grief

You may develop your own practices for offering comfort to families and friends who grieve. The following resources may be helpful to you.

Books

Robert W. Bailey, *The Minister and Grief.* New York: Hawthorn Books, 1976.

Andrew W. Blackwood, *The Funeral.* Grand Rapids MI: Baker Book House, 1972.

Paul E. Irion. *The Funeral and the Mourners.* New York: Abingdon Press, 1964.

Edgar N. Jackson, *You and Your Grief.* New York: E. P. Dutton, 1961.

Thomas G. Long, *Accompany Them with Singing: The Christian Funeral.* Louisville: Westminster John Knox Press, 2009.

W. A. Poovey, *Planning a Christian Funeral: A Minister's Guide.* Minneapolis: Augsburg, 1978.

Kent D. Richmond, *A Time to Die: A Handbook for Funeral Sermons.* Nashville: Abingdon Press, 1990.

William Powell Tuck, *A Positive Word for Christian Lamenting: Funeral Homilies.* Gonzalez FL: Energion Publications, 2016.

William Powell Tuck, *Facing Grief and Death: Living with Dying.* Cleveland TN: Parson's Porch Books, 2013.

Grangrer E. Westberg, *Good Grief.* Philadelphia: Fortress Press, 1962.

Funeral Manuals

Perry H. Biddle, Jr., *Abingdon Funeral Manual.* Nashville: Abingdon Press, 1976.

Al Cadenhead, Jr., *The Minister's Manual for Funerals.* Nashville: Broadman Press, 1988.

James L. Christensen, *The Complete Funeral Manual.* Westwood: Fleming H. Revell Co., 1967.

J. R. Hobbs, *The Pastor's Manual.* Nashville: Broadman Press, 1954.

Joseph E. McCabe, *Service Book for Ministers.* New York: McGraw-Hill Book Company, 1961.

4. Ten Beatitudes for Deacons

The Beatitudes of Jesus lift before us the high virtues of Christian living (Matt 5). The word "beatitude" comes from a Latin word that means "blessedness" or "happiness." I want to draw on one of Jesus' favorite methods of teaching—the use of beatitudes. Listed below are ten beatitudes for deacons I have used in several of my churches.

1. Blessed are deacons who confess that Jesus Christ is Lord. Deacons are individuals who have surrendered their lives to Jesus Christ in a commitment of faith. You have followed him as Lord and have experienced forgiveness of sins and rebirth. You acknowledge and affirm that genuine religion begins in your personal experience with Jesus Christ.

2. Blessed are deacons who have been chosen by the congregation. An effective deacon is one who has not sought the office but has been chosen by his or her peers. The congregation has called you out from among the others to serve in a special way just as the early deacons were chosen as recorded in the book of Acts. This congregation has needs that must be filled, and you have been selected and set apart to help meet those needs. Always remember that you have been chosen. It is an honor, but it is also a great responsibility. Labor in this position with humility, knowing that you have been selected by your fellow church members.

3. Blessed are deacons who consecrate themselves in worship. One of the most important things that you will do is to nurture your spiritual life. To be an effective deacon, you will want to be a growing Christian. Be open to new insights from God, and be faithful in your worship attendance and in your own spiritual development. Set aside time to grow spiritually.

Many of you are like I am—you like to build log fires during the fall and winter months. You know, of course, that you cannot have a fire without several pieces of wood touching each other. The hot coals of each log keep the others burning brightly. The contact of one with the other is what gives the radiant heat. Our lives continue growing spiritually when we are in contact with the radiant, glowing presence of God. We need to make sure that this strong relationship continues. You cannot help others grow spiritually if you yourself are not progressing.

4. Blessed are deacons who are committed to showing compassion, concern, and comfort. Jesus used the word "deacon" to describe greatness: "Whoever would be great among you must be your *diakonos* [deacon, servant], and whoever would be first among you would be slave of all"

(Mark 10:43-44). The New Testament and early church make clear the functions of deacons. Deacons are to be servants of Christ and his church. They are to assist the pastor in ministering to the spiritual and physical needs of the congregation. In John 17, Jesus indicated his power was to be demonstrated through a towel and a basin, which he picked up to wash the disciples' feet. He had come to serve not to be served.

Some years ago, Emily and I attended the inauguration of Dr. Tom Graves as president of the Baptist Theological Seminary at Richmond. Instead of a golden medallion as the school's symbol of authority, Dr. Graves and the seminary faculty and trustees chose the towel. "The towel signifies the pathway of power for the Christian minister," states Dr. Tom Graves, "a pathway of humility and service." The Christian minister and deacons are both called to be servants and not to be people of authority.

A committed deacon will seek to minister to people in our congregation. You will acknowledge that this is probably the most important responsibility you have. You are charged to be a minister to those people in good and difficult times. You will reach out to them and show love, understanding, and concern. You will help them as they grow in the faith. You will become pastor to them through your devotion. Support them in good and bad times.

5. Blessed are deacons who cultivate the church community. As an effective deacon, you will seek to be a calming factor in your church community. You will seek to build up the community and not do it harm. You will always seek to be fair and confidential in the way you respond to others. You will listen to the concerns, hopes, dreams, and needs of others and seek to do what is best for our community. You will not seek only what you want but will strive to do what enables this community to serve Christ most effectively.

6. Blessed are deacons who have consistent character. You will champion high moral standards and values in your own life. What you say will be reflected in what you do. What you are will be demonstrated by the actions you live. A deacon cannot say one thing and do another. In your business, recreation, home life, and all your living, you will seek to follow Christ as your guide and to follow his high ideals.

A child noticed one day that a woman had her Catholic medallion showing outside of her blouse. Looking at the medallion, the young child remarked, "Your religion is showing." In a real sense, our religion should always show. I hope it will be reflected in all of your life as a deacon.

7. Blessed are deacons who are cheerful and celebrative. The church does not need more dismal, despondent, sad-faced people. We leaders who have felt the contagious power of the God of joy and life. Jesus said, "I have come that you might have life and have it more abundantly" (John 10:10). A deacon feels this inner joy and wants to share it with others. You will be a happy force in the church community who will help build it up by love and grace. Through your attitude, concern, and words, you will seek to radiate joy and goodwill in this community.

8. Blessed are deacons who command respect. Respect is not something that is automatically given; it has to be earned. It will be earned by your attitude, service, humility, love, and devotion. The office of deacon itself commands a certain amount of respect, but that respect will be enhanced by the high standards you bring to it. May God give you strength and courage to live out the kind of life to which you have been called.

9. Blessed are deacons who have caught a vision. If our church is to continue to follow Christ, we must not look back at where we have been but ahead to the future and where we can be as we follow Christ, who goes ahead of us. The church has a wonderful foundation, but we must have a vision of what we can be as servants for Christ. We must have a vision of what this church can do in the days ahead. If we do not have this kind of vision, then we continue to drift and do not move ahead into the future. Christ goes before us, so let us follow him.

10. Blessed are deacons who are commissioned to share the good news. Remember that you have been chosen not simply to be honored but to be a worker in this congregation. You are commissioned as an apostle, one who is sent, to share the good news of Jesus Christ with others. I hope that you will do this in your home, in your business, in your recreational pursuits, and in all of your life. When the opportunity arises and can be done appropriately, I hope you will share with others the good news of Jesus Christ by word, by deed, and by your very manner as a person. May God enable you to do this.

These ten beatitudes are guidelines for deacons to serve the Lord they love more effectively. May God give you grace and strength to serve your Lord faithfully.

5. Ten Beatitudes for the Pastor

1. Blessed is the pastor who continues to nurture his or her own spiritual growth. Every pastor needs to nurture her own spiritual growth through a specific time set apart for quiet meditation, prayer, and Bible reading. You cannot guide others effectively in spiritual development when you ignore your own spiritual development. Let your spiritual nurture be always a top priority.

2. Blessed is the pastor who is open to new insights and new direction in ministry. Just because a pastor may have graduated from seminary does not mean his or her education is complete. Continue to read, study, and take new seminars and continuing education that will enable you to be aware of the latest biblical and theological scholarship and approaches to ministry and preaching. You will never arrive to the point where further knowledge is not possible.

3. Blessed is the pastor who works diligently to prepare biblical sermons and meaningful worship. Effective worship and preaching do not just happen. They require extensive hours of careful preparation and study. Commit at least twenty hours a week to sermon preparation and several hours to worship planning. Guard that preparation time carefully. It is essential.

4. Blessed is the pastor who listens to the needs, struggles, concerns, joys, and hopes of the congregation. The members of our congregations want pastors who will listen to their problems and concerns and celebrate with them in their times of births, weddings, graduations, etc. To do this, you must be involved in personal contact with them at home, at church, in the hospital, or wherever there is opportunity. This contact with the people will also enrich your preaching because you will have your hand on the pulse of your congregation.

5. Blessed is the pastor who trains and equips the congregation to use their spiritual gifts in ministry. To do their ministry, our laypeople must be trained properly to use their gifts appropriately. Simply securing a person to serve on a church committee or board does not assure that the proper ministry will be accomplished if the person is not equipped for that responsibility. One of the essential ministries of the pastor is to train his laity for their ministries.

6. Blessed is the pastor who ministers faithfully to the pastoral concerns and needs of the congregation. Preaching alone will not enable a pastor to fulfill his or her ministry. Pastoral calling in times of crises, hospitalizations, deaths, and grief is crucial for effective ministry. Appropriate pastoral counseling will enable you to assist your congregation when needed.

7. Blessed is the pastor who studies and strives to interpret the Scriptures to direct and enliven the lives of the people. The pastor is charged with the responsibility of carefully studying the Scriptures and staying informed of the latest biblical and theological scholarship. This will enable you to interpret and communicate the Scriptures correctly for your congregation. Your people have a right to expect their pastor to stay informed of the best available scholarship.

8. Blessed is the pastor who ministers faithfully to all parishioners without regard to their social or economic status. The pastor will not minimize time with those in the congregation who are less educated, from a different racial or cultural background, or in a lower economic bracket but will strive to serve all members fairly and with the proper love and attention their needs require. Nor will you discriminate because a person has wealth or prestige. Before God, all are Christians on the journey of faith.

9. Blessed is the pastor who offers positive and effective leadership. Few things can be as harmful to a pastor's ministry as negativity and discouragement in leadership. Even when ministry is difficult or the church has a conflict, maintain a positive and wholesome attitude as you seek to provide direction and vision for the future.

10. Blessed is the pastor who is caring and loving of his or her own family while serving the congregation. While ministering to the congregation, the pastor has to give the proper attention to his or her spouse and children. Neglecting your family is not only a negative example for the church but is also ignoring a responsibility that demands priority in your life and the life of the congregation. Faithful attention to your family is essential for genuine ministry and for genuine happiness in your life.

Note

1. Rudyard Kipling, "L'ENVOI," in *Masterpieces of Religious Verse*, ed. James Dalton Morrison (New York: Harper & Brothers Publishers, 1948) 602.

Bibliography

Some of these books are no longer in print, but they were helpful to me in my pastoral ministry through the years.

Adams, Arthur Marrihew. *Pastoral Administration*. Philadelphia: The Westminster Press, 1974.

Anderson, James D., and Ezra Earl Jones. *The Management of Ministry*. San Francisco: Harper & Row, 1978.

Anderson, Ray S. *Minding God's Business*. Grand Rapids MI: William B. Eerdmans Publishing Company, 1986.

Bagby, Daniel G. *Crisis Ministry: A Handbook*. Macon GA: Smyth & Helwys, 2002.

———. *Seeing through Our Tears*. Minneapolis: Augsburg, 1999.

Bass, Diana Butler. *Christianity for the Rest of Us: How the Neighborhood Church Is Transforming the Faith*. San Francisco: HarperSanFrancisco, 2006.

Bendroth, Norman B., ed. *Transitional Ministry: Successful Strategies for Churches and Pastors*. Herndon VA: The Alban Institute, 2014.

Best, Harold. *Music through the Eyes of Faith*. San Francisco: Harper, 2003.

———. *Unceasing Worship: Biblical Perspectives on Worship and the Arts*. Downers Grove IL: InterVarsity, 2003.

Blackwood, Andrew. *Pastoral Leadership*. Nashville: Abingdon Press, 1959.

Block, Daniel I. *For the Glory of God: Recovering a Biblical Theology of Worship*. Grand Rapids MI: Baker Publishing Company, 2014.

Bratcher, Edward B. *The Walk on Water Syndrome: Dealing with Professional Hazards in the Ministry.* Waco TX: Word Books, 1982.

Bramson, Robert M. *Coping with Difficult People.* New York: Random House, Inc., 1988.

Brubaker, David R. *Promise and Peril: Understanding and Managing Change and Conflict in Congregations.* Herndon VA: Alban Institute, 2009.

Calian, Carnegie Samuel. *The Spirit-Driven Leader: Seven Keys to Succeeding Under Pressure.* Louisville: Westminster John Knox Press, 2010.

Campbell, Thomas C. and Gary B. Reierson, T*he Gift of Administration.* Philadelphia: Westminster Press, 1981.

Carroll, Jackson W. *As One with Authority.* Louisville: The Westminster John Knox Press, 1991.

Chapell, Bryan. *Christ-Centered Worship.* Grand Rapids MI: Baker, 2009.

Craddock, Fred B. *Craddock on the Craft of Preaching,* edited by Lee Sparks and Kathryn Hayes Sparks. St. Louis MO: Chalice Press, 2011.

———. *Overhearing the Gospel.* St. Louis MO: Chalice Press, 2002.

Cueni, R. Robert. *The Vital Church Leader.* Nashville: Abingdon Press, 1991.

Cully, Iris V., and Kendig Brubaker Cully, eds. *Encyclopedia of Religious Knowledge.* San Francisco: Harper & Row, 1990.

Cummings, H. Wayland, and Charles Somervill. *Overcoming Communication Barriers in the Church.* Valley Forge: Judson Press, 1981.

Dale, Robert D. *Leadership for a Changing Church.* Nashville: Abingdon Press, 1998.

———. *Pastoral Leadership.* Nashville: Abingdon Press, 1986.

———. *Seeds for the Future: Growing Organic Leaders for Living Churches.* St. Louis MO: Lake Hickory Resources, 2005.

Dawn, Marva J. *A Royal "Waste" of Time: The Splendor of Worshiping God and Being Church for the World.* Grand Rapids MI: Eerdmans, 1999.

———. *Reaching Out without Dumbing Down: A Theology of Worship for the Turn-of-the-Century Culture.* Grand Rapids MI: Eerdmans, 1995.

Deusen Hunsinger, Deborah van, and Theresa F. Latini. *Transforming Church Conflict: Compassionate Leadership in Action.* Louisville KY: Westminster John Knox Press, 2013.

Diehm, William J. *How to Get Along with Difficult People.* Nashville: Broadman Press, 1992.

Dobbins, Gaines S. *Building Better Churches.* Nashville: Broadman Press, 1954.

————. *The Churchbook.* Nashville: Broadman Press, 1951.

Doohan, Leonard. *Laity's Mission in the Local Church.* San Francisco: Harper & Row, 1986.

Engstrom, Ted W., and Edward R. Dayton. *The Christian Executive.* Waco TX: Word Books, 1979.

Epperly, Bruce G. *Starting with Spirit: Nurturing Your Call to Pastoral Leadership.* Lanham: Rowman & Littlefield, 2010.

Farris, Patricia. *Five Faces of Ministry: Pastor, Parson, Healer, Prophet, Pilgrim.* Nashville: Abingdon, 2015.

Forman, Rowland, Jeff Jones, and Bruce Miller. *The Leadership Baton.* Grand Rapids MI: Zondervan 2004.

Fortune, Marie M. *Is Nothing Sacred? When Sex Invades the Pastoral Relationship.* San Francisco: Harper & Row, 1989.

Friedman, Edwin. *A Failure of Nerve.* New York: Seabury Books, 2007.

Galindo, Israel. *Perspectives on Congregational Leadership.* Vienna VA: Educational Consultants, 2009.

————. *The Hidden Lives of Congregations.* Herndon VA: The Alban Institute, 2004.

George, Carl F., and Robert E. Logan. *Leading & Managing Your Church.* Old Tappan NJ: Fleming H. Revell Company, 1987.

Gillingham, E. Leonard. *Dealing with Conflict.* Nashville: Abingdon Press, 1983.

Glick, Robert P. *With All Thy Mind: Worship that Honors the Way God Made Us.* Herndon VA: The Alban Institute, 2006.

Graves, Mike, ed. *What's the Matter with Preaching Today?* Louisville KY: Westminster John Knox Press, 2004.

Groff, Kent Ira. *Clergy Table Talk*. Gonzalez FL: Energion Publications, 2012.

Halverstadt, Hugh F. *Managing Church Conflict*. Louisville: Westminster John Knox Press, 1991.

Hammett, Eddie. *Reaching People Under 40 While Keeping People Over 60: Being Church for All Generations*. St. Louis MO: Chalice Press, 2007.

————. *Recovering Hope for Your Church: Moving Beyond Maintenance and Missional to Incarnational Engagement*. St. Louis MO: Chalice Press, 2014.

Harbaugh, Gary L. *God's Gifted People*. Minneapolis: Augsburg Publishing House, 1988.

Harris, John C. *Stress, Power and Ministry*. New York: The Alban Institute, 1977.

Hawn, C. Michael. *One Bread, One Body: Exploring Cultural Diversity in Worship*. New York: The Alban Institute, 2003.

Heifetz, Ronald. *Leadership without Easy Answers*. Cambridge, MA: Harvard University Press, 1998.

————, Marty Linsky, and Alexander Grashow. *The Practice of Adaptive Leadership: Tools and Tactics for Changing Your Organization and the World*. Cambridge MA: Harvard Business Press, 2009.

Hemphill, Kenneth S. *Spiritual Gifts: Empowering the New Testament Church*. Nashville: Broadman Press, 1988.

Higdon, Ronald. *In Changing Times: A Guide for Reflection and Conversation*. Gonzalez FL: Energion Publications, 2015.

Hoge, Dean R., and Jacqueline E. Wenger. *Pastors in Transition: Why Clergy Leave Local Church Ministry*. Grand Rapids MI: William B. Eerdmans Publishing Company, 2005.

Howell, James C. *The Beauty of the Word: The Challenge of and Wonder of Preaching*. Louisville KY: Westminster John Knox Press, 2011.

Hulme, William E. *Managing Stress in Ministry*. San Francisco: Harper & Row, 1983.

Jinkins, Michael, and Deborah Bradshaw Jenkins. *Power and Change in Parish Ministry*. New York: The Alban Institute, 1991.

Johnson, Ben Campbell. *Pastoral Spirituality: A Focus on Ministry.* Philadelphia: The Westminster Press, 1988.

Jones, G. Curtis. *The Naked Shepherd.* Waco TX: Word Books, 1979.

Jones, Jeffery D. *Heart, Mind and Strength: Theory and Practice for Congregational Leadership.* Herndon VA: The Alban Institute, 2008.

Judy, Marvin T. *The Multiple Staff Ministry.* Nashville: Abingdon Press, 1969.

Killinger, John. *Fundamentals of Preaching.* 2nd edition. Minneapolis: Fortress Press, 1996.

————. *The Tender Shepherd: A Practical Guide for Today's Pastor.* Nashville: Abingdon Press, 1985.

Leas, Speed B. *Discover Your Conflict Management Style.* Washington, DC: Alban Institute, 1997.

Lester, Andrew D. *Hope in Pastoral Care and Counseling.* Louisville KY: Westminster John Knox Press, 1995.

Lilley, Roy. *Dealing with Difficult People.* Philadelphia: Kogan Page Limited, 2013.

Lindgren, Alvin J. *Foundations for Purposeful Church Administration.* Nashville: Abingdon Press, 1965.

Long, Thomas G. *The Witness of Preaching.* 2nd edition. Louisville KY: Westminster John Knox Press, 2005.

Lott, David B., ed. *Conflict Management in Congregations.* Washington, DC: Alban Institute, 2001.

Lutz, Robert R., and Bruce T. Taylor, eds. *Surviving in Ministry.* Mahwah NY: Paulist Press, 1990.

Malcomson, William L., ed. *How to Survive in the Ministry.* Valley Forge: Judson Press, 1982.

Marshall, Myra. *Beyond Termination.* Nashville: Broadman Press, 1990.

McBrien, Richard P. *Ministry: A Theological, Pastoral Handbook.* San Francisco: Harper & Row, 1987.

Mead, Loren B. *The Once and Future Church.* New York: The Alban Institute, 1991.

———. *Transforming Congregations for the Future.* New York: The Alban Institute, 1994.

Newbigin, Lesslie. *The Good Shepherd.* Grand Rapids MI: Eerdmans Publishing Company, 1977.

Noyce, Gaylord. *Pastoral Ethics.* Nashville: Abingdon Press, 1988.

———. *The Minister as Moral Counselor.* Nashville: Abingdon Press, 1989.

Oates, Wayne E. *Behind the Masks: Personality Disorders in Religious Behavior.* Philadelphia: The Westminster Press, 1987.

———. *Pastoral Counseling.* Philadelphia: The Westminster Press, 1974.

——— and Charles E. Oates. *People in Pain: Guidelines for Pastoral Care.* Philadelphia: The Westminster Press, 1985.

———. *The Care of Troublesome People.* New York: The Alban Institute, 1994.

———. *The Christian Pastor.* Philadelphia: The Westminster Press, 1982.

———. *The Presence of God in Pastoral Counseling.* Waco TX: Word Books, 1986.

Oden, Thomas C. *Becoming a Minister.* New York: Crossroad, 1987.

Osborn, Ronald. *Creative Disarray: Models of Ministry in a Changing America.* St. Louis MO: Chalice Press, 1991.

Oswald, Roy M. *Clergy Self-Care: Finding a Balance for Effective Ministry.* New York: The Alban Institute, 1991.

Powers, Bruce P., ed. *Church Administration Handbook.* Nashville: B & H Publishers, 2008.

Rediger, G. Lloyd. *Clergy Killers: Guidelines for Pastors and Congregations Under Attack.* Inner Grove Heights MN: Logos Productions, 1996.

———. *Ministry & Sexuality: Cases, Counseling, and Care.* Minneapolis: Fortress Press, 1990.

Rowatt, G. Wade, Jr. *Pastoral Care with Adolescents in Crisis.* Louisville KY: Westminster John Knox Press, 1989.

Sanford, John A. *Ministry Burnout.* New York: Paulist Press, 1982.

Scalise, Charles J. *Bridging the Gap: Connecting What You Have Learned in Seminary with What You Find in the Congregation.* Nashville: Abingdon Press, 2003.

Schaller, Lyle E. *The Multiple Staff and the Larger Church.* Nashville: Abingdon Press, 1980.

Schnase, Robert. *Just Say Yes! Unleashing People for Ministry.* Nashville: Abingdon Press, 2015.

Schwartz, Robert M. *Servant Leaders of the People of God.* New York: Paulist Press, 1989.

Seaborn, Joseph, Jr. *A Celebration of Ministry.* Grand Rapids MI: Baker Book House, 1990.

Sherman, Cecil. *To Be a Good and Faithful Servant: The Life and Work of a Minister.* Macon GA: Smyth & Helwys, 2010.

Sims, Bennett, J. *Servanthood: Leadership for the Third Millennium.* Cambridge MA: Cowley Publications, 1997.

Sisk, Ronald D. *Surviving Ministry.* Macon GA: Smyth & Helwys, 1997.

Stafford, Gil W. *When Leadership and Spiritual Directions Meet.* New York: Rowman & Littlefield, 2014.

Switzer, David K. *Pastoral Care Emergencies.* New Jersey: Paulist Press, 1989.

Thompson, Deanna A. *The Virtual Body of Christ in a Suffering World.* Nashville: Abingdon Press, 2016.

Tuck, William Powell. *A Pastor Preaching: Toward a Theology of the Proclaimed Word.* Macon GA: Nurturing Faith, Inc., 2012.

———. *A Positive Word on Christian Lamenting: Funeral Homilies.* Gonzalez FL: Energion Publications, 2016.

———. *Holidays, Holy Days, and Special Days: Preaching through the Year.* Gonzalez FL: Energion Publications, 2015.

———. *Overcoming Sermon Block: The Preacher's Workshop.* Gonzalez FL: Energion Publications, 2014.

———. *The Forgotten Beatitude: Worshiping through Stewardship.* Gonzalez FL: Energion Publications, 2016.

Wainwright, Geoffrey, and Karen B. Westerfield Tucker, eds. *The Oxford History of Christian Worship.* New York: Oxford University Press, 2006.

————. *Doxology: The Praise of God in Worship, Doctrine, and Life.* New York: Oxford University Press, 1980.

Warlick, Harold C. *How to Be a Minister and a Human Being.* Valley Forge: Judson Press, 1992.

Welch, Robert H. *Church Administration: Creating Efficiency for Effective Ministry.* Nashville: Broadman & Holman Publishing, 2011.

Willimon, William H. *Clergy and Laity Burnout.* Nashville: Abingdon Press, 1989.

————. *Pastor: The Theology and Practice of Ordained Ministry,* rev. ed. Nashville: Abingdon Press, 2016.

————. *Worship as Pastoral Care.* Nashville: Abingdon Press, 1979.

Woods, C. Jeff. *Congregational MegaTrends.* New York: The Alban Institute, 1996.

————. *We've Never Done It Like This Before.* New York: The Alban Institute, 1994.